# *Living and Succeeding with the Divine Father*

## A Memoir

## Ida Kesse Harris

*Living and Succeeding with the Divine Father*
*A Memoir*

Copyright 2003
by Ida Kesse Harris

No portion of this book
may be reproduced in any form
without the written permission
of the author

ISBN: 1890306541

Library of Congress Control Number: 2003112835

Warwick House Publishing
720 Court Street
Lynchburg, VA 24504

*Dedicated to my father and mother
Peter and Helena Kesse*

My father Peter Edward Kesse was born September 2, 1876, in Malupe (Clayriver), on a fourteen acre farm, near timber forest. He was the last child in the family. The first was Karlis, then three daughters, Karolina, Emma, and Minna.

Their home was a wide-eave log cabin—big and comfortable. It also housed a weaver's workshop and a loom. In the middle of the cabin was a big stove, like a heating furnace. At one end was a big opening where firewood was put in. When it had reached a certain high temperature, charcoal was pushed to the sides and in the middle space was put the bread loaves and the front opening was closed. Nobody opened it but the one who put the bread in. After a certain time (hours), the bread came out. It smelled so good!

All of the walls of the furnace were warm, the bread was warm, and the aroma of baked bread filled the cabin. "And we know that soon the loaves will come out," said my father. "Yes," he continued, "Mother will put them on the white scrubbed table."

After they cooled a little, she asked us to bring the butter and put it on the table. Then we thanked the Lord for the day's good baking, cut slices of bread, and put on the butter, which melted on that hot, black aromatic bread.

"There's nothing in the world better tasting," said my father.

Seems that the family kept busy at the house, using the loom to weave linsey-woolsey cloth for work clothes, like skirts, jackets, pants and trousers. They took care of the cattle, pigs, and poultry, plus milking and churning butter. Also, there were potatoes and vegetables to be planted in time for harvesting. There was rye, wheat, and barley to sow; and the harvesting of hay, stacking it, or putting it into the barn. There was the harvesting of fruit from the garden, berry picking, and other preparations for winter.

On Sundays they walked to church in Aluksne, a city by Aluksne Lake. They carried shoes with them, stopped near the church by the creek, put on their shoes, and entered the church, which was called the Evangelical Lutheran Church.

Aluksne Lake is at East-Vidsemes Highlands. It is a deep lake, forty-nine feet in the deepest place and sixteen square kilometers (six square miles). It is rich with fish. On the big lake island there was once an ancient Latvian castle. In that place a German Order erected a stonewall castle, which the Swedes blew up in 1702 when the city was captured and destroyed by the Russians.

At the minister's house two oak trees grew, planted by the Bible translator, Ernest Glik. Their age is about 300 years (one he planted in 1685, after translating the New Testament, the other in 1689, after translating the Old Testament).

Part of the lakeshore is high and has a forest. In that spreading forest, raspberries grew. "They are so big, like cherries, sweet, juicy and so many. In no time, the bucket was full," our father was saying. "The mushrooms were easy and fun to gather and so many kinds," he added, "the forest and lake are so beautiful smiling at us. One can never forget it.

"Only in August, there was an open place in that forest where snakes came and they made a big pile. They were rubbing each other. They were so busy with each other; they never noticed we were watching them. Then when they chose their mates, the couple would go away." As he told the story we felt we were there, too.

Last summer I needed some help outdoors to take care of bushes and trees and engaged a nineteen-year old man from Aluksne, a commercial school graduate, who wished to work here in America. He came and worked and lived with us. We talked about my father, and he told us that my father's story about the Aluksne's forest, lake, raspberries, and mushrooms is still true. Over 100 years has passed since my father's time. The boy's name is Ugis Vaivods; he was a good worker.

A good size country/city market was in Aluksne, my father told us. "And still is," Ugis added. Once a week, if there were a need to buy or sell, the family would go there. Once father, at age ten, noticed there were brooms for sale. He checked and decided he, too, could make the brooms and with his parents' permission, he did, and was selling them for twenty-five cents apiece. When he was twelve years old, he was saving money for school.

Since the place had lots of forests and seven months, more or less, of snow in winter, they had ten well-cared-for horses to haul out timber. It was good income. The family was always busy, summer or winter.

In the old country a custom is that the oldest son inherits the farm, the family's property. The girls usually get married, but the last boy (the youngest) is sent to school, given an education if the family has money, or else some training in arts or trade.

When my father Peter was fourteen years old, his parents decided to look for a place for him in some trade or business, at the same time preparing him for probable necessary changes. The family all agreed.

The family lived with God, the Bible, and Church. Since they belonged to the Evangelical Lutheran Church, they arranged for him to take a class for confirmation. It required two weeks preparation in a class, meeting every day, taught by the minister in the church.

He did not miss a day and did all that was necessary. Then the big day came, Sunday in the church—confirmation, ceremony, and certificate. After that was the celebration at home, the dinner with family and friends.

Now he was a member of the church and prepared to live and work by God's law.

At this time he continued to work on the farm and do what was required of him at home. He prayed and trusted that our Heavenly Father-God would provide everything that he needed and by God's timing.

After awhile, the end of April, his father was telling that he was in Riga and there was a big hardware store. The owner was Mr. Popovich. He also had a bigger store in Moscow and had more stores in Russia, but his main store was in Moscow. His home was there also. He had apprentices who started as delivery boys. He could live with his household. The housekeeper would show him a place and he would help some with housework in the morning, then work in the store. When the customers bought something, the delivery boys delivered the purchase to the customers' homes. He said that they had several boys. Someday they could work up to being a salesman.

Now that was something to think about. Moscow was far away. Father did not know the Russian language, he did not speak or read in Russian, and it was so far away. Finally, he decided to go to Moscow.

In April, while there was still snow on the ground, Father and his brother Karl would leave by sled. He started preparing a traveling bag (I think, actually a carpetbag that was called that, rather than calling it a carryall).

Then Mother came in asking what and how he was packing. It seemed she was satisfied, but asked, "Peter, have you put the Bible in?" "Yes," he replied, "but it is so big, it takes up too much space."

"Peter, do remember that if you have the Bible in the bag, you will always have all you need, but if not, you maybe will have the last pair of shoes, the last shirt, the last coat on your back."

Peter never doubted what his mother was teaching. He knew that she was doing it for his own good. When the time came, he and Karl were ready, along with the horse and sled (kamanas). Early in the morning they took off for Moscow.

In Moscow they found Popovich's place. Masha, the housekeeper, came out to meet them. After resting awhile in the Popovich's big kitchen, Masha fed them a bowl of soup and bread. Next morning Karl left for home. Peter started to work in the store.

The store was big. He had never seen one so big. He became a delivery boy. The Russian people almost always gave a tip when purchases were delivered. He was kind and helpful to the housekeeper so she put a cot in a corner behind a wardrobe and a big stone stove and a little table behind the cot. He put his Bible there. It was very small but warm.

Because of her kindness he got up early and started the stove. She also started helping him with Russian language.

The other boys were local; after work they left for home. One Saturday after work, one boy asked Peter if he would like to come with them to the tavern. He was not used to taverns. He was still young, but after a few weeks he went along. They sat at a table. The boys ordered beer and they insisted that Peter do so as well, so he took a cup, but did not drink, just touched it to his lips. By the time they were leaving, Peter's cup was still almost full and he had to help the boys get home. They were not steady on their feet.

Since he was not interested in drinking, he started to listen to what other people were talking about. He noticed a man sitting at the counter talking and drinking. He found that the man was a teacher and a good one. Peter started to think, some people are needy and poor, and some are not. Mr. Popovich has a nice home and has a summer cottage at the lake and uses horses and carriages, so it must be the education that makes the difference.

He decided to find out more about education from the teacher. He said to him, "If one plans to go to the university you have to have a high school diploma." "How do you get a high school diploma?" was Peter's next question. "One can study, then when you are ready, you go to The Education Ministry, pass the exam and you get a diploma. With it you can then go to the university, but it is very expensive; or you can go to the Military School and it is free," was the teacher's answer.

By the time the teacher had finished telling him this they were at the house where the teacher lived. He was a single man and he was renting a one-room apartment.

After praying and thinking, Peter had an idea. The next time he met the teacher, he asked if the teacher could prepare him for the Education Ministry exam. He offered to pay him every weekend, after he brought him home from the tavern with a bag of groceries and a little money. The teacher accepted and they had an agreement.

Two years later, Peter passed exams and had a diploma. He was sixteen years old, but Military School would not take him because he was not seventeen years old yet.

He continued working at Popovich's with good pay. A year later he was accepted in Military School. Four years later he graduated from the Military School and became a lieutenant. That was in Moscow; he was twenty-one years old. He rented a nice apartment in Moscow.

Then he received a letter from his sister, Karolina, who lived in Baltinava, telling that her husband had died. She needed his help. He took the train to Latvia; the junction was at Rezekne, a good-sized city, where he had to stay for a day for the next train to Baltinava.

He got a room in the hotel and went out to a restaurant to have a meal. There he found that the city of Rezekne was for sale, and the price was 2,000 rubles. There was a suggestion that if you bought one side of the main street you could buy just half of the city for 1,000 rubles. Peter had in his pocket 2,000 rubles, but his sister was a widow, who would help her now?

Next morning he continued to Baltinava. There at the station, Karolina's oldest son, Alfred, met him with horse and cart to travel over the marshy road for three hours to the village. The road was very rough, it needed constant filling; the marsh was just sucking it in. The day was sunny and bright.

Peter asked, "How is the hardware store? Who will be taking care of it?" "I," said Alfred.

"But how about school?" asked Peter.

"I'm already in the store, I dropped school," Alfred replied. "The store was in debt; Edi will have to help me. I hope it's only on the weekends so he doesn't miss too much school. He wants to be a teacher someday," said Alfred.

So, while talking, they neared the village. "Oh, you have a bakery?" said Peter.

"Yes, they are Russians. After the war they stayed and started to bake bread in their kitchen. Then they got married and now the whole family is baking good bread. They are good people," Alfred said.

Finally they reached their destination. Karolina with her other children, Edward and Milda, greeted Uncle Peter, whom they had not seen for a long time.

Peter found that the house needed many repairs, so while he was there he got busy with the repair work. He also paid off some of the store debts. At the end of the week he gave to Karolina and Alfred what was left of the 2,000 rubles to repair the house and barn. Then he left to return to his work in Moscow. He also decided to keep in touch with his sister and her family.

About a year later he received a message from his father that his mother was sick. He hastily set out on the journey to Aluksne. Nobody was at home when he arrived. As he stood and prayed, he heard the cemetery bell ringing. He hurried to the cemetery, but was too late. She was already in her grave.

He missed her, she was his mother, but she was also his friend and he loved her and always trusted her.

After the funeral, he noticed a little boy. He also noticed that the child was holding close to his sister, Minna. Since everybody was busy, Peter tried to get the boy's attention and to play with him. The child liked it. After the boy was put to bed Minna came to Peter and thanked him for taking care of the boy.

"I would like to talk to you, I just have to," said Minna. Peter noticed that she was sad and grieved and said, "Let us go out for a walk."

"The boy is mine," said Minna, and she started the story. "I was in love with a man and he with me. We wanted to get married, we told my father, but my father forbid."

He said, "This man's family is not good; he didn't want his daughter's life to be ruined. He said to forget about that man." As much as she tried she could not; so she and her man decided to have a child without marriage. When the child arrived, her father would let them marry. But it did not happen that way. Gossip in the village, bad names about her, and shame kept following her. The father of the child left the village; people said he went to America. She said she didn't know what to do.

Peter was praying about what to do. Where will the child go to school? How will the people and other children treat him? What can my living in Moscow do for the child? For my sister, Minna? She could marry somebody, but what about the child? Peter expected Divine Father's help and guidance. He was always trusting and trustful to God.

Then the idea came; he would take the boy, Adolph, with him to Moscow. He had an apartment and a housekeeper who could take care of the boy. Then he would go to school and later to the Military Academy.

Peter's father and Minna liked the idea and the rest of the family, too. So soon Peter and the boy left his home in Malupe for Moscow.

Peter found that traveling with the boy was very interesting. In Moscow the boy seemed to get along just fine with the housekeeper. With time the boy started to show his likes and dislikes.

One time Peter and Adolph were sitting at the table having dinner. The housekeeper brought in soup; the boy did not like it. He just sat at the table. Peter left for the kitchen. Suddenly through the open window came screams and loud voices. Peter came back into the dining room in a hurry. Adolph was still sitting at the table. Peter went to the window of the apartment, which was on the second floor, and on the street was a lady with her big hat dripping with tomato soup. Adolph's bowl in front of him was empty.

Father remembered another time. He had a date, a dinner date with a nice lady in a fine restaurant. Everything was good, and there were lots of people. When they were served, the soup was brought in; Adolph did not care for it. The lady started telling how good it was. The next moment Adolph hit the soup with his soupspoon and the soup flew all over the place. After that my father never took the boy along on a date.

Meanwhile the boy's mother Minna married a good man, Resgals. They went to Baltinava, near her sister Karolina. John was a good worker and very talented in the arts and built for himself and the family a nice two-story house with all modern conveniences in it. They had three children. Their daughter, Anna, was beautiful, industrious, and was a dressmaker. She passed away with T.B. before her thirtieth birthday.

At the age of twelve, Adolph was sent to pre-school in the Military Academy, and he was home only on holidays. Since Peter's work assignments were often to eastern, southern, and other parts of Russia, he felt the boy would be well taken care of. Later, with time, the boy went to the Military Academy where he graduated as a surgeon's assistant. He used that profession as his life's work.

At the age of twenty-five, my father was an army colonel. He traveled a lot, but did not forget his duty to the boy. He was in China, Japan, Caucasia, Turkey, and other places. He quickly learned several languages: Chinese, Turkish, and Polish, as the need came.

He was in the Russo-Japanese War (1904-1905) and was leading an army to China. They proceeded on the road through steps to the Ural Mountains to cross them. The road was level but they hardly were moving. Peter realized that this problem must be solved. The troops were given vodka three times a day. They were drunk from day to day or sleeping. The barrels were on the wagons. He ordered to shoot all the barrels to destroy. The vodka was flowing over the road and into the shallow ditches and the men were crawling on their knees, licking up the vodka along with the dirt.

Then they fell asleep. The next day they were up and the army was moving.

My father, being the colonel, was responsible for the army. They reached China in good condition, and there was no vodka in sight.

In China, he was stationed with the highest-ranking officers. They were nice, well-mannered military men. His meals and living quarters were with these men. They were all Chinese.

Every day they took a bath in the bathhouse. They first undressed, taking off their topcoat, then seven layers of underwear. Then they rubbed themselves with soap, rinsed with water, and then they went to another room where barrels were filled with water. Each stepped into a barrel with water to his neck. They stayed for a while, then came out, dried, and started to dress. They left the bottom layer of clothes to be washed, put on the second layer, then all the rest, then a clean (fresh) layer. Now this was the seventh layer till tomorrow. Then they put on their topcoats.

Papa had a hard time sleeping at night with a certain man in the lodging, something about the smell. So he explained to them that for his health reasons he would sleep outside in his sleeping bag. It was sheepskin and he said it was warm even in the winter.

After the war he went to Japan. Papa still was young and unattached. He dated some Japanese girls; the dates started in the midday.

He arrived at her parent's home as they were leaving. A woman called Nanny was following them, keeping her distance of twenty feet behind them. They went to a park; it was immaculate, with beautiful trees, flowers, and many different chrysanthemums, big as a child's head. In the middle of the park was a square, encircled with flowers and plants, and in the center was a pagoda. Poles supported the roof and a bell.

In the center were several bowls, one on top of the other. On the second bowl a man was sitting. The bell rang monotonously; the man seemed to be asleep. In the bottom bowl coal was burning, in the top bowl was a rat. The rat was gnawing the man's bottom and the blood was dripping down to the lower bowl.

It was explained to Father that they do it this way to punish some criminals. They said that the man has no sensation, and they used the blood as fertilizer to feed the chrysanthemums. When we heard this story from Father we did not like those big flowers anymore, and never had them in our home.

After the Russo-Japanese War Father returned to Moscow and later was transferred to Kiev in the Ukraine. There he rented an apartment and had to walk to his work. Often he was passing a beautiful lady who did not seem to notice him. He wanted to find out who she was, and how one could get acquainted. He found that it was not possible on the street, but there were right ways. She was a teacher, her father was a notary public, and he and his wife were von Verchovskys. They lived by the lake in a large house with fourteen rooms. Father started to take walks on the described location. One weekend he noticed a gentleman working on a boat. He stopped and greeted him with, "Good morning," and started to talk about the boats, but he never had any boats nor knew anything about them, still he offered to help. The man thanked him and said, "It would be good and I hope to see you again." So the acquaintance continued.

But one time he was coming, he noticed another man with Mr. Verchovsky, he recognized him as one of his officers, and thus was introduced to Mr. Verchovsky. The introducer was the husband of Mr. Verchovsky's daughter, Kate.

Then he was invited to a picnic. The island on the lake was nice, comfortable and had trees and bushes for an inviting shaded area; it was wonderful for swimming and also had tables and chairs and some stumps for sitting.

That's where the boat came in handy. And that's where Peter was introduced to Helena. He was now accepted by the family. He was very happy, finally he could converse with Helena; he had waited so long.

Helena was a teacher in the primary school; she loved her work and the children. Often she instructed some children after regular school hours in reading, writing, arithmetic, and other subjects.

There was an expression by some students, "I don't want to learn, I want to get married." Such laziness!

Peter and Helena found that they had mutual interests; they both loved to read and listen to music, classical and folk. They also liked the theatre, opera, and good food. They often went to nice restaurants. Peter often was a guest in Helena's home.

In that two-story white house was not just fourteen rooms, but also a big kitchen. They had a kitchen maid and a maid just to keep the house clean. Upon the arrival of Christmas or other big holidays, two cooks came two weeks ahead, one for pastry and bread and the second for roasts and other meats. The table was overfilled with rich and diverse foods and fruits.

After a couple of years they married in the Orthodox Church in Kremenchug and moved into an apartment, which they beautifully furnished. He told our mother never to serve duck. We wondered why, but he never explained.

After several years they had a daughter, me. I never learned to crawl. When they put me on the floor I just sat there, if I was close to a chair or other furniture, I pulled myself up, but did not walk. Once the maid tied a rope around my middle and said, "Walk." I never stopped.

I remember one time Christmas was coming. Papa (Peter) and Mama (Helena) dressed up the little girl (me, Ida) and left the house. Papa carried me. The sun was shining and Papa's shoulder was

*Ida and her father by the canal in Riga, 1937*

warm; I fell asleep and awoke in a big room with many people. There were tables, standing people, sitting people, talking people, all greeting more people. Then Papa put me down, telling me to stay, not to go away.

I sat next to a big Christmas tree and it had many little things on it. It sparkled and shined, with beautiful birds, wee cups, wee teakettles, stars, silver bells,

*Ida's mother, Helena*

and small white candles. I forgot all about Papa and Mama. I wanted to be by this tree and look and look and see this beauty. Somebody came and picked me up. I did not like it. Then I was carried to my mother and put onto her lap. She offered me food, but I did not take it. Next morning I awoke in my bed at home.

Later Papa left Kiev with his family and got a small apartment. Mama was teaching at a school. During the day I was left with the maid. Sometimes the maid took me out for a walk. The maid was to clean the house and kitchen. It was a warm day and I asked for a drink; the maid said, "Later" but forgot. In the kitchen I saw on the floor a bucket with water. I was happy and drank from it. The maid came in and saw what I was doing and got angry. "That water is dirty, I washed the floor with it; now you will be sick." I still remember that threat. I was still thinking about the water in the bucket. There was so much I noticed. Papa did not wear uniforms, but he was at home more.

The next morning I did not awake. Papa brought another man; he carried a black bag. I did not like this man; I only wanted to sleep. Papa talked to this man and then he left.

That night Papa did not sleep. He had me in his arms, walking around the kitchen. All I wanted to do was sleep, on and on. Then suddenly I said, "Burn, burn." He put me on the bed, opened the blanket I was wrapped in and then put another blanket on me. He sat up with me all night.

Several days later Papa was walking on the street and saw

the doctor. He went up to him and asked why he didn't come back to see his little girl as he had promised. The doctor was coming toward him saying, "I am so sorry about your loss, but there was nothing that could be done. She had brain meningitis; there was no medicine to cure that disease. I am sorry for your loss."

"She was up and running around in a couple of days," Papa said.

The doctor, the man with the black bag, looked at Papa with disbelief. "Nobody lives with that sickness!" he said.

"Come and see," said Papa.

The doctor came and saw me; then asked how this happened.

So Papa told him that he did as the doctor told him to do. Put ice over the head and put hot water bottles around the body. One of the bottles burst and she cried, "Burn, burn." So he changed her and put her to sleep in the bed.

The doctor said, "She must be one of God's selected children."

I still have the burn scars on my right leg and smaller ones on my bottom.

Then the family moved to Odessa on the Black Sea in the Ukraine. The new house was on a corner of Main Street and a street that came directly down from the mountains. In the spring when the snow melted the street became a river. Water jumped from stone to stone and then ran into Main Street, continuing down to the Black Sea.

Papa had rented two rooms and a kitchen with big windows facing both streets. I liked to sit in the window and look out when there were parades. First came the camels, some had one hump, some had two, and on some was a man all dressed up. Next came the music player. Then came pretty girls in transparent trousers and under them tight fitting shorts in green, blue, red, and golden colors. On top was a sheer blouse and fitted vest in colors, embroidered in gold and silver and pearls. They were holding and playing tambourines. Mama said they were Tarters and had something to celebrate.

I found a little paper on the street. The maid who was with

me noticed too, and asked me to give it to her. I did and the maid said it was money (two Kopeks). When I asked what to do with it, the maid answered that I could buy some candy. "What else besides?" asked I.

"You could buy water," said the maid.

"Can you come with me after water?" I asked. We got a bucket and walked up the stony mountain road to the spring.

That was the water station and one could buy water. Around this well were sitting older Tarter women. They were dressed like the girls at the parade, but not so nice, and they smoked funny looking pipes.

I paid the money and the bucket was filled.

The maid wanted to take it, but I said, "No, that is my bucket."

I lifted it, but it was too full and too heavy. So I poured some off and carried a little, but it still was too heavy. So on again and off again. Then I carried the rest home and gave it as a present to Mama. The maid explained to my mother about the water.

My little brother Misha was walking unsteadily toward the bucket. He probably was one year old. I was three years old then.

He had been away out in the country. He had been sick and needed a mother's milk. On the farm was a nursing mother who was willing to nurse Misha, too. He looked well and happy. Now the family was together. One day Mama said we would both go to visit Aunt Katy. We went to Yalta. It is by the sea. We had to climb up the high stony steps. On both sides of the steps between the stones, right and left, were yellow and red blooming roses. The sun was setting just a little and the dolphins far out in the blue sea were jumping up and spitting out water, like fountains. The sky, the sea, and the dolphins were beautiful. Even all the roses with their big blooms smiled to the sky and the sea. The roses were naturally planted by God.

Then it was midsummer. Mama and Papa brought big baskets of tomatoes and fruit to the market to sell.

As a young girl, Mama embroidered many beautiful things, like tablecloths, blouses, pillowcases, and so on. Now she was selling them at the market, and all the items were selling well.

In the evening when they came home it was all sold.

One day Mama took me to the beach. I thought we would be swimming, but we did not. We only climbed the mountain. On top was a round house in which all the walls were made from glass. All around we could see the sea and the ships. Mama said it was an art studio. Then I noticed the pictures from everything that we could see outside. The ships in the sea were the same as on the pictures. It was a wonder to me how one could do that. Mama explained to me that the artist-painter was Ivasovski and he had painted the pictures. I wished I could do that, too.

When the days and nights became hot, Papa decided that we would have to sleep outdoors. We went deep into the backyard and put our blankets on the grass. I looked up into the sky. It was a deep, velvety-blue and richly "embroidered" with gold stars and I knew all were alive. They were mostly smiling, but not all, because some were thinking. I fell asleep.

One night, Papa took me up while I was still sleeping. I put my head on his shoulder. Mama picked up Misha. He, too, was asleep and had his head on Mama's shoulder. We left "our" place, walked out on the street, which was stony and rough and we never returned.

When I woke up we were in an abandoned place with several railway tracks and a few red cattle carriages (wagons). There were a couple of run-down cabins and a fence at one side.

Papa went to a cabin, somebody opened the door and he went in. After a short time he opened the door and Mama went in with us. It was simple and clean, just a table and a couple of chairs and benches. Mama went to the kitchen and with another woman prepared some food. Mama started to feed Misha. Papa brought tea and cups and we all were eating.

After we had our meal, a few men came and Papa went out. They opened the door on one cattle carriage and Papa and another man got into it. They stayed there a long time.

Then Papa left with those men and Mama was with us. She told us children's stories and we sang together. Later, Papa came back and said that he found a little cabin for us. He said there was one room and a kitchen. He said there were two large beds and a small one, and a maid was willing to come if Mama and Papa would have to go somewhere.

This time Papa took Misha, and Mama held me by my hand as we walked along with Papa. That night we all had a good night's sleep.

So we were living in the little cabin, usually just Mama and the children, but at night Papa was home too.

We did not have any place to go. It was like a desert, just sand, not even bushes. We were in Bessarabia.

After some time we left the cabin and were standing at the door of a school.

I don't remember how we got there. Papa rang the bell; a man opened the door and we went in. I think it was a summer day, because there were no children. We went on the second floor. We were told to stay by the window wall and be very silent. It was getting dark and we fell asleep. We were sleeping on the bare floor. In the morning we left. Papa left one way with Misha and Mama left another way with me.

We walked a few street blocks toward a big open place. It was a harbor with ships and boats, large and small, but mostly fishing boats. There was a very tall pole in the sea supported by two posts. A man in a small boat came to it and climbed up to the top and took a seat. He was watching the sea. He did not move for some time. Then he stretched his arm and made a sign in the air. We were standing near the edge of the stone coast. Mama said, "Look in the water near the pole, the fish are coming, lots, a school of fish." Now the men in boats were coming and encircled the school of fish, pulling the nets into their boats and to the shore. There was a long row of warehouses. When the fish were on shore, more people were coming to buy or to take to the warehouses.

We stayed in the schoolhouse some more days. One morning, we left very early and later we were back in the same place with the run-down cabins and railway tracks with red cattle carriages. Doors opened on some. Yes, it was more than one carriage, and people were around. Some people were climbing into carriages. So Papa and Mama did also after Papa lifted

Misha and me. Near the middle was standing a potbelly stove and a big pot was on it. There was firewood next to it and a sack with potatoes. At each end of the wagon were bunks with hay sacks, side by side.

Papa said that women and children would be on top bunks, men on the bottom. Mama said that Misha would sleep between her and me. So I chose to be by the window. It was small black iron, like an oven door on a stove. It was easy to lift up and I could see outside and listen if somebody was there and talking.

Mama was putting pillows and our blankets on our hay sacks. Other mothers did the same. Every place on the bunks was taken. The door was almost closed; just a narrow gap was left. Somebody said it is only for the good air.

I was looking through the window. People were coming and going. Some carried boxes, bags, and blankets. Some came with the children and some carried hampers. They all bypassed our wagon and were talking in low voices.

Then Papa and another man made a fire in the potbelly stove, took off the big pot, and put on a teapot. When the steam was coming, Papa offered people hot water if anybody wanted to drink or make tea for himself or herself.

"As you know, each one has to provide his own bread and food," said Papa.

Mama had a little aluminum bowl, she put in a little hot water, and then some bread, sugar, and cottage cheese, mixed a little and fed it to Misha first and then similar for me. It was good.

We had only one cup, which was aluminum also. With a little sugar and hot water, Mama made a drink for Papa and gave him a sandwich. Then she made something for herself.

That night we slept in the wagon, but it stood in one place. In the morning I asked Mama why we were still here in the same place. She said that a locomotive would come and hook to our wagons and its engine would pull our wagons and we would travel.

Then Papa and another man got out and were talking. There were some from other wagons, too.

Papa came in and put the big pot on the stove with potatoes

and water and put in some firewood. "After the potatoes are ready we will eat. The children will have smaller or a half potato, adults a large or make a choice. Then," he continued, "we have hot water for tea if one wishes. In about three hours, the engine will be here and we will travel.

"As you know we will not stop for many hours and we only have a latrine here for the children. The rest of us have to go out before the engine is here," he said.

The potatoes were cooking with the skins on. When they were ready we had to take out the small ones. The children ate first. Then the rest of the people ate. The water in which potatoes were boiled was not thrown out.

Later we heard a hit on the wagon and then the locomotive and engine noise. They were hooking our wagons on.

It felt so good that we would not stay in one place. This train was going through Bessarabia, along Carpathians and some lower mountains. Our train was standing so that everybody could do that day's chores. I was looking through a window to the top of the mountain; it was high and I saw little horses pulling little wagons and little people running in front of them and in the back. "Mama, Mama," I called. "There are toys, somebody playing, children playing, on the mountain top."

"No," Mama said. "They are soldiers going back home, the war is over."

"Why are they so little? Those are toys!" I insisted. "The mountain is so high, and they are far away. The farther away something is, the smaller it appears to be," Mama explained.

When everything was done, the train took off. So we were traveling on. Sometimes the train stopped and the men went out and brought back water, firewood, food items, and some fruit.

Finally, after weeks, we crossed the border to Latvia and we were in the back of the main railroad station of Riga. Papa and other people from our wagon and others left for the main station.

When they came back they told us that there is a big place where we would move in.

The place for us to move in was across from the main station where the seashore station was. On the first floor was that station's assembly hall with double stairs to the seashore station. Another big door was to a room to the right like a big auditorium. It had many big windows and many bunk beds placed in squares of fours or six separated by two feet for walking space.

We had to keep our things like bags, boxes, and such under the bunk beds. Papa reminded, "Under your bunk beds."

Mama was putting our blankets and pillows on our beds. Misha was so little that he would sleep between Mama and me. We used only three beds. Papa used the fourth bed to place our clothes and the Bible.

After we got settled, a man came and said we would be served a dinner. We had to go down the corridor to the dining room. First, the mothers and children would go. When they were finished, the men would go.

As I remember, we had soup with milk, white bread and something more, but I do not remember anymore. Then Papa went to dinner and other people too. After dinner all were silent.

After the long travel from Odessa in wagons and then to move our belongings from the train, and helping each other with bags and boxes, we were all exhausted. Misha was asleep and Mama, too.

Papa asked me how I was feeling, if I would like to go back? I asked, "Back to train?" "No," he said, "not to the train, but to Odessa." I said, "Not tonight, I want to sleep."

The next day was very busy, but people were looking happy, hopeful. We were home—our country, our home.

We were called to breakfast. After that Mama took Misha and me to the bathhouse. I loved warm water running over me. When Mama called me, I did not want to go. I just wanted to stay in the water forever. When we returned back to the camp Papa was not there. There were only women and children, hardly any men. After we had dinner, Papa came and was telling Mama that he was looking for work. He was willing to do any kind of work but that day he did not find work.

Like always after our meal, when we were in our bunk

bedroom, somebody came. I think a lady said to come to the dining room without the little ones, that they would have some clothes for us. So Mama went and took me. The tables were full of clothes, shoes, coats, and underwear. Mama was looking and picking some dresses my size. I did not like any. Then she said, "Then you choose what you like, you know that you will have to wear it."

There was one dress I had noticed. Of all the dresses, there was only one that I liked. I picked it and put it on. It fitted me perfectly. Black, it had a collar and buttons up the front to the neck, and it had long sleeves.

Mama looked at me and did not say anything, but she looked sad. When Papa saw me in that dress he did not say anything, but looked at Mama and she, too, had nothing to say. Sometime later, maybe the next day, we were going to the dining room through the corridor. We met some adults and children coming from the dining room. Papa seeing a girl my size said, "Look at that dress, blue and white print, so pretty. Would you like something like that?"

I looked at the girl and the dress and said, "No, never!"

How long we stayed in that camp, I do not remember. Papa did not have any family members living in Riga. His family lived in the country. Yes, they were peasants. So he was planning to stay in Riga. One day he came and said that he had a job working on the railroad in Riga as a railway man, probably as a switchman to change rails.

We were happy that Papa now had work. He also told us that one railroad man with whom he would work told him about an apartment in the same building where he was living. It was across the Daugava River. It was on the fifth floor, with one room and a kitchen including a stove and sink, water, and bathroom.

After talking with that man he decided to wait until he finished the work, only one more hour. They took the tramway and in no time they were across the river.

He saw the place. Excitedly, he said, "The kitchen and the room have a window. It is small, but the view is beautiful. It has no furniture except a table by the window that has a broken leg. I can fix it. There is also a small grocery store down the street."

Mama was listening attentively. The rent seemed reasonable. Papa reassured Mama that as he would be working, in time they would find something better.

They rented that apartment and we moved in. It was just like Papa had said. I looked through the window; the view was beautiful. We were above the treetops. There were many, many treetops, probably woodland, and a far away white castle rising over the green woodland and contrasting with the beautiful blue sky and sunshine. What a picture!

Papa fixed the table. Mama was cooking something on the stove. I don't remember what we ate that day. Papa and Mama washed the floors in the room and kitchen, so it could dry before it was time go to sleep. As we had no beds, that night we slept on the floor.

The next morning Papa's new acquaintance, the railroad man, came and also another man. They brought some planks, an axe, some tools, and nails.

Mama said that because they would be busy, she would take the children outdoors for a walk. So we went downstairs and out to the street. Mama turned to the left and we walked

*The Daugava River runs through Riga*

along the riverbank. We had the entire river in view, and it sure was beautiful.

Misha and I could run and jump as much as we wanted. There was green grass and there were a few stumps. Mama took one to sit on. Misha attempted to scramble up on one but rolled down from it. Then Mama said it was time for us to go back. As we walked back, we saw Papa standing at the door looking for us.

"You look so happy," he said, and picked up Misha. He told us that they had just had finished the work. They made a couple of bunk beds and small benches. His coworker friend said they had just bought a new dining room suite and that he had a couple of old chairs in the cellar.

Papa carried Misha upstairs. He was so little, not yet two. As soon as we were in our apartment there was a knock on the door. Papa opened the door and there was his friend Mr. B with the chairs, his wife and a girl, some years older than I. Mrs. B put a pan with hot soup on the table. "I hope you like it. I just cooked a big pot of green peas, carrots, onions, and meat," she said. "Thank you so much for your kindness," said Mama. The little girl, Amy, had in her hands a small bag. She gave it to me saying, "This is for you, apples, we have apple trees." I thanked her in the same way that Mama did.

"Do you have any toys?" Amy asked. I shook my head no.

"I have two dolls. I will bring you one so we can play," Amy said.

Both mothers agreed about our playing together.

Then the "B" family excused themselves to go home before their dinner and our dinner would get cold.

They departed saying, "We will be seeing you. If there is anything you need, come to see us. We will help you."

Papa said, "Now the soup time." We sat at the table and enjoyed our meal.

After the meal Papa and Mama talked for some time. Then we went to sleep on our new bunk beds. None of the beds had padding, but we were satisfied.

We were living in that place for some time. Amy brought me the doll. She had a porcelain head sewed on a rag body filled with something soft, as were the arms and legs, and she had on a pretty dress. Sometimes I played with Amy and the doll.

Once Misha and I were on the street in front of the house where we lived. I had to go back to our apartment for a minute. On the corner of the street was a square metal box about two feet high. I put my doll on it and asked Misha to guard her. He promised. When I came back I saw my brother walking at the opposite end of the street. When I asked him about my doll he said he did not take it. So I learned my lesson, never trust the two-year old. I never found that doll or even had another one, but Amy's present is still remembered as if it were just yesterday.

Month after month passed. Then one evening when Papa came home from work he was smiling as if he had some secret. But he said that he was hungry and asked if dinner would be soon. Mama told him to wash up and change his clothes, and dinner would be on the table. So he did and dinner was on the table. Papa said, "We have lots to thank our Lord for taking care of us all the time and each day providing for us what is the necessity," and he prayed the Lord's Prayer. After dinner he said he had something to tell us.

Just today when he was very busy he heard a voice behind him. "Peter, is that you, Peter?" Papa turned around and recognized the man, one who also graduated in Moscow from Military Academy. After the war was ended he returned to Latvia.

He asked Papa what he was doing here at the railroad. Papa told him that he was working and that just a few months ago he returned with the family from Ukraine.

Papa's friend, Colonel Ranka, told him that he could do much better because Latvian military needed a man with his education and experiences. He suggested that Peter go to the War Military Ministry.

Mama, hearing this story, asked him if he would do what his friend said. Papa answered positive. So he asked from his employer one day off for family matters and went to the Ministry. He was given a good position in the military. He went back to the railroad, gave a notice and worked one week, according to his employment agreement, then left.

Since Papa's new work was across the city, we had to find another place to live. He found a place on Matisa Street. It was in the backyard, on the first floor. The entrance was from the yard. It had a large kitchen with one window and another large room with no windows. That is where we all slept. There was one electric bulb hanging from the ceiling, but it was too high for me to reach.

We did not stay there very long because transportation from that place to Papa's work by Forest Park was not convenient.

Our next apartment was also on Matisa Street but closer to the streetcar. It was on the second floor, a kitchen and two rooms. One we used as a dining room and family room. In the center was a good size table, which belonged to the landlady. She had no place for it in her home. I also started to first grade. Mama taught in Russian. Some girls (it was a girl's school) spoke loud and only Russian and acted boastful. They were bigger than I, but they could not read and the teacher was more occupied with them.

Then arithmetic was added. It was not hard for me, but I did not like the book and tried to avoid it. When Mama found

*A square in Riga*

out, she asked me why I did not like it. First I did not talk about it. She insisted. Then I said angrily, "It is a dead book, there are no pictures, just numbers, dead numbers."

Later when I learned to understand math I had no problems. It became quite interesting. The next year my brother started school. Father put him in elementary school on Bruninieku Street #8. It was a new school with big windows and a large playground in the back surrounded by big trees.

When I saw this school and the children with parents registering for the year, I liked it all and said to Papa, "I want to go to this school too."

"I can learn with Misha; we speak Latvian anyway," I said. So Papa registered me too after talking with some teachers.

In September, Misha and I went to our new school. I liked everything there and everyone. So did my brother.

One day Papa came from work and just before dinner, he called us together and said, "When I come home from work at 5:00 p.m. we all speak Latvian. All day long when I am not at home you can speak any kind of language you like. We start it now. That is today. Vai pusdiena ir gatava?"

"Ja," said Mama.

"Paldies!" said Papa, and took his place at the table.

When Mama taught me to read, she did it in Russian. Now she was teaching Misha an ABC book in Latvian. Russian alphabet is Cyrillic and is used for writing in Russian and various other Slavic languages. The Latvian alphabet is Latin, coming from Latinus. Latium is related from Latins, members of the people of ancient Latium.

With all that, Mama did not speak Latvian fluently, just some different words.

Playing with the children, Misha learned Latvian. As Mama was teaching him to read, he was teaching her what each word meant in Latvian. In one month, the ABC book was used up. It looked like an old used up rag and they had to buy a new book.

Within one school year, that is nine months, they both could read and write in Latvian and understand it.

After that time our family very often went to the library, and brought home books to read and talk about.

As the spring came, Papa began making plans for summer. He had been in contact with his sister, Karolina, in Baltinava. He asked now if we would like to be in the country this summer? I asked if we would just visit like a weekend? Papa said, "No, we would live in the country all summer until school starts."

I had never been in the country, but had seen it when we were on the train. It looked so empty. Here and there were a cow, horse, and a sheep. I was doubtful and asked, "What are we going to do in that emptiness? You and Mama will forget us."

"No way," Papa said, "Mama will travel with you, and Karolina has her children. Milda is only about twelve years older than you. Adolph is seventeen, Edward, twenty, Alfred, twenty-six. He is the storekeeper. You could help him in the store." That sounded more interesting.

"Then she has two cows, and plenty of milk to drink, chickens to feed, eggs to gather, and berries and apples to pick," he told us.

It sounded good. Misha listened carefully and asked, "Are we going there now, this week?"

"No," Papa said, "but soon."

Mama thought it would be good for us children, but she was still concerned about Papa. "Who will do your laundry? Who will cook for you? Who will iron your shirts?"

"I was a bachelor for some time before I married you," said Papa, "and I know how to do those things. Sundays, after church, I can go to the officers club for my dinner.

"We will think about that some more," said Papa. They did talk about it, but slowly prepared us and everything for the journey.

At the beginning of June, Papa took Mama and us children to the train station. We had only one carryall for all our things. We kissed Papa goodbye and soon the train took off. We had a nice bench to sit on and a window to see outside. We had to travel many hours.

As we traveled and looked out of the window, the view was nice. We saw forests, green fields and rivers, farmlands, and busy farmers driving farm machinery. Apple trees were in bloom. We passed small towns, clean and neat. People were nice and clean at the small railroad stations. Even the herd on the pasture grazed peacefully.

Blue sky and warm sunshine looked down on everything and everyone was happy because there was peace. We had peace in my country.

When our train reached the station where we had to get out and travel to Baltinava by horse and buggy, I saw one. As soon as we were out of the train a man from that wagon came to us and turning to Mama he said, "You must be Ms. Kesse, and you, Misha, my cousin and you cousin, Ida. Welcome in our corner, but we better get in the wagon, we have a couple of hours on the road to our home. Everybody has been waiting for you. My name is Edward," he said, helping Mama in the wagon and putting in our carryall. "Is this all your luggage?" Edward asked, and took a seat in the wagon and the horse took off.

Edward was silent while driving. It seemed that this horse knew the road. We had been on the train a long time, and this quiet unpopulated, swampy road made us drowsy.

When we reached Aunt Karolina's place and stopped by the gate, we were met by Karolina's dog, Reks, jumping and barking. He was a little under medium size, black with white spots and it seemed happy to see us.

*Daugava River*

Edward was opening the gate and Karolina, Milda, and Alfred were coming to meet us. The house was divided in two parts with a corridor between. We were led to the back part. There were three beds, a sitting room and a kitchen, but Karolina said we would eat all meals in her home.

I don't remember what we had, but the food was good. Misha and I sure liked milk. Reks, the dog, seemed comfortable not only outside but in the house, too. All of Karolina's family were sitting at the table. They were asking questions about our life in Riga, about our school, and about Papa.

Karolina was telling us that some years ago she had a bad time when her husband died. The house needed repairs and Alfred had to leave school to work and restore the family business–the store. They were in debt. "Your Papa came. He had just graduated from Military Academy and helped us out." She wanted us to feel at ease in her home; without Peter's help she would not have this home. They probably would have starved.

Aunt Karolina was very good to us. We really felt loved by her and my cousins. Milda took me under her wings. She worked at the store and took me along "to help her there," she said.

Alfred's store was at the village square about a half-mile from Karolina's home. The road stopped at the square. On the right was a drugstore and next to it was the druggist's house, very pretty with trees and flowers and a white picket fence. The druggist was very kind. There was along his right side a babbling river and a bridge only one horse-wagon wide.

At the bridge, to the left along the riverbank, there was a vacant place, then Alfred's store. It was big. The first floor had hardware, seeds, fertilizers, and farming equipment. Then some foodstuff, even all kinds of candy. The end of the store and downstairs had small and large farm machinery. Alfred was mostly busy with that big stuff.

At the corner of the square the road to the bakery took off to the right and the square continued. There was a post office, then some buildings, and a bookstore. Another road led to a water mill and a butcher shop. That belonged to the Jewish family. Their home was across the street from Karolina's home. One of their daughters was my age and we became friends, and we spent time together on the babbling river outside the village. The deepest water was four feet deep and we had fun in that water. Bramble bushes were growing along the river. They had berries, big, black and juicy, and they were so good. We ate as much as we wanted but never told anybody about it.

I think it was some Jewish holiday and in my friend Reva's home everybody was busy. At midday Reva came running from their home, keeping her hands under her apron. I opened the door to let her in the kitchen. She came to the table, took her hands from under the apron and on the table put her kitchen towel filled with wonderful honey dipped cookies. "You did not think that I will forget you today? I just had to bring these to you. Nobody at home knows it," Reva said.

I found that Papa's brother, Uncle Karl, was living in Baltinava on the same road as Karolina. He had built a log cabin. It was so cozy and beautiful that I still remember it. Just across from the Greek Orthodox Church was another beautiful building surrounded with pretty trees that he had built. Karl sure was a good builder.

He never got married. Papa told us when Karl was young he wanted to learn how to dance because when he was in the village there was music and others were dancing and he wanted to dance too but was ashamed to ask any girl.

So he learned the tune by heart. He picked up a log, went into the room, and hugging the log, he was learning to dance around a room. If it seemed not right before he finished the circle, he went back to the same corner and started again and again. I don't know if he ever learned to dance, but when he finished that beautiful cabin he still was single.

Karolina's one kitchen window was looking out on her vegetable garden, which was fenced in. Her vegetable garden was about 40 by 60 feet and stopped where the house started. It was beautifully neat. Onion beds, carrot beds, beets, cucumbers, tomatoes, bean salad, and tasty pig-beans. When they were almost ripe she baked them in the skins in the oven with butter and sour cream till they were almost melting before you put them in your mouth.

A white picket fence ran along the road in front of the house starting with the post of the vegetable garden until it reached the neighbor's property. Along the fence from the corner of the house she had planted maple trees 15 feet apart and had gravel paths and flower beds. In the middle of the house, the corridor's front door opened to the porch with a roof and two side benches. It was wonderful to sit there and listen to Adolph play on his guitar. We often did it on the weekends.

In the morning Karolina was very busy preparing breakfast for the family. Then the pigs and chickens had to be fed, and she had to take the cow out from cowshed and walk her out on the road to a pasture where there was an agreement with the owners. The cow would be with their herd until afternoon when Karolina would go and bring her back to be milked. Sometimes her daughter helped in the house and milking.

Part of the milk she would let turn sour and then she put it in cheesecloth to strain for cottage cheese, fresh and so good.

Several times when Karolina was leading Browny the cow out from the shed, I was watching her and wishing I could go with her. So my aunt asked me if I would like to come along. Of course I said yes and I liked it.

Later Mama said, "Now since you know where the pasture is for Browny, we could both take her there." Karolina liked the offer and once a day, either morning or afternoon, we did it.

The hardest day was when we did laundry. There was no water in the house. In the yard was a well and with a bucket one could draw out water. In the kitchen she always had a bucket of water. They had no washing machines. All was done by hand and with this size family they had lots of laundry, but eventually all was done and was hanging on long lines in the yard. Mama always was willing to help.

Uncle Karl was always on the go. That summer I only saw him once when he came to Karolina's home and then only for a short time, as he was just leaving.

After he was gone, Karolina gave a pair of shoes to my mother. She had none.

I had not noticed that Mama did not wear shoes in Baltinava to save the ones she came with from Riga. We all had a hard time in Latvia, and Mama was willing to economize to help Papa any way she could, even with bare feet.

Karolina brought out two pairs of socks and gave them to Mama. One pair was cotton and the other wool knit. She said, "The shoes are new, it may be better for your feet to wear with socks on. The woolens are softer, but this is summer and warm; maybe cotton will be better. They are yours. You do as you like."

In the kitchen/family room by the window facing the maple trees and white picket fence was a chair and small table. On that was the Bible, as old and big as Papa's and some knitting things. Misha told me that he had seen our aunt knitting a sock and reading the Bible at the same time.

"She could not," I insisted, "she would lose the stitch and the socks will have holes."

He still insisted that she didn't lose the stitch, the needles, or reading the Bible.

Aunt Karolina was very fond of five-year-old Misha. She loved to have him with her a lot. She even wrote letters to Papa telling him what a good, honest, and bright son he was.

Yes, he was bright. Later he went to technical school. No subject there was a problem to him. He made a couple of inventions. One was something about high speed in airplanes. It was so good that the school bought it from him. He saw some engineering literature, but did not know English. He got some magazines and taught himself and in no time he could read and understand English.

After graduation, his teachers wanted to speak to our father to tell him that his son was an unusual young man, that it seems he is quiet and slow. He passed all examination finals so good that the exam board decided to test him with additional questions. He passed all splendidly.

"You sure have a son there," the teacher in charge said, and others agreed.

At the beginning of September, Papa came after us. He was only there a few days. We all were very happy to see him again.

Karolina and her family were happy too and treated him like a king. The best seat at the table, the best piece of meat, fresh churned butter, and so on. After the meal everybody was sitting and talking. Misha and I lost interest in grown-up talk and went outside.

Later Mama was telling us that Papa found a new apartment for us on Peace Street near the small park. The apartment was on the second floor. It had two large rooms, a real bathroom, and a nice kitchen. Every room had big windows on the sunny side. He also has bought some new furniture and we could play in the backyard.

One day Karolina said that it was mushroom time. Papa heard it and became very lively for he loved to gather mushrooms. He was ready to go.

Karolina and Milda gathered baskets and short sharp knives and some little things for us.

Papa decided that Mama should stay home and Karolina also should stay, because she had plans for a special dinner. So Milda, Papa, Misha, and I took off. We had a wonderful time in the forest. Milda and Papa indeed knew the forest and the places where different kinds of mushrooms were growing. Not only mushrooms but also the bilberry patches were still growing. There Misha spent most of his picking and eating time and half filled a very small basket with berries.

We soon filled our baskets and left for home. "One thing," said Milda, "now we have to clean all the mushrooms, steam, and prepare for winter."

"Will we have none today?" I asked.

"Oh yes, we will. The best, the buttercups," said Milda.

Our summer vacation was ending and we were ready to leave. We arrived with one bag and still had it except it was much fuller. Karolina had knitted socks for Misha, Mama, and Papa, as she said, "for winter, you might need." Then she had a couple of boxes. Papa did not want to take them. He said that he was very grateful to her family for taking us in and providing for his family during the summer but the gifts in boxes were too much.

"Peter, never say to me that I give you or your family too much. When I was in need you helped me. You saved my home, our store, and family. At least take these boxes. There is just my homemade preserves, homemade cheese with caraway seeds, and baked chicken. When you arrive home you will not need to run right away for groceries," said Karolina.

After hugs and kisses, we stepped in Edward's buggy. Milda came along with us to the station. "So that Edward will not be lonesome coming back," said Milda.

At the station, we had to wait for the train and Edward and Milda did not want to leave us alone. Finally, the train came. They carried our things into the train and we were off to Riga. While on the train we saw the sunset painting the fields and forests pink, then it got dark and we were napping. We arrived in Riga early the next morning and we went directly to our new home on Peace Street.

That street was nice and on the right side was a small park, just as Papa said. Then we went to our apartment and all was just as he said. Mama liked it too. He bought beds for us, army metal with four-inch mattresses, a chest of drawers and some other furniture. Then he explained that each of us now had our very own bed, plain but healthy. The army used them to keep the men healthy.

So we settled in the new place. Soon we started school and homework. Since Mama was once a teacher, she knew how important school was for our life so she observed our homework and checked it over. If we did not understand something she explained it thoroughly.

*Doma Square in Riga*

One day we came home from school and the door opened for us not by Mama, but a lady dressed in white and on her apron was Red Cross. She let us in and asked us to be very quiet. I asked where our Mama was and she said that Mama was busy in the room and another lady was with her.

Misha wanted to go and see Mama but was told to wait. He asked what was the name of the other lady. Nurse said, "Midwife." (In Latvian =vecmate=grandmother.) Soon she came and went to the kitchen, then back to Mama. Mama screamed, after awhile she was quiet, and then a baby cried. I did not know it was in Mama's room and my brother and I did not understand. Then all became quiet, only midwife moving from Mama's room to kitchen and the bathroom, back and forth, doing something. The nurse with us in the other room was reading to us, but with one ear I was listening to what was happening with Mama.

I think the midwife in the kitchen was making something, or maybe cooking a big pot of soup. Misha and I were getting hungry but could not ask for anything.

Then Papa came home. We heard him unlocking the door. We jumped up and in one second we were at the door as he was opening it.

"Papa, Papa," Misha was all excited telling "we have a grandmother with Mama all the time and a nurse playing with us. Is Mama sick? Why won't that woman let us see our Mama?"

Meanwhile the nurse and the midwife came from the room into the corridor and told Papa that Mama was now sleeping and asked Papa to come with her in the kitchen, that she had something cooking on the stove. The nurse went into Mama's room and after a short time she came out and took us back to the storybook.

After awhile Papa came out from the kitchen and asked if we were hungry and we said yes and he admitted that he was too. He asked the nurse to set the table in the room and excused himself saying that he had something to do first and he went to Mama's room. The nurse set the table and brought the soup.

We started to eat and Papa came too. He asked how we did today in school, if we got some good grades and so on. He also thanked the nurse for her good work. Then came the midwife and Papa got up and invited her to dinner, pulling out a chair for her, and serving her.

After dinner the midwife and nurse were ready to go. He thanked them for everything and asked for the bill. When they left Papa said to us that he had something to tell us, if we were grown-up enough to listen.

"Yes, we are," Misha and I answered, and we meant it.

First, Mama is all right, just a few days in bed and she will be up. I hope you will be helpful to her. You know that there is a book named Bible. It is given to us by divine Father, God. In that is the first Moses book called Genesis, chapter I, how God created everything.

"Aunt Karolina has that book, too," interrupted Misha. "Yes," said Papa and continued. "That book tells us that He created you, Misha, Mama, me, Ida, Aunt Karolina and your grandfather, grandmother, and all people.

"Now divine Father has given us through Mama a little girl. Do you think you will like her and love and help her?" Papa asked us.

"Can we see her, can we see Mama now?" asked Misha.

"Sure," said Papa, "but you have not answered my question about loving your new sister."

"Yes, Papa," said Misha, "I want to play with her now. I know, Papa, when God gives us something, we never say 'no' to Him, Aunt Karolina told us." So we entered Mama's room, Papa asked if she was ready for visitors.

Mama smiling said, "Anytime, anytime." Everything in that room was clean and on the two plain side by side chairs was a square basket about two feet long by one-and-a-half-foot wide and about one-foot deep. Inside it was a pillow and on that lay the baby asleep. Our sister was born 15 October 1922 in Riga, Latvia. We all were happy for Nina's arrival.

As a child she was good natured, bright, and beautiful. When Papa and Mama took her anyplace, people stopped and admired and gave endless compliments.

With a new baby at home, some adjustments were made. I had to help Mama more. Then I had to watch my sister all the time, even when I was doing my schoolwork. When Mama took her in the basket to the backyard, I was ordered to watch. So no more playing or jumping around for me.

Once two girls who lived in the front house came out and were standing by the door. I saw them and ran to them just to ask if they are coming to play here now or if they were going to the park.

All of a sudden Mama was calling me when I was already coming to the basket.

"You left baby all alone, you know I said never, never to leave her alone!" Mama was saying it very angrily and went back to the apartment. She scared me. I felt all alone. I looked to the sky, then across the neighbor's wall and above that I saw a tall electric pole, and wished to be one, then I could see everything. I was only seven years old.

When Nina was about three months old, my parents decided to baptize her. Mama was a member of the Orthodox (Greek) Church. Papa was Lutheran. The Orthodox Church they selected was small, but nice and very close to where we lived on Peace Street. Across to the left is the corner of Peace Cemetery. Continue that street (I don't remember its name) along the cemetery's fence, about 150 feet to the wide iron gate, go in and you see that lovely chapel.

Alfred, Karolina's son, and Milda, her daughter, were asked to be godfather and godmother. They accepted and came to Riga for the baptism.

We all arrived on time at the Chapel. The priest came in too. He was regally dressed in white headdress with silver and gold embroidery on his coat. A big gold cross lay on his chest. The prayers were said and crosses made on the baby and everybody who participated. With water from a spatial dish the priest made a cross on Nina's head.

When the baptism was over and thanks and gratitudes were expressed, we all walked to our home. Milda, the godmother, carried her goddaughter.

Since the ceremony was not far from our home we reached our place quickly. Mama had left our meal in the oven so everything was warm.

With Milda's help, the table was set and the roast and all other things were placed on the table and the family sat at the table. Everybody felt good and grateful to God for His goodness, love, and blessings to all.

In the morning, Papa left for work. Milda and Alfred were finishing breakfast and were ready to return to Baltinava. Misha and I had a day off from school.

So life was progressing on. We were moving to another apartment and again to another and again and again. I think four or five times. Papa even bought a piece of land in Sigulda. He built a log cabin with two big rooms and a brick stove to keep it warm in winter and to cook a meal anytime, summer or winter. He planted a good-size apple orchard and made a place for vegetables and lots of strawberries. Now we had our own place and cabin where we could go in the summer.

I remember that the grounds were being prepared for the foundation and basement for a two-story house. The architect's drawings were beautiful, but the progress was very slow.

As the summer was coming to an end, September was rushing us to return back to Riga and schools. Mama packed up everything we would need there and it was much. She had big jars with strawberry jam and dried apple slices. Our apple trees were too young to have apples, but Mama was buying and slicing and drying outdoors in the sunshine so we could have them in the winter. In the winter, she cooked apple-prune soup and served that with cream of wheat custard. Sometimes she soaked the apple slices in sugar, then covered cake pastry, added more sugar and baked it the oven. It sure was good.

We were back in Riga and school. Besides our native language (Latvian), a foreign language was added, which was German. Papa decided to help me, so he engaged a tutor. She was German and a retired teacher. Once a week I had to go to her home. It was all right, but since I thought that I would never use it, I did not have enough interest and the progress was slow. I passed the fourth grade, but my parents were not happy.

Papa had an idea. If I could be with a German speaking family for a few months that summer I would easily learn the language. He put an advertisement in the largest local paper: *"A young student would like to work during the summer months as a mother's helper where there are children in the family."*

He received a few responses and he selected one. Mr. Stubendorf answered that his daughter and his son-in-law had a young baby. In the summertime they lived by the river Lielupe in Melluzi, a summer resort. Her husband worked in Riga during the week. His daughter Greta and baby were there alone, plus two girls from her sister. On the weekends the working family all went to Greta's place.

Papa made an appointment to meet Mr. Stubendorf. They lived on Raina Boulevard, across from the park and canal. He was a jeweler and his business was in the Vec-Riga (the old Riga). The apartment on Raina Boulevard was on the fourth floor, five or six rooms, large and nice but old.

It seemed we were satisfied with what we heard and saw. They asked questions of us: Who are we? What kind of work Papa does? If my mama works? I answered, "No, she brings up us, her children, but before she was a teacher."

Mr. and Mrs. Stubendorf liked our answers. We decided to think it over and then let each other know. When we arrived home, everything was told and explained to Mama. Papa and Mama talked between themselves, then it was all settled.

At the beginning of June, Papa took me by train to Melluzi and Lielupe where Greta was living. Papa looked all around, and then left to take a train to return home. The house was two-story, with grounds around, the front faced the street and there was a pine grove and a picket fence. It was landscaped with lots of roses, fruit trees, and berry bushes.

I was given a bedroom with three beds, which I shared with two girls, Ilze and Trude, daughters of Greta's sister. Greta's father and mother, the Stubendorfs, stayed with us only on the weekends.

During the week Greta and I worked in the vegetable garden, cleaned the house, took care of the rose and flower beds, gathered berries and made preserves and sometimes two times a day we went to swim in the river. It was only about 150 feet from the picket fence gate.

Fridays at 7 p.m., we went to the river station to wait for the boat to meet Grandma with baskets with the next week's provisions. When we saw the boat there was such fun and excitement. Grandma was so kind to everybody and she and Greta took me in like their own.

As soon as the boat came and a man tied it to the landing we watched urgently to see if Grandma was on it or if there was just the groceries and only a note from her. When we saw her there was joy and she would come hugging and kissing everybody. We piled all packages in the wheelbarrow and slowly walked home. After opening the gates, Grandma stopped by the rose bed and admired each blossom and the other flowers. When we entered the kitchen she gave compliments to our cleaning and keeping the place in apple pie order.

Greta set a coffee pot on the stove. Grandma took the chair by the window and baby Dieter was in his high chair. Greta and I unpacked packages and stored everything in the pantry.

Then we put a white and red checkered tablecloth on the table and set the table with fresh country butter, honey, jam and fresh bagels, which Grandma just brought from the city and served hot coffee with milk.

Grandma told us all the news of what happened during the week in the city. Greta told her that we had our first carrots and strawberries. Baby Dieter laughed as if he understood all along. Ilze and Trude ran in and out and the setting sun gilded the table, the bagels, and us in gold and rose.

Early on Sunday Mr. Stubendorf would be in the garden working, trimming, and weeding. He had come late Saturday after closing the store.

At 9 o'clock I had to set the table for the family's breakfast in the sunroom. Ilze and Trude helped me. There were soft-boiled eggs, little fluffy pancakes, jams, small smoked fish, lots of milk, and coffee hidden under a quilted warmer to keep it hot.

Grandpa took his place at the end of the table facing us all and the garden pines and the river were seen behind him. Grandma was sitting on his right, Greta on his left, her husband, then the rest of us.

Since there was no church nearby Grandpa prayed, then we had breakfast. After that Trude and I did the dishes. Margaret Stubendorf's oldest daughter, Ilze and Trude's mother, started dinner with Grandma's help sitting under currant trees, cleaning vegetables. We had a big dinner at 2 p.m. After dinner the oldest people took a nap and Dieter also. Some went swimming in the river and others were reading.

In the afternoon we had visitors. We served sandwiches and strawberries. Sometimes we had a clambake, sometimes we crossed the river to the island and just played hide and seek. Then we had a swim in the river and came home tired and hungry.

Usually after such a day we had cottage cheese dumplings with hot brown butter and cinnamon sugar, some berries, egg sandwiches, milk or coffee.

Sunday night we went to bed early because the working family had to return to the city early. With them also went Grandma.

Every evening I had to go for milk, about one mile to a small farm. I often met two young men, students. One of them had a tech school beret. We started to speak, like "good evening." After awhile, we would stop and exchange some words. Then the farmer where I was getting milk introduced us. After that he sometimes walked with me home till we reached the gate.

Once when I was coming with the milk can he met me. About halfway between the house and the farmer, he grabbed me and tried to kiss me. I wanted to get away. Just like that, as an apple from a tree on the roadside, you like to take it, I thought.

I hit him with my fist. The milk can rolled from my hands to the road. He was a foot taller than I. He would not let me go. After some struggle, I got free.

"What's the matter? Girls are for kissing," he said.

"I don't want to see you ever again," I said. His face turned red and he said, "Neither I you."

After that, when I saw him coming, we passed by like two strangers. I hoped we would make up but I was too proud to make the first move.

Summer was ending. I learned German quite well and returned home the first of September. That fall I started my first year in commercial school (high school).

Though I enjoyed summer very much, it was good to be home with my parents and my brother and beautiful sister.

I lived in a city where there was cleanliness and beauty that was hard to find in other cities. Between the canal and the river Daugava and the castle was the old city that was rebuilt in 1002, but research gave evidence that this city is 5,000 years old at least. All the buildings were built with thick walls, solid wooden doors, and windows with small panes. Streets were built with cobblestones with very narrow sidewalks. On the block corners were beautiful gas light posts made of iron. They were a pleasure to look at, especially at night when their greenish lights were on. On some block corners, gas lanterns were hanging from iron scrollwork fastened to the house corner. The roofs were made of red tile shingles.

The names of the streets told another interesting story. A street called "Little Smidth" had plain houses and meant that here lived only young smidts, trade beginners, who were not masters and so did not own the shops.

Shop owners and masters lived on "Big Smidth" Street. So did the Big Tailor and Small Tailor. The Shoemaker lived there also, but those who made shoes were on Cobbler Street. There were Salesmen and Master streets and so on.

The Big Master connected Canal Bridge straight through the city to the river Daugava. That was the only wide street, which had two-way traffic with slow speed and no passing. That old city was and is very busy.

The canal was built to protect the city with drawbridges and was eventually changed for boats with farm products. Then it was changed again to develop the surrounding land which included a beautiful resting place with benches, walkways, trees, lawns, flower beds and a quaint boat station where one

could rent a boat by the hour and row from one end to the other. I have seen high school students in long boats compete in rowing matches. High school and university students loved this sport from early spring to late fall.

On the old city side was a small high hill called "Bastion Hill" with a coffee pavilion on top. Old spreading trees covered the sides of it and it had a path like a ribbon going around and around leading it to the café. Between the trees were small tables where you could sip your coffee or enjoy your ice and look over the city, the canal and the park. Across the canal and park starts the new city with Raina (a poet) Street (boulevard).

From Masters Street you cross the canal bridge and face Freedoms towering monument on Freedom Boulevard. That street runs through the city into the highway on which you can travel through the country, Estonia, Finland, and Leningrad, Russia.

Raina Street runs along the canal and has beautiful trees and four-story buildings. These buildings are mostly apartments. In front are small gardens with evergreens and flowers. Some of them are foreign ambassadorial houses. One whole block is the University. On Kalpaka Boulevard, across the esplanade, is the city Commercial School, which was my school. There were several high schools, trade schools, classical schools, technical schools.

On the other side of the esplanade was the Greek Orthodox Cathedral with its golden cupola and golden cross high in the blue sky. Big trees and shrubs surrounded the Cathedral. Many army parades, song festivals, and other big size events were performed on the esplanade. A skating ring and Christmas markets were there when the season came.

Near that was Elizabeth Street and Verman park and across it the court. It was Peoples Court near the Supreme Court. At the end of Voldemar Street was an old, small but beautiful park with lake and swans called Kronvalda Park.

Then there was Gertrud Street with an art theater, where we saw many good plays. In the center of this street was the old Evangelical Lutheran church of St. Gertrud.

One beautiful June day, when all was in green leaves and blooms, we had a chemistry exam for the entire two-year course. We had one week to prepare for it. I never was good with it. In fact I had only passing grades.

Mr. Caune, our chemistry teacher, told us on the last school day, "Work hard for exam. I may ask you criss-cross the two-year course. If you had just average grades and happen to pick the 'lucky ticket,' you know before I give you top grade for that I will test your fundamentals and hard."

At home I locked myself in Papa's den with the books in the morning at 5 a.m. and I studied till 12 at night, with short interruptions for meals. I started from the beginning and concentrated so hard that steam was coming from my head. I forgot the spring, beauty, everything but chemistry.

Tuesday came and the week was gone. I was to be in school at 11 a.m. That morning I did not touch the books. I dressed, had my breakfast, and left home two hours before the exam. I did not take the bus or streetcar. I just walked.

Now noticing the warm air, the beautiful sunshine, and the blue sky, I walked block after block, bypassing the store windows with their goods. During all that time I took stock of my knowledge about chemistry. With all the time I had studied, I

*A panoramic view of Riga, Latvia, with the Greek Orthodox Cathedral in the foreground*

did not know much. I needed help, as always before and after in my life.

I was approaching the Greek Orthodox Cathedral with its golden onion cupola and cross high in the blue sky. I wondered if this church was ever closed. Wide steps led up to the door of the light stone building. The thick walls of the cathedral shut off any outside noise. In the front hall was a table with candles in all sizes and prices for sale. I could only afford two thin ones and turned to the right niche. There was a painting of Jesus Christ on the cross. I knelt in front of it and set my candles after I lighted them. Kneeling, I prayed for God's help and guidance in my exam.

There were two or three other persons in quiet corners who also meditated in their prayers. Though the space made them appear insignificant, I think they felt the same way about me. In this splendor I felt the Lord's presence.

When I got up and was about to leave, the golden altar doors on the right side opened and a person in blue robe with gold and silver embroidery came out. He had mires burning in a little gold container that was hanging on a chain. He was swinging it left and right sending sweet smelling fragrances flowing in the air.

I did not want to leave the church, but had no choice. At school that day I had a different feeling.

"Did you prepare for all the course?" somebody asked.

The three chemistry teachers and the secretary of the school were sitting in the room. Only one student was let in at a time. Somebody came out. "How was it?" "Who is asking?" "Did you pass?" questions were coming from us who still had to go in.

My turn came to go. "You sure are cool. Don't you worry at all?" somebody asked.

I don't remember if I was worried or not. I just felt that there was a work to do and I would do it, and I went in. On the table was a box with folded tickets. I took one. It was #24 and the question was one I did not go over. Still I did not panic. When I came to the blackboard and started to write formulas, it was like a miracle. I wrote and wrote until the board was full.

"Please, can you tell us what you wrote and what your ticket is about?" asked my teacher.

All of a sudden I had so much to tell about #24. I knew they were pleased with my answers.

"Since you did not do so good the past year, I will ask you a few questions in general," he said.

And did he ask! I answered them all as fast as he asked. Then they were talking between themselves. Finally my teacher said, "Five for exam and four on final, you did excellent."

Five was the highest grade. It was unusual to right away tell the grade to a student. Later he called my father and told him that I had surprised him on the exam.

After the exam we all walked through the park and crossed the canal. Damp, young leaves on the trees sent an aroma. We stopped at the pavilion and bought ice cream. Then we parted in smaller groups.

My girlfriend and I were passing the Cathedral. I knew I had to go in and thank our Heavenly Father. "Can you wait for me?" I asked Alla, my friend. "May I go with you?" she said, "I have never been in this one." "Sure, if you like," I said. We both walked up the steps. Once inside my friend stopped, surprised. I left her there and walked to the place I was before. I knelt and thanked our Father for his help with the exam.

*Latvian National Opera House*

When we walked out, Alla said, "It is beautiful but so strange."

"Believe me, there is nothing strange about religion. Our Lord is wonderful."

"Do you always go there?"

"Especially before exams," I answered.

"Now I understand why you are so good at exams," she said, "but I have so little time and my protestant church is closed all the time, except on Sunday."

Alla took the bus on the next corner and I continued on my way home alone, through parks, rose beds, and busy streets. In reality, I was not alone then nor after. I often felt some presence with me.

Summer was at the door. My brother decided to go to Baltinava and help Aunt Karolina and Alfred. Sister Nina and I would stay home in the city and spend lots of time in the library. We looked at children's books for my sister and other kinds like what was in cinema or popular books translated from other languages. Papa, Mama, and I were all reading and at the end of the week after a good supper we would discuss what we read. It was very interesting.

Then it was July and Alla, my friend and classmate, invited me to visit with her a month or two in Gulbene. Her parents had a business there. After school year ended she returned there. When school started she came to Riga and lived in a rented room. We always liked being together. So I left for Gulbene. She was waiting for me at the station. She told me that her mother left that morning for a health spa in Kemmery and since I would be with Alla and her brother, she feels good that her children would not be alone.

Their business was ready-made clothes and yard materials. In the morning, Alla was in the store but I went to the lake to swim and get a suntan. We went back to the house for lunch, then she went back to the store, and I went back to the lake.

At the lake one day, we met Alla's ex-teacher and her brother Karl Praice, a cadet. I was introduced to them and we sat by the lake and talked. That evening we had a short visit by Karl in Alla's home. When he was leaving, he asked permission to call on me. The next night we had a date. After that we had more dates, but I never fell in love with him. Our acquaintance became friendship and respect and brought me many introductions among his friends.

After graduating from Military Academy, Karl married a teacher from Gulbene and they had a baby. In the summer of 1943, communists from Gulbene deported him and many other officers to Siberia. Karl had so much goodness in him and his soldiers liked him. The communists did not like his popularity. Their code was to destroy all leaders and all possible leaders.

At the end of August I returned home. Everybody was getting ready for school, including my brother and sister.

This year I changed school from night to daytime classes at Riga city's Vila Olava Commercial School. I really liked daytime school better because the teachers and students were alert, not tired like in the evenings. The quality of teachers was better. So I was doing very well and liked the students in the class.

Once walking home from school along Verman Park, I noticed across the street by the university a group of about twenty-five cadets standing and talking. I did not recognize anybody and almost bypassed them, when I heard a voice, "Where are you going?" I looked where the voice was coming from and saw cadet Karl almost on my side of the street and another cadet following him. When I recognized Karl, I stopped.

I don't remember what Karl was asking me or was telling me, it has been so long ago, but as soon as the other cadet had reached him, Karl introduced him as Jahn Buda. Then Karl said to Jahn B., "I know that we have to return back to school, but this little girl I have not seen for some time and wished just to say hello to her."

"Come visit us one Sunday," said Karl, turning to go back to his group.

Jahn Buda, smiling and looking at me said, "We will be seeing you," with an expression as if he did not know what to say or what to think. He then followed Karl to the group. I continued on my way home.

When I arrived home, Mama needed my help in the kitchen. So I changed my school uniform for house clothes and went to help her.

That day we had a very nice dinner and Papa came with two guests, cadets. One was Dzirneks and one was his friend. Dzirneks was Papa's family line, whose family still lived in Malupe, in the home where Papa grew up. So they had lots to talk about their forefathers, their works, their lives and so on. His friend was from a different corner. His family had a bee farm. He told us about the care of the bees, which was interesting.

Our guests had to return to the school and they thanked us for the dinner and we thanked them for their visit with us, inviting them to come and see us again.

Spring was approaching. Politically, many things were going on in the world. Papa was nearing the time to retire. Since Latvia was such a small country, they had to retire higher-ranking officers so the younger generation could advance and be promoted. So his aim at home was to lead us, his children, to think and plan for more education.

My brother Misha knew what he wanted to do—engineering. He was strong in sciences. Always reading, always drawing. When he graduated from school, he had an offer to go to the Ford Company in America. Since Nina was seven years younger than I and so beautiful, nobody bothered her about such things. Maybe we thought that a prince would meet her and marry her. She would not need to work.

Papa suggested that maybe I would like to continue school for higher education, maybe the university, "you are so good with mathematics." I knew what I wanted, but I also knew what my father thought about it and what the answer would be. Thinking about it, why not? And I said, "There is in this city the Arts Academy. You know I like colors, forms, and nature. You now that in arts class I had top grades."

Papa thought for a while, then he finally said, "No daughter of mine will ever go to that school. They all become tramps."

My father was a militarist. There was nothing I could do. A couple years later I met Voldis and found that his birthday was coming. I had seen his rented room and noticed the empty walls so I drew a picture of a statue, a woman standing by the water and dropping a cloth on a stump. It was in pencil. When Voldis saw it he liked it and took it to a framing store. When he went to pick it up it was in the store window and he was told that several people came in the store and asked if it was for sale. Later on in America, I took art classes (at evenings) and participated in an art competition and won top prize.

Riga, our capital city, was growing in size and people in quantity and quality. Papa decided that this summer I must improve my German language. I had not planned it. I did not say yes or no, but I hoped he would forget it.

One Saturday, Jahn Buda called me to go with him on Sunday to the natural science and history museum at Baltezers Lake. Lots of people were there. I felt so good with Jahn, as never before with anybody else. When we were in the last cabin all by ourselves, I wished Jahn would kiss me, but he let the chance get by; I was disappointed. I did not understand why, because I never liked to be kissed by anybody before and did everything to avoid it. Once when it happened I disliked it so much that I said to that

*Latvian Museum of Fine Arts*

boy, "It is nothing, give me a sandwich anytime." The boy's face looked unhappy and I never saw him again.

Papa said one day that he had put an advertisement in the newspaper that I would like this summer to work as a mother's helper where there are a couple of children.

We got some answers. I remember one someplace by the lake. The family had three or four children; one was ten and the others were teenagers. He called them but when he found that one boy was eighteen, he destroyed the letters and said, "That will not do."

One letter was from Majori, a popular summer resort. This was a German family from Berlin. He was a representative for a big firm in Riga. The mother with three children were in the summer cottage in Majori. Mr. Zimmerman was nice when we met him and on Saturday we took the train to Majori to meet him and his family there. His wife was a pleasant woman and the children were a boy, nine years old; a girl, seven; and one was two-and-a-half. Two older children were from his first wife and the little one from the present wife. The family was nice and harmonious. They were a loving family, well mannered, polite. I was given one bedroom upstairs, called "maid's room." It was simple, but nice and with a window, the stairs went up from the kitchen. I liked everything and arrived to work the beginning of June.

Her husband worked all week in Riga, but Saturday and Sunday he was with the family. The weekends gave me more freedom.

I had two schoolmates who lived year-round in Majori, but attended the same commercial school as I did during the school year. One was Zenta, whose father was a fisherman; the other was Veronica. Her father and mother owned a property with several summer cottages for rent. Her father had bad health. Most of the time I was with Veronica, especially on the weekends. We went to the sea to swim and suntan. Veronica's place was very close to the river called Bigriver. Most Majori inhabitants lived by the river all year. The soil was richer than by the seashore and they had vegetable gardens and fruit trees.

Also on summer weekends was a place where local people had built a wooden dance floor. They even had musicians.

What is better in the summer evening than to be out of doors with music and a partner to dance with? Sometimes we both would go there just to listen to the music and watch how others danced.

One time when we went there were many people in a circle around the dance floor and we could not see the dancers. Veronica, being taller than I, could see some over the people's heads. I tried, but couldn't see anything. In front of me was standing a tall man in mounted police uniform. Veronica whispered to me, "Ask him to move aside." I just could not. First, he was a policeman and I was just a kid. Veronica was a little older then I, so she said now, "Just push him aside with your hand!"

"I cannot do that, it's getting late, I'd better go home," I said, and stepped back, but now the man in uniform stepped back asking, "Am I in your way? Why, you can come in front of me!" Veronica looked at him and had a happy smile on her face. I was behind him and did not care to see him. Now she pushed me in front of him, she was now by his side. They started to talk. I did not think that it was right for me to be there and said, "I have to go home!" He right away offered to take me to my home; I did not like it. I think I was afraid of him, a stranger and I said, "I live with Veronica, it is near. We don't need any help."

I was really afraid that he would find where I lived and I did not like it at all.

She and I started to walk away, but he followed us. We came to the gate of Veronica's place. She said goodnight and thanked him for coming with us. Then he said, "We will be seeing each other again." "That would be nice," she said. He departed. I let Veronica into her house and right away felt safe, believing that I would never see him again.

Everything was fine with the Zimmerman family. Often Mrs. Z and I took the children to the beach for swimming and building castles with wet sand. The children liked it very much. After that we went home for lunch and then the children took their nap. Since the boy did not care for a nap, I played some children's games with him or read some children's books.

Sometimes I went to the beach alone and sometimes I joined Zenta. We would sit in the sand and talk. Once when we were walking she noticed two policemen walking ahead of us. As we were nearing them, Zenta said, "I know them." I did not pay attention to her or them. When she called one name, the policemen stopped and turned around toward us, "I want to introduce you to somebody," said Zenta. I wanted to turn back and walk away, but it was too late. She said, "Voldis, meet my schoolmate, Ida." That was the same man that Veronica and I met at that dance by the river. I wanted to vanish in the air.

Voldis, smiling at me, said, "So, your name is Ida?"

I had nothing to say, so why should I talk. Zenta was busy telling them about yesterday's fishing in the sea. They asked if anybody could go and fish if they like.

She was explaining that fundamentally one had to belong to the fishery, because fishing is an industry. If fishing just as a pastime one would have to get a permit. They went on and on.

I had to get away from them and turned around as fast as I could and said, "I just remembered something I have to do," and I ran away from them.

One afternoon I wanted to see Veronica and had time to do that. It was a beautiful day, sunny, and mildly warm. We were sitting on a blanket in the grass and talking. Then we saw Voldis by the gate, but it looked like he would pass by it. Veronica noticed him too and asked if he was in a hurry. He answered that this was his day off. We noticed that he did not have on his uniform but blue pants and white tee shirt. So she asked him to come in, saying, "We still have a corner on the blanket for you to sit on."

I realized that Veronica liked him, so I decided that because she was my friend and she liked him, I had better be civil to him. We were talking about horses. He loved horses and had them on the farm in Cesis, then in the army where he had served three years. Now he worked with horses, that is saddle horse, grooming them and riding in police escorts and in sport riding over obstacles, in hurdle-races, and steeplechase.

Veronica asked, "Did you ever get a prize? Maybe a million dollars?"

"The million dollars, no, but prizes, yes," Voldis said.

I do not remember how it happened, maybe I pushed him, but he was flat on the blanket on his stomach and I said, "You will be my horse," and I sat on his back, calling, "Jump! Jump!" Veronica was laughing; he was laughing. I stopped, rolled off his back and said, "I am sorry, but I don't have oats to feed my horse, so no more riding." We talked for a while then I had to go back home. He insisted on walking home with me, because he lived that way. That's what he said.

About a week or more later I went to the sea for a swim. There were very few people on the beach, though it was warm and sunny. I liked it when the beach was so vacant. I had on my swimsuit and a skirt, took off the skirt and sat on the warm sand, enjoying the view of sky, the sea, and the constantly moving waves, ripples, and billows. Then I went in the water. When I had enough and went to get my skirt to put on, Voldis was standing in front of me. Needless to say, I was surprised. He did not have his uniform on, just pants and a tee shirt. He asked me if we could talk, I said that I had had my swim and had to go home and stepped back to go. He asked very kindly, "Just ten minutes?" He did not move from his place, so I said "ok".

He asked me why I disliked him so much. I said, "You are a stranger. You are grown up. I am just a schoolgirl. I came here to Majori to work as a mother's helper. They are good people."

"Why do you have to work like that? I know that you go to commercial school," he said.

"I am not working for money, I just get a couple lats a week, but I wan to learn German language, so that I can read all various kir s of books," I answered.

"You like books to read?" he asked, "I like to read, too." I was surprised. "You like to read?" "How about tomorrow, after lunch, here on the beach," he was saying. I was not sure, but was feeling some interest. I answered, "Ok, maybe, if I have time."

Then he said, "I go to night school in the winter to improve my education."

Since Veronica, my dear friend, liked him so well, I went to the beach. He was on guard duty along the coast. We walked and talked. We stopped by the ice cream cart and he bought me an ice cream. After licking ice cream and walking along the beach for an hour or more, I had to go home. He thanked me for coming and said, "Hope we will meet again." I said, "Maybe, thank you for the ice cream," and left.

After that we were seeing each other here and there. The time came for me to return home to Riga. The Zimmerman family was also returning to Riga and the children to school. Voldis had to stay in Majori till the end of September.

Summer was gone and I was back home. It was so good to see my family and be together. Mama was preparing a big family dinner. There were questions and talk about our summer experiences. I talked about Voldis and Veronica. My sister, now ten years old, was asking if Voldis was good looking. I said that Veronica thought that he was. My sister again asked, "How does he look?" I said, "Tall, but Veronica is tall, too." "Will you see him again?" "He is with the police, with horses," was my answer to sister.

The dinner was over and the day was gone. Tomorrow was Sunday and we were planning to go to church. Papa was a member in Doma Cathedral. He was Lutheran and also a member on the board. He took church very seriously and also was passing his test understanding about God and life to us. Through all my life I found that this preparation for us was the best and strongest foundation in our living.

Since we were again in school I heard from my friends, Jahn Buda, Karl, and some others. Jahn reminded me not to forget that soon they would have a dance at the military school. I was so happy to hear from him. When the time came, he called to say that he would send a cadet after me. He could not come himself because he was on duty.

What should I do? What to wear? What would other ladies wear, especially the faculty ladies? I was told not to worry about it, even the dress length was not important.

I had long hair and went to the beauty shop. They shampooed and plaited my hair into a braid on one side of my head, then wound it like a crown. Then my beautician took from her vase two pieces of Lily of the Valley and put it in the braided crown.

At home I put on my taffeta white, full-length skirt and on top a taffeta blouse, checkered green-blue, gold, and cream with full sleeves to the elbows, mandarin collar, buttoned in the back with extended pleats about seven inches. The blouse had a silky, shining glitter. My family said it was beautiful. Soon Karl came after me.

The academy was about three blocks from my home so we walked. It was still sunny and was warm.

"Jahn is delayed," said Karl, "he will join us shortly. You know he is cadet-corporal, more duty."

We went to the school cafeteria and took seats at a four-person table. Jahn came with another cadet. After supper we walked upstairs. There was a large hall with many windows. In one corner the floor was elevated for a stage where there was a piano and the band.

When the colonel, his Mrs., and faculty members were upstairs the band started to play. Then he started the polonaise. First we went one circle in that room then down the stairs to the second floor where we meandered in the cadets' bedrooms, which were large, all beds made up clean and neat. Then we meandered down stairs to the kitchen. There were big and small pots and frying pans, clean, and shining like silver, as if they were just bought and never been used. The walls were white and the floors were cream color tile. Then the polonaise meandered upstairs, where the band was playing and we waltzed.

After that Jahn did not dance. We were standing by the window and talking. Faculty members' wives were sitting by the wall and sometimes dancing. I did too when some cadets asked.

At about ten p.m., the band members picked up their instruments and left. In a little while some cadets with violins in hand and other instruments came on the stage and with a piano player they began playing dance music. One or two couples started to dance. Then a nice tall cadet came to Jahn asking him permission to dance with me, and we danced.

I danced with that cadet one circle around, and then at the same spot where we started, another cadet came and touched my partner's shoulder. My partner left and I danced the circle with the other. Then came the next cadet and touched his shoulder and my partner left. Then I asked, "What is going on? I have to know."

"I cannot tell you," my partner said, "you will be angry with me."

"I promise not to be angry, but I have to know," I said.

"We wanted to dance with you all evening, but we did not. Then the band left, so we organized our own band and agreed that each of us can dance with you one circle," he said.

"Look," I said, "there are so many ladies sitting along the wall. Why not dance with them?"

"Be not angry," he said, "we wanted to dance with you."

"I am not angry, but you are now the fourth cadet I am dancing with. How many of you are there?" I asked.

"We are forty-two," he said.

I counted in my mind forty-two means thirty-eight more circles and I said, "I am not angry but it was a long day for me. I am thankful to you and all the other cadets, you all are so kind to me, but I am tired."

"So you want to finish with this circle?" he asked.

"Yes," I said, "it is time for me to go home." We finished that dance and said goodbye and I went to Jahn so I could go home.

Monday we all went to school again, and we all were very busy. Papa was in charge of armories near Riga and some nearby places. When the police obtained some small arms and other weapons he had to go there and collect them. One time he brought three or four. It was late, after 7 p.m., so he brought them in the dining room and put them on the table. They were pistols, big, gray and ugly, but there was a small one with an ivory handle. It looked handmade, with cut-in ornaments.

I said, looking at it with admiration, "It is so beautiful."

Papa's face was somber looking. He called my brother and sister and me into dining room.

"These are weapons and are evil. They do only harm to anybody. You say 'beautiful'. Evil, small arms and bullets are not beautiful and will never be, and anything what harms anybody is not good. Do not ever touch them, not even with a finger. They are stupid and bad things."

I looked at the ornaments on the ivory handle and did not see any beauty anymore, only repugnance. The same disgust was on my brother and sister's faces.

The next morning father left for work and took the weapons with him to put in the armory.

We children grew up not having any interest in weapons as protection or hunting tools.

Papa was talking again about retirement. Latvia, being a small country, had to prepare opportunity for progress to the younger generation.

He was reading in the papers so he could make some choice about what to do. There was one offer to participate as co-owner of the watermill. It was out in the country by a medium size river. The possibility was that we would have to move there too.

Papa did not like that part because of schools and education. In Riga, the schools were very good. Educating his children was very important to Papa.

He decided we would stay in Riga, but he would go to the mill and come home over the weekend. So for a while we lived that way. The business was doing well. After a couple of years, Papa's co-owner bought him out.

Then Papa found a little milk store for sale. It was only two-and-a-half blocks from our home along Ziedona Park. It was opening before five in the morning and closed at five in the afternoon or before if the milk was sold. His helper was Mrs. Menna, a widow lady. She knew the business well and the surroundings too.

Everything was going fine. Usually she was opening the store in the morning. She had an apartment about a hundred feet from the store. One morning Papa arrived a little past five. The milk cans were outside by the door, but not Mrs. Menna. He unlocked the door, brought the milk cans and all other products inside. He assisted the customers with all that they asked for. People were asking for Mrs. Menna and he answered, "She will be here later." By four o'clock all the milk and other products were sold. Papa closed the store and went to see Mrs. Menna.

He knocked at the door, but there was no answer. He knocked again—no answer. He waited, nothing. He turned the doorknob.

The door was not locked. He opened the door more and called, "Mrs. Menna, are you home?" No answer. He called her again and as he turned to leave he heard some kind of noise. She had a one-room apartment and kitchen. He was in the hall and the door into the room was opened. He moved to the door and saw that the room was empty. All the furniture was gone except for one broken chair and one box like we used in the store for apples. Then he saw in the corner on the floor a coat, a blanket, a corner of a pillow and something moved under it.

He said, "Mrs. Menna, are you sick?"

No answer. He uncovered her face a little. Her face was hot. He thought that she had a fever and decided to help her.

He knocked at her neighbor's apartment door and said that he thought that Mrs. Menna was sick. He asked if they knew her doctor, then asked permission to use the telephone to call the doctor. Then he asked what happened to her furniture. "Where is it? Why is the elderly lady sleeping on the floor?"

The story came out. There came a Baptist minister, Thompson, from America, preaching that he can forgive all sins with Jesus blood and then they will have everything that they wish for.

So people started to give what they had, furniture, sewing machines, and so on. They had little money. Papa asked what that preacher did with those things? They took those things to the backyard and the preacher vanished. "Well," Papa said, "we just have to go and bring some of the things back to her place."

Papa and some neighbors brought her bed and other things back to her apartment, set them up and put Mrs. Menna in the bed. The doctor came and took care of her. Papa found Mrs. Menna's friend and brought her in to stay with her until she was well.

That evening Papa came late home. He was very tired. After the meal and several cups of hot tea with lemon and sugar he was refreshed and told us the experience of Mrs. Menna's place and the Baptist preacher's promises unfulfilled.

I wanted to ask questions about that stupid preacher, but Papa said, "It's late. Tomorrow is a working day for me, and school day for you." But, seeing my disappointment, he said, "We will talk about it."

After a week Mrs. Menna came back to work and her friend came with her to help. They were doing fine. Papa had a long talk with Mrs. Menna and her friend about many things.

With his kindness to people and his life's experiences, everybody liked to hear him and many people's lives had changed for the better.

Papa had many friends, some military, some not. Some were well educated, some were not, some were Jews, and some practiced other religions. Colonel Bruveris, a fine family man, living just two blocks from us was retiring. His family had a big, prosperous farm. So Papa and Bruveris had some plans. They decided to buy the tobacco factory "Riga." Colonel Bruveris was the president; Papa was vice-president.

They were buying tobacco from several places. I remember from Greece, Egypt, and Virginia in the USA. I am sure there were other places, but I don't remember. They also bought a good size farm in Olaine and raised tobacco there. They built a barn in which to dry it when harvesting. Their main product was cigarettes. Their market was in New York and other places. They employed in the season 2,000 people and off-season 1,000. Most of them were female. Many had families at home, but it was not easy to get food. The business was doing fine.

I was about eighteen years old and I told Papa that I would like to join our Lutheran church in Doma Cathedral. He agreed. I had to take a class in the church for two weeks taught by our minister Terinsh. In that class I asked the minister several questions.

"When we die, where do we go? What really happens to our life?"

"We don't know," said the minister, "maybe after we die, we will find out."

"Why can we not know that now while we are alive?" I asked.

"Only God knows," he said, and immediately changed the subject.

I still wanted to ask more like, "Why God created death? Why it is not in the Bible?"

But Minister Terinsh turned away to the side. I was sitting in the first row.

Mama and I went to store to select and buy material for a dress to wear on confirmation day. We selected white chiffon material and white shoes. Then she took me to a dressmaker. The fashion we chose was a simple, long, full skirt and three-quarter sleeves.

The day of confirmation came and it was a beautiful sunny, early spring day. We went to church on time. Minister Terinsh met us. When the service started he grouped us two by two, girls first and boys the same behind the girls and he led us to the altar.

After the service and hymns were sung, we were grouped the same by two. We were twelve girls and ten boys.

I was put in the first row with another girl on my left, Anna. She was taller than I. Then the boys and our minister were at the end. We were walking towards the main door.

We were just about in the center of the church. The people were standing. There was one man standing to my right, he was so clean, middle age with a gentle, sweet smile saying, "Be thou blessed," and he made a cross on me. Anna asked, "What did he say to you?" We both looked back, but there was no man anymore, nobody. Just a second before the rows were full with men, women, and children. They had vanished. After that I never saw Anna anymore.

It has been many years since that happened but I see that man and hear his blessing as if it were yesterday. Outside were our friends and families waiting for our coming with greetings, flowers, and presents.

Mama had prepared a wonderful dinner for this occasion. Most of it was done ahead of time. We had some invited guests. Voldis came and gave me a gold bracelet. I still have it and it is beautiful. My father's friend, Colonel Blumental, had come too, bringing me a present but it has been so long ago I don't remember what it was. He had a degree in pharmaceutical chemistry and had a large apothecary in Old Riga. He used to be in Russia; in tsarist time he was Ceremony Master in Tsar's palace.

He told us interesting stories about Tsar, the family and endless lines of visitors. So many people wanted to see or visit with Tsar. So they wrote the letters. Colonel Blumental was in charge of that. He read the letters, answered them and then appointed time when each one had to meet Tsar. When they arrived he started to prepare them for the reception. For thirty days they learned manners–how to enter in the room, when and how to take the seat at the table, when and which spoons, forks and knives to use and so on.

If they could do all perfectly in thirty days, then one had a chance to see the king, but if not they had to go back home. After a year they would have another chance. If one failed the second time in thirty days, learning could not come anymore.

"Does really somebody fail after sixty days learning?" my brother asked.

"Yes, many," said Colonel and got up, "it is getting late; tomorrow is a workday. Time to go home."

After we thanked everyone for the presents and for their visiting us, our guests left.

Everybody was tired and Mama said she would do the dishes tomorrow. So we all were ready go to bed.

With the spring coming, summer work was on our mind. Misha, my brother, found work on a small ship. It was navigated on the lakes Yugla and Kisezers. It was just a plain job as a deck hand, mostly delivering timber, but he liked it and the pay was good. He started to save some money. He hoped to save enough to buy an accordion.

As we were living in an apartment house with many apartments, we communicated with some younger people who also lived there. Misha had heard an accordion being played from someone's apartment open window.

Eventually he found the young accordion player and they became friends. With this friendship Misha had an opportunity to learn about that instrument and to play it and play it well. We loved to listen when Misha played on the borrowed instrument. With time he saved enough and bought an accordion. He was so happy as I had never seen him before.

The next year Misha graduated from State Technical School. He had some kind of plan, but he did not tell me. It was not long before we found out, and it sure messed up my brother's life forever.

He had two friends attending the same school as he. They also graduated with him. They, too, were living in the same apartment complex, only in the back. They had been friends for a long time and they had some secrets. They found out that merchant marine ships take on men as workers just before they navigate to England or America and so on. That night Misha was to go with them. Stankevich and the other boy waited a little while and then took off for the ship.

That night my brother went to bed early. I was reading in my room. I went to the kitchen for a drink. Sister was reading in the living room. It was late. When I looked at the big clock on the wall it showed more than two hours later.

"It's wrong. It cannot be that late!"

"No," she said, whispering and putting a finger on her lips, "Papa did that to other clocks, too."

I wanted to change them but sister shook her head and said, "No, Papa said no." I still wanted to change them. It was Misha's choice to go. He was grown up. Why did Papa not want to let him go? I felt bad, very bad, but we were taught to obey our father.

In the morning brother got up and went to the ship, but it had left. The ship reached America with both his friends. They found good jobs, married, and had a home and families.

My brother was always helping somebody, always forgiving, never complaining. He went to the army for three years and was stationed in Daugavpils, close to the Russian border.

Voldis was after me to get married. His work was very demanding. Long hours. I had noticed his jealousy. Then he explained that when we were married he would know that I belonged to him and he would not worry about losing me. We talked about marriage and I said we would have children.

He answered, "Why? We don't need children. Many people marry, but don't have children. They have more fun without children." No, he definitely didn't want children.

Since we had talked about his opinion regarding children previously and his mind about it had not changed, I was getting angry and said, "You do not understand, if you do not want children, you do not have to marry. You just bring a woman from the street, jump with her in the bed, do what you want to do with her, and then kick her out on the street. You don't have any responsibility to her, if that is what she wanted from you."

"I love you and want you," he said.

"I want a family. A real family with children and husband and real home for us," was my answer. I stopped seeing him.

I entered the housekeeping school. Besides housekeeping and cooking, we had other valuable subjects about health, diets, bookkeeping, finance and so on. Our school was selected to prepare dinner and serve for the president's party in the castle.

I graduated from that school after one year. The school prepared a graduation party with dinner and invited guests and we finished that with two hours of dancing. Everybody was so happy. The guests were thankful for dinner and all asked to be invited again.

I found employment in the office of Tradesman Guild (historical organization). There were builders, blacksmiths, bakers, tailors, dressmakers, confectioners, cabinetmakers, carpenters, butchers and so on. To become a member of this guild you choose one of the trades, pass the exam, continue the second year as zellis (journeyman), pass the exam, then the third year pass an exam and you become master. They take you in the guild and you can open your business. My work was interesting and I liked it.

Voldis wanted to marry and agreed to have a family. We were married in the Doma Cathedral Octo-

*Voldis and Ida were married in the Doma Cathedral in October 1939*

ber 30, 1939. The wedding was nice, but small. At that time we had (country) problems with the Russians. They were "contracting" to use our Liepaja harbor, because the Baltic Sea harbor never froze.

By that time Misha was in the Latvian army and had little time left from his three-year service. He was driving a heavy-weight tractor for the army.

I had left some money in Papa's table drawer, about 40 lats ($40.00), for Misha; he had called, promising to drop in. Mama was gone, but Nina, our sister was home. I told her about Misha coming and asked her to give him the money. He told me that he had none. Later I found from Nina that our brother came, but she did not give the money as I asked. She bought lace under panties for herself and spent the rest of the money too.

Papa was not at home. So brother left with not a cent in his pockets and only four days was left from his army duty, but we did not see him. Russia took him. For 18 years we had no knowledge about Misha.

Papa found for Voldis and me a three-room apartment in an apartment house at the corner of Artillery and Marijas Streets, on the third floor. My family gave us furniture. It happened this way.

One morning Mama said to me that she had to go someplace and if I could come with her, afterward we could go to the city market to buy our groceries. I thought she needed my help. So we went, crossing a couple of streets. Then she said, "There, down the stairs we go." So we did and it was a carpenter's workshop. There were all kinds of furniture. She would stop by some pieces and look and then ask my opinion. There was an elegant, beautiful desk, then a couch and a bookcase with glass doors. This all was so beautiful.

"What do you think?" Mama asked in a careless way. "We'd better go to the market."

That's what we did, but she did not mention our visit to the carpenter's shop while we walked home with groceries.

In the meantime our apartment was repaired and painted. Now and then I would drop in. I noticed the comfortable bathroom and good size tub and hot water tank. The kitchen had an electric stove. A window was at the end of the room and was the perfect place to put a small table for two to have breakfast in the morning. I found there was one more room. Through a door from the kitchen was a cozy maid's room with a window.

Voldis and I went to look for some furniture. First we would buy bedroom furniture, maybe a dining room table and chairs. We could not find what we wanted in ready-made furniture, so we elected to have custom made from Karelian birch a wardrobe, beds, and all the other bedroom furniture.

Finally our apartment was clean and shining. Voldis learned that our beds were ready too and all could be delivered when we wanted. Since Voldis was working that day we chose the next afternoon.

We went to the apartment a little earlier and walked from room to room. When we opened the door to the room next to our bedroom we were so surprised. The room was furnished. It had a sofa, desk, bookcase with glass doors and a couple of chairs. On the desk was a card, "Welcome home, Papa, Mama, and family."

That was the same furniture I saw when Mama and I were going to the market and we stopped by the furniture shop. It showed me how much my parents loved my husband and me, although Papa was on pension.

When our new bedroom furniture was brought in and placed the way we liked, we rushed to my family's place to thank them for the present.

"That's what you liked in the furniture store! We hope you still like it!" Mama said, "Dinner is ready, we hoped you would be coming."

The dinner was wonderful and we celebrated our new life and apartment with my family. After dinner we were all sitting and talking about Easter and how we would celebrate it. Misha said, "Wouldn't it be nice if all people in the world would celebrate it at the same time?"

"Maybe some day they will," Papa said.

"But in old days, when you grew up the people were more religious, they all attended church," my sister Nina said.

"Not exactly so," said Papa, and then he told us the story about what he saw as a nine-year-old boy when living on the farm.

"Oh, this farm was nearby. You could count all the apples on the trees in the fall. You certainly could recognize every member of the family. That farmer always attended church, but people were talking that they have seen that he never swallowed the special Holy Communion bread at the church, and as soon as the preacher turned away, he would take it out. What he really did with it nobody knew," he said.

On that particular Easter morning when my father was nine, they had a swing at the apple orchard and they were enjoying it when they heard a shot. They all looked in that direction and saw the neighbor at the edge of his apple trees with a gun. Something white was hanging on the trees. In the middle of the gun smoke stood Christ, just as He is seen in the books.

The neighbor threw the gun and ran away. My father and the other boys wanted to know what that was all about.

When the vision vanished, they ran to the place. On the branch was hanging a white kerchief with a couple of bullet holes and in it they found what was left of the Holy Communion bread.

"What happened to the man?" my brother asked.

"As I recollect," Father said, "one famine after another followed that family and their place burned down. We never saw them anymore."

It has been so many years now since I heard that story. My children are all grown up, but I could never forget it. I still feel sorry now, as I did then, that the man had never learned to love God. In his ignorance he blamed our Heavenly Father, God.

I did not feel so good and went to see the doctor. He asked some questions. I answered. Then he said for me to come back in thirty days.

Thirty days later I did go to see the doctor, but not to him. I went to see Dr. Peter Abele, obstetrician, and he said that we would have a child. That was such good news for me and for the family. When I told the family, Mama happily said we would have to get a baby cart.

"No, not just a cart. We have to get a perambulator," Papa said. "First we have to get a bed. Not just any kind. It must be a good one and beautiful. I know somebody, a craftsman. I have seen his work. It is beautiful."

"Maybe we will not be able afford it," said Mama. "Well, he is a good man," said Papa, "all things are possible with God."

"You sure have proved that, time and time again," said Mama.

Voldis, my husband, was even busier in his work as a criminal investigator with the police. The working hours were long. Often he worked on the weekends, too. Most nights he was home, but he left early in the morning, sometimes before breakfast. When I was just waking up he was leaving.

Since about September 1939, we saw Russians on the street and shopping in the stores. The men were in uniforms.

The talk was that they would use our harbors here and there. Papa was still working in Riga's Tobacco factory with Colonel Bruveris, but when we went shopping in the stores for sugar, butter or clothes, they asked for our passports and stamped on the last pages the shopping date, the things purchased, and the prices we paid.

At that time the city markets had plenty of food to sell. There were all kinds of goods in the stores too. Russians were buying a lot. Eventually stores became empty.

I remember the time to have my baby was coming closer. I needed baby things: clothes, linens, blankets, but if the store had it, they could not sell to me. We had to go to city hall, ask for a permit to go to the stores and if they had what we wanted to buy, then we could buy, but if not, we had to go to another store, hoping to find it there.

There were lots of people waiting in line at the city hall. Some were old, pensioners, and not well. I was in my eighth month of pregnancy, but was not showing so much and the people tried to push me out. I had to tell that I was near the time to have my baby. Then they left me alone, but still argued among themselves that I did not look pregnant. Since I had my doctor's note, when it was my time to go in, I received a permit to go shopping. I was surprised at how empty the shelves were in the large stores. Then I started to look for less popular stores and found almost all that I needed, but they, too, did not have much.

April 20 was such a nice sunny day. Voldis was working and about dinnertime I went to see Mama. Her apartment was on the fourth floor. I felt so light and joyful, I felt like flying. I was running over a couple of steps at the time. I felt so free. That evening after supper with Papa and Mama I left for home alone, thinking maybe Voldis would come home, but he did not.

About 9 p.m. I was preparing for bed. Suddenly I felt water running down my legs. What now? Since it was near 10 p.m., all the doors and gates to the street were locked by government order. I knew I had to go. I called Papa and told him that I was coming and also told him about the water.

He said to come right away but stay down by the door. He would get a cab and call my doctor and would meet me downstairs. In no time Papa and the cab were there and they took me to Voldemar Street to my doctor's clinic. I was put in a room with my bed facing a huge window through which I could see only dark night sky. I was there many hours. The doctor came, then a nurse, now and then.

April 21$^{st}$ was ending. My doctor came and said we could not wait any longer. I had no pain. I pushed and he pushed. On April 22, 1942 at 2 a.m. my baby Maija arrived.

But the placenta, the afterbirth, did not come out. The doctor tried to get it out but with no success. He explained that he would have to operate because the placenta immediately dissolves and is a most dangerous poison.

The doctor, midwife, and nurse were preparing me for surgery. They gave me an injection to put me to sleep. Then seemingly I fell asleep, but I found myself across the room standing by the door. I saw the midwife and nurse standing by that bed-table doing something, but I was not there. I could see the table was empty. I saw only the doctor's back. My arms still were on my chest. I was telling them "I am not there anymore but here (by the door)." They did not pay attention. So with my hand I pinched my arm and felt the pinch and thought, I am alive! I looked then to the right, the sky in the window was light yellow. There was no night darkness, but it was 4 a.m. in the morning in April.

Then I woke up. The midwife was asking me, "What did you see, what did you see?" I answered, "Why are you waking me up? It was so good. There was a door on the right," I said, looking for the door, but I did not see any. It was a solid wall.

"How do you know? There used to be a door there a long time ago," the nurse said.

"I am glad," said my doctor "that we still had that German adrenaline injection (the last one). It always works."

Later, the midwife said that the doctor first used a local injection to bring me back, but it did not help. Then he used a German injection, which was the last German one they had at that time in his clinic.

I will never forget what he said, "It always works." His words sounded so powerful. Then later when we came to America and I was led into Christian Science, I understood why that German adrenaline injection was so effective. He had an absolute, total trust in it and it became effective.

My doctor, Peter Abele, later came to America and lived and worked in New York many years. He passed away and left his inheritance to the American Latvian Association.

In 1962, I obtained the book *Science and Health with Key to the Scriptures* by Mary Baker Eddy. I read it and understood why I am alive. This book also explained to me that absolute trust in something we do is good and positive expectation with no grain of doubt will bring the right result.

Dr. Abele never married because he had diabetes and an apparent belief that diabetes was an inherited disease in the family.

I still tried to get back to that "door" where I felt so good, but the nurse would not let me continue to sleep. Finally by dinnertime she explained that my doctor ordered her not to let me sleep because I may not come back. Then she also told me that I had a healthy and beautiful seven and a half-pound daughter that I would have to take care of.

I did not remember anything, why I was there, anything about the birth, the baby—my baby. Later they brought her to me. She was a beautiful child; she even smiled to me.

Still then and for many, many years when life here was hard, I had that feeling to go back to that "door." I think that feeling of duty for child helped me to live in this world.

Later Papa and Mama came to visit me in the clinic. After more than a week Voldis came and took me home to our apartment.

He still was very busy with work and soon left. So there never was any help from him, but I was happy with my baby. She was such a good baby and slept at night. Papa found an elderly lady to come and help me take care of the apartment and my baby.

Mama came often, even brought meals. Then one day my parents brought a beautiful perambulator for my baby. It was almost impossible to buy anything in the empty stores. Through a friend Mama found that a couple was selling the perambulator—not for money, but for a good size smoked ham. Their child did not need it any more, food was scarce and the ham would help them. Yes, the wartime years of 1942 and 1943 were hard and limited living in many ways.

As he said he would, Papa gave us a new custom-made baby bed. It was a very safe and beautifully carved ironwork so that our child could be visible from all sides.

Our little girl Maija was baptized in Doma Cathedral in Riga. We had guests in my apartment and served dinner. Then we had music and dancing. I think at that time she was six months old. Our guests were family, friends, and some were dear workers from Papa's tobacco factory.

There were presents, too, including a couple of beautiful oil paintings and some toys to play with. And there were three large-size fabulous cakes. One was from the famous Schwartz confectionery. People were happy and harmonious. Maija was put to bed about 8 p.m., but the guests stayed and we shared interesting stories. By 10 p.m., our guests left to go home.

Colonel Bruveris and Papa's business, the tobacco factory, was doing quite well. They were importing tobacco from other countries: from Virginia USA, Egypt, Spain, and others. They used local tobacco, too, but still the need for more tobacco was increasing because the demand for cigarettes and cigars was growing. The German Army and Soviet Army were coming and going to Russia then, blundering around to and from. Lots of them that were stationed in and around Riga used a lot of tobacco products.

The men then decided to use the farm for the factory's benefit to help the workers. So they planted vegetables and raised some pigs, cattle, and chickens. They employed a couple, a man and his wife, to manage the farm.

They employed Russian war prisoners on the farm who lived there till all the crops were harvested. In the factory kitchen they had a housekeeper in charge of cooking breakfast and dinner for the workers. The meals were very good and very reasonable. Workers who had families at home could order dinners ahead of time and after work they took home a hot meal.

One Sunday Papa said, "Today we will take a train to the farm." So Papa, Mama, Maija (she was about sixteen months old, very alive and strong in her walking), and I went to the station. On the train Maija was "fastened" to the window watching the scenery glide by.

The farm was very nice, well kept and well organized. We saw the new tobacco barn and the main house, which had a large kitchen with a big table where many people could comfortably sit. There was a cattle barn and poultry house and pigs in the pigpen. There was a bathhouse and another longer new house. Our hostess said the new house was for Russian war prisoners who were working there. They have beds and tables and all that they need for living.

When Papa asked about their work and their attitude, she said they were hard workers, kept their places clean, helped in the kitchen, in the garden, and were always ready to help with the animals. They had told her that if it could be possible they hoped to stay on this place even after the war.

When we finished walking among the apple trees and currant bushes and other berry bushes, we were asked to come in the kitchen and on the table at one end a meal was set for us.

There was tossed salad with dressing, bacon and eggs, cottage cheese, new boiled potatoes with skins, milk, linden blossom tea, and country bread. For dessert we had cream of wheat topped with currant juice jelly (kiselis). We sure enjoyed this simple country meal.

Maija had no time even to take a nap. She was busy, holding her on with the grown ups.

As soon as we reached our train to return to Riga, Maija, sitting in her grandmother's lap, fell asleep and woke only when we were at home. Papa was very satisfied with the farm.

The Germans were getting more and more involved in our daily living, especially going to the opera, theatre, best restaurants, museums, and so on.

Not too long after our visit to the farm my baby and I were visiting with Mama. It was the end of the week and she wanted to make a special dinner. All was ready; the table was set and waiting for Papa to arrive at about 5 p.m. He didn't come, neither at 6, 7, or 8 p.m. We were worried. In the morning there was no news.

Mama called Colonel Bruveris at the factory, but they too did not know his whereabouts. So my husband went to the police to find out about Papa. He learned that Papa was arrested by Germans and put in the police jail. He could not find the reason.

After a day or so, Voldis attempted to do more investigating and at least had permission to see Papa in jail. They talked a little. Papa said that he had been questioned, had answered all, but still did not know the reason for his imprisonment. When Voldis asked who arrested him, he said, "Germans." Voldis promised to investigate more.

Voldis told how bad looking that cell was and that there were many men in it. It seemed that the case had nothing to do with Latvian police.

I think Papa was in that cell about three weeks. Voldis finally found that there were some Germans in charge to control cars and tractors on the highway connecting the city and other highways in use with the war zone. What they were looking for we still did not know.

Papa's workers were also worried about not seeing him around for such a long time. One of Papa's young secretaries, who knew the German language well, had an idea to solve the problem. There was talk that any woman, if she was pretty, could get anything she wanted just by talking to a German soldier. She found a higher-ranking officer who was responsible for army road transport.

She learned that there was a tractor on the road approaching Riga with hay on top. The soldiers wanted to stop it, but the tractor driver did not want to stop because it was a private factory tractor and had nothing to do with the German army. Latvia was not in war.

The soldiers insisted. For peace sake, the driver stopped the tractor. Soldiers looking under the hay found a pig. They ignored the driver's explanation about it being the tobacco factory's property. The driver did not understand their language and they did not understand Latvian. They arrived in the factory with the soldiers and took Papa with them and put him in jail.

What Papa's secretary told the officer had answered the question from a higher-ranking officer. She told us that he was a nice, educated man and after her explanations about the factory and farm being the factory's property, the officer was sorry for this unnecessary misunderstanding by his soldiers. So he ordered Papa freed to go, but the pig did not return, nor money for it.

When Papa came home he did not look the same. His hair was gray. He looked so tired, but the next day, as I remember, he went to the factory.

The young secretary was really a student of law and near finishing her studies. Neither Papa nor anybody at work knew this.

With spring drawing near we were happier. Maija's second birthday was on the twenty-second of April. Papa loved that girl so much, if she had asked for the moon I think he would have done anything to get it for her.

He was bringing toys for her. My mother was baking cookies. Somebody sent a wonderful cake. Papa bought a white teddy bear as tall as

*Ida and Voldis with Maija, age 2*

she was. He played with her, crawling on his knees just as she did. Sometimes she was on his back and he was her horse, laughing, sliding down on the floor. Later when we were in the refugee camps, Papa and Maija were inseparable.

In 1939 the Russians came to Riga, Latvia. The Baltic Sea never froze over and they could then use the harbors in Liepaja, Ventspils, and Riga. In no time the Russians were all over Riga, the city and the country. Yes, they also brought communism. There were meetings on the streets and shootings.

Then came 1940 and 1941 and more bad things were beginning to happen. The Communist Party of the Soviet Union placed itself in Riga and the country. In 1943 the stores were empty. There was no milk, no bread. How would you feed your children?

On the railroad there were more and more cattle wagons, like baggage cars. They had two doors and four windows by the ceilings, about two feet by two feet, with black metal openings. There was nothing inside to sit on or to lie on. People were arrested without reason and brought to these train cars. The doors were shut and Russian soldiers with rifles on their shoulders marched back and forth in front of the wagons. The people had nothing with them; they were just taken from their homes. Families, including the elderly, sick people, and the children were immediately taken to the railroad and forcibly deported to the vast slave labor camps of Siberia. Most never saw their homeland again.

At about the same time as the Russians had dropped the bombs on the bridge over the Daugava River in Riga, people were leaving their towns, farms, and cities, hoping to return.

The Russians were gaining ground. People had nowhere to go. Some headed to the forests; the majority moved towards Germany and the sea with hopes of getting on a boat or any ship that may be leaving. There were German ships in the harbor waiting on their wounded soldiers that took on some of the refugees, helping them as much as they could.

It was June 1944. Voldis went to work in the morning but about 11 a.m. he returned. He told us that the German military ordered some of the men to board the bus in an hour. He hardly had time and had no knowledge what to take with him. He took Papa's very old briefcase. He put in a pair of shoes, a shirt, and a sweater. That's all. When I asked about this trip, he did not know anything. I was told that four church ministers and about twenty men like him had to be on that bus—reason or destination unknown.

"If we meet again we will not live like we did. We will change a few things. Do with the things what you want." He kissed me and left. The furniture and dishes he mentioned were given to us as wedding gifts by my parents and some smaller gifts by his relatives Mr. and Mrs. Priede.

I felt numb. It was like a stranger had left. He did not leave me any money, but it was in the middle of the month, so no pay.

Yes, his work with the criminal police and court was time consuming. Yes, Latvia was a new state after World War I and needed all the men to work hard to rebuild war-destroyed land. But for a young couple with a first baby this was not beneficial. I felt alone.

Russians were pushing in. After his departure, we heard that many people were leaving our country. Some were Estonia refugees and some were our people, mostly farmers from the north part of the country along the Russian border lines. Horses, wagons and other possible and impossible vehicles were passing our city through the Main Street. I saw them standing by the new St. Gertrud church. Their faces were sad. Even the children were sad. Babies were held on mothers' laps sitting on the bench in front of the wagon. These wooden boxes looked like little coffins. If they died while traveling, they would be buried in them on the roadside.

At the end of September 1944, father insisted that we pack what we could take with us and leave Riga, crossing the Daugava River for the country. I did not like it. I loved my country. It was beautiful and good. To make such a decision I needed to pray, and I did.

Then something unusual happened. I was with my child in Mama's apartment. The weather was sunny and warm. The windows in the apartment were opened. It was such a beautiful day.

Suddenly I heard screams on the street. Quickly I was by the window. There were many people on the street. It was work-ending time. From the fourth floor window I could see everything on the street.

Directly under my window was standing a formation of Russian prisoners coming from work. In the last row the second prisoner from my side was lying on the pavement; his head was bloody. A German soldier with a rifle stood behind him and with the butt of the rifle continued beating him mercilessly.

People were screaming on the street. Stop, stop! I was thinking. God, do stop it. I was looking at the sky. It was blue and there was a white cloud and I hoped God would stop this. These prisoners looked so young, just kids.

Two prisoners lifted the lifeless-looking bloody man, supporting him on both sides under arms. His feet dragged helplessly on the pavement.

I looked at the sky again. I felt so lost. I could not help that beat up, hurt man, but God did not do anything for him either.

After praying for a while I thought that God could live up on that cloud and I would live by myself and somehow manage.

Papa was packing. Mama bought loaves of black rye bread and cut the crust into pieces about one inch wide and two inches or less long. Then she cut the soft part off, leaving the crust about a half-inch or less thick. She dried the crust in the oven on low heat. The next day it was cold and she put it in small pillowcases and tied them up. She did the same thing with sweet-sour bread (saldrabmaize, fine rye bread), and when it was dry she put it in a pillowcase.

She explained that when we traveled from Odessa, people could not find bread and we can use this. It was not only for grown ups but for little children, too.

The grocery stores were getting empty. One morning I went after milk and they had none, but they said to come back later. I went later and got the milk.

I was so sure that we would return in a couple of weeks. I packed a couple of suitcases, mainly for my child, adding two pounds of sugar, one pound cream of wheat and some oatmeal. Also included were one aluminum cup, a couple of candles and a small box of matches, soap, two towels, a couple of blankets, sheets and pillow, and her clothes. All these things took so much space. There was hardly any space left for my things.

The next morning I took a bath and put on all things new: underwear, blouse, wool sweater which I had just finished knitting, pants, socks, ski boots, and a soft, warm, winter coat in case we had a need to use it as a blanket. Then I walked out of the apartment, with two suitcases, Maija walking ahead of me. She was small and if need be, I could carry her too. She was two years old. We walked to Papa's place. It was September 27, 1944.

Early in the morning a few days before this final decision, I was still in bed and it seemed that I heard a strong knock on the door. I got out of bed in a hurry and swiftly was in the hall and went to the door. Before I reached the door I saw it opening and in it was standing a very tall being, the face covered. I looked down in front of him and there was a small oriental carpet on the floor. I never had that carpet.

I was not troubled, and had a feeling that it was not just a dream, but a message that inspired me to leave that place, pack and join Papa.

I had never doubted nor ever was dubious all these years. I also have never forgotten that apartment, the place of that vision, that dream experience. It definitely was a message for me to leave. Moving on roads, through cities, forests, countries, lands, and oceans and sea, nothing happened to me. I was protected by divine law but at that time I did not know.

The factory pickup truck arrived for us at Papa's apartment. Colonel Bruveris and his lady friend were in it. The driver and his wife, a younger couple, a workman from the factory, were sitting on the tobacco boxes, but there still was a place for Papa's baskets and suitcases and mine, too. Papa helped Mama to get in the truck and then he got in. They put me, with Maija on my lap, in front with the driver.

We went towards the Daugava River, crossed the bridge and continued seaward, passing farms, forests, and fields. We saw very few people on the road.

The first stop was by our driver's sister's farm. The sun was setting. We paid them with cigarettes. We had our own food except milk.

Father insisted that we all work on the farm, just for our "spirits" sake. It was potato-harvesting time. The soil was red clay. I wanted to save my snow boots for winter's bad weather so I had on my new custom made crocodile shoes with low heels. Every night I cleaned the red mud off between the crocodile skin on top and the leather sole. Two weeks later the tops came off the soles. The red clay's acid had eaten them off. So I was left with just snow boots.

They gave Maija and me a half-finished room in the attic. At least we had privacy there. But it had so many fleas that we soon looked like we had measles, especially little Maija. Yes, she was scratching, but she never complained.

After a couple of weeks Papa decided that we should move to the seaside, with the hope that we would get a boat and go to Sweden. When we arrived there, we found one big room in a fisherman's home that we shared with other people like Mr. and Mrs. Ratsep, who were of Swedish descent like my father. We all slept there, cooked, and ate. Their oldest son was a shipbuilder (as I remember her telling us) and was awaiting them. We all were from Riga. One of her sons was a doctor taking care of soldiers in Kurzene on the war fields. Later we found out he was killed one hour after the war was stopped.

Before the week was out we found the coast, in reality the open seashore. On the beach were some German SS and they would not let us go there. So no boats. On Saturday a German messenger came to tell us that we had to leave the place in twenty-four hours and move at least forty kilometers from the coast.

We had a hard time finding a horse and wagon to move us, but almost at dawn we found one, not for money but a few bottles of liquor. We fastened our things on the wagon. In front was sitting old Mrs. Ratsep. At the end of the wagon on top of all the things fastened with rope, was sitting my little daughter. The rest of us walked on foot.

Maija did not cry or complain. She was just sitting there. When the time came to eat I gave her a little piece of dry, black, rye bread crust and water, and she was satisfied. That was some of the crusts Mama prepared for travel when we were still at home. The child had a sad expression on her face as if she knew what was going on.

We were on the highway, but in all our travel we met only two farmers with wagons. We were going uphill, but as we were fresh in the morning we made it all right. Then we were on level road. Occasionally it did have a slight roll. The sides of the road were lined with trees and further out there were abandoned fields. I soon found out that these people, who with their serene, almost rugged looks, lived in seclusion and at the same time had immeasurable hospitality toward their fellow man—a soldier, a refugee, a neighbor or homeless. They were fishermen and farmers. Their homes in the midst of the forest were wide, very comfortable, and warm.

We were asked to the table for the meal. It was good country food. The host took his place at the table. He put his hands together as for prayer and said a gratitude to God for the food we were about to receive. There were ten or twelve people at the table. There was fresh baked piragi (baked pastry with filling of bacon and onion). At our end of the table was a plate piled up with them. Somebody from the other end was asking for piragi. At my end nobody paid attention. So I picked up a couple of them and lifted up my hand as if to pass, but no one paid attention. So I moved my hand as if to throw to the other end of the table.

My host noticed that, took the piragi out of my hand, put it on the table next to his plate, and with a somber face said, "This is God's gift to man never to be tossed around." Then he took the plate with piragi and turning to one sitting next to him said, "Pass the plate around."

I understood the man was living, working, loving, and trusting God, honoring him. So his family too was used to it. No wonder that his place was so comfortable, warm, and loving; these people lived with God, the best provider.

These people along the seacoast have lived there a long time. They were descendants from the same branch as Finns and Estonians. In Latvia, they were called Libiesi.

After that meal we had to continue our travel. The road from the farm was not wide, but long to the main road. It wound between trees in the woods as if to protect peoples' private property and life.

Then we were on the big road again. First we did not pay attention to kilometer posts. But after fifteen, we began to notice. We were glad when we saw twenty. Our mother took a seat on the wagon next to Maija. The rest of us were still walking.

I remember twenty-five posts. The forest started to grow rich, dark, and tall on the right side. The left side opened in fields; here and there a haystack was left. After post thirty the forest ended and we saw open fields. Soon after that we left the main road, turned right to a smaller road in the forest and continued through Dundagas forest. There were no kilometer posts, but it did not matter. Before we often asked my father, "How far do we have to go?"

"Soon we will be there," he would say. Our father was sixty-five years old, but he never showed it, at least not on this trip. He worked and worked.

The forest was beautiful, sometimes dense; sometimes there was a field with a haystack in the middle. A doe slowly crossed our road with a young one. Sometimes a farm road would turn to the left or right off our traveled road. The fisherman whose horse and wagon we were using was leading our party to his distant widowed relative's farm.

Finally we turned into a farm road and followed it between balsams, maples, and birches. The road broke off in front of a rustic gate and

*Sigulda, Gauja River*

fence, showing smaller fields and pastures, barns, cattle shed, stable, pigsty, hencoop and a sprawling farmhouse still in good condition. There were about a couple dozens fruit trees on the left side of the house edged by various berry bushes, lilac, and jasmine. Most of the flowerbeds were naked at this time.

The house locked snug and one of its two chimneys was smoking. The roof had wide eaves. The buildings in the middle were situated on several acres, with cattle in the pasture, horses drinking at the well and chickens picking in the garden, all surrounded by forest in green, gold, and red in the soft fall sunlight, and above was the smiling picturesque blue sky. The view had not only beauty but was welcoming at the same time, like only a home can look.

My father, another man, and the fisherman left us at the gates and went to the house. After awhile they came back to us.

"We can come and stay as long as we want, but we will have to help her with work. She has only one farm hand, husband and wife, and they are backed with work." Father opened the gates and we walked to the house. The landowner came out.

She had on a brown heavy skirt, covered with a big striped apron with large size pockets and a home knit sweater opened in front, sleeves rolled back to her elbows. Her head was covered with a white scarf tied in a knot under the chin. Careful eyes in a time-lined face were looking at us. She was of medium height and slim, between forty and fifty. I don't know how best to describe that woman. She was a widow and mother whose son lost his life in the war, and she lived with her daughter, who was under twenty when we met her. She had brought up her children after her husband passed away. She kept the house, farmed the land, and did it well. She forgot herself and took in everybody else's troubles. Yes, she was a farmer in every sense of the word.

Meeting us she said, "Come in, I'll show you where to settle."

We went in and were in a large room. "The left door is to my farm hands' place." She opened the door on the right. "Lisa and I live here, and now you, too."

We were in a long room, dark with age. There was a long table near the window and long benches on both sides.

A door split the left wall. Between the corner and door there was a long bench with two buckets of fresh water, an aluminum bowl to wash hands, soap, and a hanging towel. On the right side of the door was a big cooking stove with a large cast iron kettle with wooden cover at one end. Water was boiled in this for the pigs and the laundry. That place was ruggedly built and old fashioned but gave one a feeling of welcome.

On the left and right were shelves with dishes. The windowsill had red potted begonias all in bloom.

Low heavy beams supported the white plaster ceiling, where golden onions were hanging plaited in wreaths. Near the stove were hanging various sizes of frying pans and other cooking utensils.

On the stove also was a big cast iron teapot, which was always ready to use, as I remember. The table was built like a picnic table, but the boards were thick and close together and it looked like one board had been scrubbed with sand and soap until it was bone white.

The opposite wall had also a door and on both sides of it were brown cabinets, where sugar, salt, and bread stayed. Also there were a few brown chairs. She opened that door and we were in a big room, we went through that and then she showed us a smaller room with two windows and a couple of made-up beds. She said, "This is for your family. Do you think it will be enough? One more bed we will bring in."

We thanked her for that room and I said, "I like for my girl to sleep beside me."

The beds had sheets, pillows, and blankets. Everything was very nice. We did not have to unpack our things. After we were settled in our room we were invited to the kitchen to have supper. We were all very tired and after the meal went to sleep. Only Papa stayed behind to take our things off the fisherman's wagon so he could return back to his home early in the morning.

My sister Nina who worked in a large drugstore (aptieka) in Old Riga left her work and came along with us. Though she was with us on this farm she was keeping more to herself and looking for young people her age and participated with them in farm work.

When harvest was done and everything was in the right places, the farmer prepared to celebrate. The food was prepared, musicians arrived, and neighbors with their families, too. By the old custom they did not come empty handed, but brought the best in food that they had.

Two soldiers from the German army came too. One was Austrian with a musical instrument and he was a wonderful singer; the other was Czech, whose family owned a dairy in Prague, Czechoslovakia.

They were usually buying food for the army and were invited. So we all enjoyed the good food, the music and singing, and also the dancing.

I noticed the Austrian only danced with my sister Nina and talked a lot with her. I did the same with the Czech from Prague. He would not let me go. He was an interesting man. We started to talk. I could read, write, and speak German because of my father's insistence when I was in school. He told me about Prague, the family dairy, and his family. It was as if I were there too. After that ball we saw each other when he had some business on the farm, or if he had some business on another farm where nobody knew his language. He would come after me and we would go there. It never took long and he brought me back.

From him we found out when the Russian army would come to Riga. I remember his saying that he would never let the Russians take him as a war prisoner. He was telling how merciless and cruel they were with their own soldiers. He would rather die.

After hearing about Riga, Papa and our family had to reconsider about change. We may be free after the war, but the war was not over yet. How it would end no one really knew. Big countries, political greed, and personal ignorance would decide. We could not stay in Kurzene. We must go.

We found out that in the Ventspils harbor there were German ships where the wounded soldiers were received to take them to Germany. Also some refugees, if they had space on the ship, could be taken.

Now we had to find out. The Czech from Prague came on his bicycle and said that early in the morning he could take me to the railway station at Dundaga. He said I should go to Ventspils and find out all that we had to know, then spend the night in the railway station and return in the morning. He said I could make it in one day. He insisted that he would meet me in the evening in Dundaga and take me to the farm.

So this is what we did. In the morning he took me to the train. There were not many people. I arrived in Ventspils at the middle of the day. I found a house in the city where refugees could come and wait until the ship would take them on. I went to the harbor and saw the ship, but did not see any life on it or around it in the harbor. Then I went to the part of city where there were stores, looking for a grocery store for bread and foodstuffs. There were some but not much inventory.

I noticed soldiers, Latvians-legionary in uniforms. They looked busy enough, but I did not bother any with questions. Then I went to the railway.

Since I could not find any place to stay at night, I hoped I would find something there.

On the side rails I saw some passenger coaches. These were vacant. A soldier, middle age, went in and stayed there. I thought since there was nobody around I would ask him if he knew of some place to stay and wait for the next train to return back. He said there were no other places to stay. People took a seat wherever they could. So I took a seat along a window wall. I was hungry. My hosts had given me a sandwich and an apple. I took it out from the bag. It was big, like two palms side by side. The sandwich was made with that black tasty country bread with fried bacon, an egg, and fried onions. Indeed it was a meal like for a king.

After that I felt sleepy and I stretched out on the seat. That soldier came to me from the other end of the coach, took off his topcoat and covered me with it.

I said, "I am not cold, you need it yourself."

"You keep it now until our train," he said, and went to the other side of the coach where he sat near the door.

I fell asleep and awoke when the sun was setting. The soldier saw me getting up and said, "It is good that you are up, the train is coming."

I thanked him and went to the train. When the train stopped in Dundaga it was dark. I had no watch and had no knowledge of time. It definitely was late and I was very surprised when the Czech of Prague was waiting for me with his bicycle. He took me in front on his cycle and in the moonlight we went to the farm.

Though my hosts had prepared some food for us, she knew that this man would bring me back. He took some milk and bread and left. The farm was very quiet; all were asleep.

In the morning after breakfast my father and mother remained sitting at the table to hear what I found in Ventspils, the place where refugees can stay until there was a place on the ship.

There were some Latvian officers in charge who organized the refugee departures. Hearing all that, my sister decided not to leave Latvia. She would go with us to Ventspils and stay there. Maybe later she would go too.

A few days later our hostess took us to the station. We said goodbye and expressed gratitude for her loving care. It was a sad parting.

When we arrived in Ventspils and I entered the refugee place it was not empty anymore. Some people were settling in. By the entrance door was a table and a woman sitting there was writing down every arrival. Papa stopped there and registered us. Mama, with my girl, was still outside with our things.

While I was looking around to decide which place or corner to take I suddenly heard a voice saying, "Colonel Kesse…"

I did not pay attention, thinking they were some old acquaintance, so I should let them talk.

"Ida," Papa called to me. I turned and saw a Latvian uniformed officer. "Look, your friend." I still was lost in thoughts. "Ida," he said. Then I recognized that he was Jahn Buda, my dear, dear friend whom I had not seen or heard from for about five years.

He said, "Just wait for a minute here, I will be right back," and he left.

He walked fast to the end of the room and through a door on the right side.

"Well, we have to wait," said Papa, "have nothing to choose. Well, there he comes."

"I have something for you," Jahn said, leading us forward to a door, "come in."

We were in a small room with a window facing the back yard that had a couple of trees and some grass. In the room were a couple of army beds. "This will be a better place for you," said Jahn.

My father had some objection about our undeserved privilege while the other people were ahead of us.

Jahn explained that this was his room because he had responsibility regarding refugees but he had not used it because his friend, also an officer, had a room facing the street where they both could see outside and who was coming and going. While we were still in the room, somebody knocked at the door. Jahn opened it and Mama and Maija came in. He greeted Mama, "I still remember you," he said. "I remember you, too," said Mama.

"What is this all about?" asked Mama. Papa and Jahn were explaining to her about the room. Maija was standing and observing the room and Jahn and the officers in uniform, with questions in her eyes. He noticed her several times looking at him, then remembered to ask, "Where are your things?" Papa too remembered and they both went out to bring our things inside for us.

Maija took off her warm coat. Jahn come in and seeing her still in the room asked, "And who are you?"

"She is my daughter Maija," I said.

Jahn looked surprised. "No," he said, "it cannot be," then he looked lost.

"I asked Adis Krumens why he did not marry you and he answered that you told him that you cannot have children," said Jahn.

"I don't remember telling him such a thing, but I did not love him and knew that I never would. I told him that I wished he would find a right companion. After that we never saw each other."

We settled in that room, Jahn brought hay filled sacks for the three army iron beds so we could sleep on them. Sometimes he would come and visit us but his eyes were on Maija.

The time came for us to go on board the ship. He had prepared everything for us. All our things he made sure were put on board. He was holding Maija in his arms. My mama and father walked up the board, said goodbye to everybody, and Nina. She had decided to stay in Ventspils and work with Jahn and other repatriation officers taking care of and helping all refugees.

They were Latvians, all our people. Most of them were farmers. Some were young mothers with children. There was an old man, lean and bent, and sad. There was a crowd, not dressed up like going to the church, but in everyday clothes. I did not see any young men either. Nor much luggage. Just farmers and working class people.

I walked up the board, Jahn was behind me with Maija and he gave her to me saying, "God be with you all, take good care of her," and left the ship. This was an old German ship prepared for the wounded soldiers.

We were told to go down and choose the bunks (plank beds) where we would stay and sleep. Mostly we would navigate at night, with no lights on the ship. Sometimes the ship may stop if there was a need. They would give us some meals. In a few days we would harbor in Danzig.

We went down into the ship's belly. I took a bunk not too far from the exit steps up. Papa and Mama were a little farther from me; they said it was less traffic and warmer.

I understood, they were older people and had suffered so much, the changes from World War I and now leaving their country, their home. "Just trust God, just trust God, He knows what He is doing," father reminded us.

"I hope, I hope so," Mama said. She always was such a good mother to us, educating, bringing us up, the best cook, too. Her husband and we were first in her life. I remember she needed a dress. She asked me to come along to the store to help her decide on a dress. When we were there she saw me looking at one my size. She insisted for me to try it. I did not feel comfortable because it was she who needed one more. She took it and said, "Just try." It was perfect on me. She bought it. My father did not like it that she did not buy anything for herself.

The next day she went to the fabric store, bought a beautiful chiffon, took it to a dressmaker, and a week later she had a beautiful dress. Mama was a beautiful woman and people passing by liked to look back, especially men. She was thrifty too. About her purchase she later said to me, "See how we did it? I have a new dress and you too and still we have money left over."

Sometime that night our ship moved very quietly. In the morning it stopped. They brought down a little breakfast. There was cream-wheat, milk, bread, and coffee (ersatz). I liked it very much, made from roasted wheat. Then again at dinnertime we had some food from the ship's kitchen. Some refugees were asked to come to the kitchen to help prepare food and to clean. They were glad to help.

One night on the ship, the captain asked all to be very quiet because they had received a message about warplanes flying in that area. That night we barely moved. After a while we reached the Danzig harbor. As soon as the ship stopped, the captain asked us to leave it and not to worry about our things, that we would get them later.

Down on the ground a woman in uniform asked us to follow her. It was a very dark night and there were no lights any place. I had to carry Maija. Then we entered a large dark building with very little light and it was subdued. There were many uniforms and army men. They asked each of us for our passport and questioned our names, places where we were from, then stamped the passports. I think they gave them back to us. Their manners were polite, really nice.

After that somebody led us to the tramway and even there were no lights. The tram was full with mothers and children. We had to stand. It had no seats. Holding my child, I was in front by the door on one side and the driver sitting in his compartment on the other.

The drive was bumpy and crooked. Sometimes the driver blinked a blue light on the road here and there. We were also warned to be quiet and we sure were.

Yes, the children are the best people in the world. They never complain, even when they are hungry. Their eyes are pleading and sad, but the minute you look at them, they look down or turn their head away.

The tram stopped by a gate. We were told to leave the tram and go to the gate. It was opened wide. The fence was barbwire, about ten feet wide, as well as I could see in the dark night.

Somebody was ahead of us and leading someplace. Here and there I saw some small buildings. Finally we were stopped by one wooden house. It was a barrack. They opened the door and let us in and turned on lights. One electric bulb hung suspended from the ceiling, near the door was a single table four feet by two and a half feet and double bunk beds. Choice—top or bottom. Wooden legs from floor to ceiling. Bunks had wood boards and nothing more. Then I noticed on the nearest bunk leg a pink streak. Could it be paint? Then I noticed it was moving slowly. Why was it moist? I came close and saw bed bugs. They were pink and my middle finger nail size and moving up in uninterrupted lines. I told and showed what I saw. The question was, what will we do with the children? Everybody had to make a decision about this problem.

When we came in I sat Maija on the table. There was not a chair in the room. Another mother's six-month old baby was lying on the table too. Little Harry, two years old, was sitting.

We decided that we would put the little ones side by side with all clothes as they were on the table and let them sleep there. Since there were no side rails to protect them from falling down, two mothers would stay close by the table till the morning. We had six children sleeping on the table. I knew that we had to do something for the children's sake.

Then we heard the bell outside. It was morning. Somebody said "breakfast." So we decided to go for the morning meal, but we were so new in this place we had no idea where to go. When we asked somebody, they did not know either. We decided to look where the majority was going and in this way we found the dining room.

The room was big. It had long tables and long benches. Then I saw my parents sitting at one, and Maija and I joined them and took a seat on the bench at their table right opposite them. It was so good to be together again.

Somebody from the kitchen brought us food. Maija was given a bowl with manna and stewed fruits. She liked it and ate it all; then she had a glass of milk and a small piece of bread. I had a cup of ersatz coffee and a slice of bread. I noticed she had finished all she had and was looking down to her empty bowl. I broke more than half from my slice and gave her. She took it and without looking ate. I was not hungry and had enough.

When we were walking to the dining room I saw a man walking past holding in his hand a mess kit. He had laced boots too large, no socks, legs purple, thin as a broomstick, loose, old worn out pants that did not cover his legs, and a worn out jacket. His face was only skin and bones, hair not gray. It was so cold that the mud and dirt was frozen hard and was bumpy. An old hat covered his head. He was walking to the same place as I, the dining room. That's probably why I was not hungry, though I had had no food for more than 48 hours.

After breakfast, I told my parents about the place we were last night. They were concerned. Then they told us about the place where they had been this night. It was a long, long barrack, and then Papa said, "Why should we talk about that, come and you will see."

We went and saw a barrack about 100 feet or more long, with only two doors but many windows and lots of ten-foot long tables, no benches, no chairs, and no bunks, just a wood floor. Papa said for Maija and me to join them in their place so we would be together. So we did. I asked Mama where there was a privy or latrine. She said it was right behind this building and impassable with overflow. People were using it outside, and with the water the same.

Last night Papa found a bucket by one vacant barrack, there was water from a turned off tap. It looked clean so he brought it with some water. "If you need any," he said, "just ask." He showed it to me in the corner behind my parents' things.

For midday dinner, we went to the same place to eat. It was watery soup and a slice of bread. I broke my girl's bread slice into pieces and put it into the soup and she ate. I think Papa did the same with his soup. It was so wonderful that Mama still had black bread dried crusts. A couple of those helped, but Papa wouldn't take them, saying, "Save for my baby." I am sure he was hungry.

That night after returning to the long barrack, I put my child on the long table to sleep. Since it had no protective edges around, I was sleeping with her. Papa took one table too. For Mama he put our three coffers side by side and she slept there on the floor.

The next day was the same except Papa was walking around, "just to see this place, maybe we will meet somebody we know."

That night we were sleeping again on the tables, but Papa said, "It will soon be some change."

The next day he was gone most of the time except that at meal times he came back. In the evening, just before sleeping time, he arrived but he did not tell us anything that evening.

In the morning after breakfast he quietly said we will change and he left. After the midday meal he took Maija and said we will go for a walk and you can come along. We were passing several barracks, then turned to the right and then we were not too far from the gate. There was a small house barrack. He knocked at the door. A young Latvian soldier in uniform said, "Come in, we are ready to depart." Then he continued, "Everything is scrubbed, all bunks and floors are washed, windows, and potbelly stove are in order."

Papa asked if they were satisfied with the reward, and the soldier said, "Yes, we are. All is good."

Papa thanked him for the work. The other soldier came in asking if everything was all right. Papa thanked him too and they, saying thanks and goodbye, left the place.

That evening we moved in and with us the six months' old baby with mother and aunt, two-year old Harry and his mother, then another young mother with a baby and her mother, a farm family whose son was the baby's father and at present in the army and still in Latvia. Then there were more people and some children.

That night we all slept on the bunks. In the middle of the room was a large table and on both sides of it were two benches.

Now we had water very near in the bucket Papa found one night, a stove, and some wood. We started to clean up, first the children and then ourselves. It felt so good after such a long time.

After a few days some mothers and I decided to go to the city, the famous, historical Danzig. I think we took the tram.

When we left our barrack house and were approaching the gate, from the left side a little ahead of us three young SS uniformed men were also approaching the gate. They saw us coming and stopped, looking at us. One asked if we were going someplace. We said yes. Then one asked if we had husbands. We said yes, "Where are they?" again one asked. They said nothing more and left ahead of us.

I went to the old part of Danzig with narrow streets, which for 5,000 years had seen pedestrians walking upon them and living century after century there. They lived in peace and did their work. Why now it shall be so changed? After seeing the old city's beauty, I walked out to the new city with broad alleys and parks where new government buildings were visible. Lines of trees still bearing some foliage, though it was November, showed their rights to be in this beautiful, important place. I was touched with gratitude to see all this beauty. I had never forgotten it, though it had been more than fifty years ago.

As I was walking I noticed a school building. By the door was standing a guard in SS uniform. People were going in and out of the doors, not many, but they looked just like me. So I smiled to the guard and entered in. Inside on the left was a separating wall with a small window like where the station tickets are sold. Behind the window was a woman talking to another woman just ahead of me, with a small packet in her hand and saying, "My husband was taken in a month ago, here is a packet with his underclothes."

I did not hear what the woman behind the window said, but the one with the packet was Polish and repeated, "It has been thirty days, he needs this." This Polish woman was ignored, there was no answer.

The next minute the woman behind the window asked me what she could do for me and I said, "I want to know where my husband is." She asked where I was from, and I told her from Riga, Latvia. That moment from outdoors came in an SS soldier and she said to him to take me upstairs. He unlocked the glass door by the stairs, let me in, and locked the door behind me.

I asked, "Why?" then answered myself, "ah, for safety." "Yes," he said, while walking upstairs to the first floor. Then he let me in the room, which definitely used to be a classroom. There were some uniformed men sitting. They were mostly middle-aged and looking tired. Not just tired, but used up.

They asked me where I was from and what I was looking for. I told them that I was from Riga, Latvia, and would like to know where my husband was, that he was ordered to be ready in one hour and be by police on the waiting bus, and there would be twenty men with him. "When did he leave?" I was asked. "It was June," I said. They said that he was in Munich (or German Mun-chen).

After that I left that place, and walking back to the refugee camp I kept thinking, "Voldis is alive, Voldis is alive…"

I do not remember how long we were in that camp. Everything was not better nor worse. Then one day they put us on the passenger train. They really filled it, though we all had seats. That train was going to Berlin. We were traveling a long time. Not too far from Berlin the train stopped. It was some kind of a station as a part of the Berlin station. We were offered hot coffee, clear, thin. Maybe ersatz, but after such a long time we liked any liquid.

A man, thin, lean and graying, took out from the inside pocket of his jacket a crust end of a black bread loaf, took out a pocketknife and cut a slice of bread and ate it. Just one slice. There was so little left. He wrapped it in the same cloth and put it back in his pocket. It was sad.

Mama gave Maija a couple of dry bread crusts that we still had from home. We were saving them and using them only for her when there was nothing to give.

After the stop by Berlin we were turned to the left and went to Brandenburg. We left the train and were walking toward the camp.

The fence of the camp was made of new wood boards ten feet high and close side by side. The gate was of the same wood and height. Outside the fence on the right hand side were many small graves with small crosses. Later we were told that every day they had funerals. Little children were buried there. Also we were told that the previous camp had burned down.

They opened the gate and we walked in the camp. All we could see were barracks and inside were two-story bunks. It was built not like beds side by side, but as the floor. So people were sleeping as herrings in a barrel.

Papa went in and took a place in front, big enough for five people to sleep side by side, and near the door and window. Since it was in front we could sit on the edge like a bench and our feet would be on the floor. We did not have to walk over the people sleeping or sitting like at the beach.

It was very uncomfortable. After people reasoned it out and divided into squares, leaving spaces between each square, it was not so bad. At meal times we had to go to the kitchen, but there was no place to eat.

That afternoon my father and I went after our food. There were two big, big kettles. In one was soup, in the other water. One of the workers had a large soup "spoon." With that she spooned soup and people passed their dish or something that she could pour it in. The soup looked watery, hardly any vegetables or potato, and a couple slices of black bread. We were happy for the bread; at least it was bread.

What we received we took to our barrack. Mama had taken two soup bowls and spoons. Papa and my daughter were eating first, then Mama and I.

A few days later I met little Harry's mother by the kitchen at the mealtime. I asked how Harry was doing. She said not good, that he was in the infirmary, she had to take him there. The doctor there said he had diarrhea. They gave him medicine, but it didn't help.

Hearing what the little boy's mother was telling I did not like it, and asked again, "What does the doctor give him?"

She said, "Castor oil."

No! No, it cannot be, I was thinking, and I asked her, "Where is that place, can we see Harry now?"

"Yes, we can," she said and we went there.

Harry was lying on a small bed. He was very pale. Then two young women came in. When asked who she was, the answer was, "She is medical doctor, from Moscow." I knew it was a lie and I told them. "How do you know?" one of them asked. "Because I am a doctor from Riga. In this situation you don't give castor oil ever. You are killing him, I will make sure that you will never work as doctors, but dig ditches. We will take the child to the hospital."

They helped to dress the child and we were told to take the tram right outside the gate and after a couple of blocks were the hospital and the tram stop.

The tram came to our camp stop at the same time as we and it was almost empty. Holding Harry in her arms, his mother and I were sitting near the door so that we would not miss the hospital main door. When we arrived there, we went into the main entrance and waiting room, which was very full. We turned to a nurse standing behind a table. She was elderly, small, lean, and tired. I told her about Harry and asked that he be placed in the hospital. She refused, saying that they had no place and to go back to where we came from.

We moved back, almost to the middle of the place, standing frozen, not knowing what to do. I couldn't even think. Then the lift from upstairs stopped and the doors opened, it was full. We were about eight feet away and looking directly into it.

The people coming out were public, but then my eyes saw a man in a white coat. He looked at Harry and us and without asking anything said, "We have to take him upstairs."

He spoke German but with little accent. I asked where he was from. He answered, "From Estonia," and he asked us where we were from. I said from Latvia.

Then we reached the fourth floor and he said something to a nurse. She took Harry from us and they went to a room. His mother Anna and I were standing in the corridor just waiting. The Estonian doctor came out, said they would take care of Harry and that we could go in to see him. We both went in. The room was small, filled with small children's beds. In one was Anna's Harry. The room was so full of beds located close together. Only a one-foot wide space was left for walking so the nurses could take care of the children.

When we came out the doctor asked what was done for Harry in the camp nursery. We told him about the castor oil. I told him that I too have here a child the same age as Harry and about ten months ago while in Riga she had a similar problem. I took her to the children's hospital in Riga and Dr. Gartje said to give her very light tea with very little sugar, one teaspoon every five minutes. Stop when she was asleep, when awake continue. The next day he described what I had to do and told me to add rusk. In a few days she was well.

So we left Harry in the hospital and returned to the camp. Anna said she would visit with him tomorrow. Most of the day I was absent. My mother was angry. She rebuked me that I was only interested in other people's needs and forgot about my child. I had to explain to her that she was my mother and my child's grandmother and the best that both of us could have. That's why I trusted my child to her and Papa and I was grateful to both of them.

"Sometimes there are people who need help, but there is no one to help. You must remember little Harry is sick and his mother is all alone. She has nobody to help her. So we found a hospital and took him there and an Estonian doctor saw him and admitted him to the hospital."

Papa sitting and listening said, "This is the right thing to do. If we cannot help each other we aren't worth our own salt."

"Yes, you are right," Mama said softly, "I hope Harry will be well soon."

After a while, more than a week or two, Harry came back well. I was so glad about that and my mother and father were too.

We did not stay in this camp long, but were transferred to Mecklenburg, to Schwerin. It was a school but there were no students; at least we did not see any. We were let in the school hall, something like a gymnasium or auditorium and around the walls were plank-beds two stories uninterrupted, just like in the Brandenburg camp. But here they had a water closet with several sinks with water where we could wash our hands and some of our things.

Then we had a big surprise. Nearby there was a bathhouse and we went there with the children and we all had a good wash. After that we received food coupons. Mama, Papa, and Maija returned to camp after their bath, but I went to have coffee with a little milk and sweet bun. It was enough for me, but not for our families.

We started to look for a store and found a fish store. They had all kinds of fish—pickled, smoked, smoke-dried, and fresh, ready to fry. Frying would be the best, but in that camp there was no way for us to do that. So we bought smoked and pickled. While we were paying for our purchase we asked if there was a place near where we could buy bread and she explained that just around the corner was a store. We went there and bought what we needed and returned to the camp.

While we were home in Riga my girl was given presents. There was a big white bear taller than she and other toys. We had to leave them behind. I had a coat with a collar, light brown, soft, artificial fur. I took it off and went to a lady who made teddy bears with eyes and ears that could sit and stand.

Maija never asked for toys, she never complained or cried, but she was happy having her bear. So long this bear had traveled with her. In the Schwerin camp one day the bear was gone. When we were talking about it some people started to offend each other. I stopped asking. The bear never came back to her. That was her only toy in her lifetime after infancy.

I noticed Maija scratching herself and I asked her not to scratch. She stopped but she was sad, not moving. She looked very unhappy. I said to my mother, "Something is not right, look at her, Mama." She looked and said, "You are right, maybe something is wrong with that dress."

I removed the dress and Mama turned it inside out and said, "Look at the seams on top of her chest. A whole row of lice are resting on the dusty seam ready to attack the little girl as if she were their enemy." This was the only wool, warm dress she had. We had to put on her baby jacket that was too short and small, keeping her on the bunk until the dress would be dry after washing.

Then we heard that we would be sent to the country where there were farms and small towns. We hoped that it would be better than in the camps.

One day we were put on the train and our family arrived in Pokrent, a small railroad station in the country. Somebody met us with a horse and wagon, put our things on it and us too. It was midday so we could see the road we were traveling on. There were no houses or farms on either side of the road.

Only here and there was a large tree. Finally we came upon a farm with a large log cabin, log barn and a big log cattle shed, but no cattle were outside. It was winter.

We bypassed that and suddenly we were in a small village. There were a couple of houses, a store, a church, and a cemetery partially enclosed with three feet or less of old iron fence. In the village the road turned to the right.

This road was hard surfaced and on both sides were big trees and then on the right side behind the trees was a long line of horse stables. On the left side behind the trees was a byre, big and long, almost as long as horse stables.

Then in front of us was a green lawn protecting a big house with large doors in the center. Our wagon turned to the right, along the side of the house and we were in the backyard of that house, and nearby was a regular door. A hostess came out to meet us. Another woman came too who I think was a mistress in charge of housework. They greeted us in a friendly manner and introduced themselves. The place was called Majorat and belonged to the family of Colonel Klitzinger (I think this was the name). Mrs. Klitzinger invited us to come into the house through the back door, which the mistress opened. So we did and we were in a beautiful large room with many large windows, but not much furniture. It looked like a ballroom. Then she opened the door to a smaller room and said, "This is the room we prepared for you. We hope you will like it."

There was a double bed and next to it was a baby's bed big enough that my child would be comfortable. Across from the big bed was a nice single bed. All the beds had linens and blankets. There was also a small table and a couple of chairs.

It really was very nice and we thanked them, then the mistress and driver were bringing in our things. They showed us a bathroom, but it seemed cold.

In the big room, almost by our new room's door, the mistress and a worker were setting a table and she said, "We had finished our dinners, we thought maybe you had not eaten and maybe you are hungry, so we still have something in the kitchen and just will warm it up."

The table was set with a tablecloth and napkins, plates and cups, forks, knives, and spoons. Then somebody brought the meal of mashed potatoes and gravy from turkey but not even a wee piece of turkey. There was also bread and butter, tea, and milk. The only food we had that day was before we left camp that morning so we were hungry. This meal with not a scrap of meat felt empty, tasteless. We should have been used to it by this time and be satisfied, but I was not. Still we did not complain, nor talked between ourselves. We were guests.

After the meal we were tired and went to our new room and beds. Mama and I were to sleep in the big bed close to the baby's bed so that at night I could take care of my child. Papa took the single bed. The place and the night were very peaceful.

In the morning the room was very cold. Papa decided not to complain to the hosts but checked out the window, door, floor, and all corners in the room. All seemed okay except an outside corner of the house. He went outside and found that this corner of the house had deteriorated and the bricks were loose and had dropped out. Seeing that, Papa offered to fix the corner if they had some cement and a man to help. They sent a Polish man and the material Papa asked for and that day the house had a new corner. Papa had a way with people. He was kind, patient, and accepted all with whom he had to work with as good workers, able and capable. So he did that way with this worker who was a prisoner, and found out that he was a professional builder from Warsaw. He knew how to do this work right. Papa found this when he spoke with him in Polish. Papa lived in Warsaw several years and had friends, good, dear friends there. When I was baptized, my godfather was his best friend, Polish Tadeush Kezinsky, a colonel, like Papa, in the Russian army.

Now our room was fixed and the warmth stayed in the room day and night.

When Colonel Klitzinger found that my father was also a colonel, though retired, he asked Papa if he would like to join him twice a week in the village inspection duty. He said that all the village male population participates for the community's safety.

"His part," he said, "was only two times a week." Papa had not much to do, so he agreed. After his first time, he told us that it was nice. They walked around the village for a while;

everything was peaceful. This village had neither collective dairy nor tavern. Then they came back to the colonel's office. The mistress of the house brought hot coffee and for Papa hot tea and a plate with ham and sausages that Papa said he liked. Then they talked. "How?" Mama asked.

"Well," Papa smiled and said, "why not? The old colonel speaks as good Russian as I. He was stationed near Russians in Munchen and had some friends."

Mama and I were asked to do some work in the Klitzinger household. There was a separate laundry house with great big cauldron-shaped washing pots. It was filled with dirty clothes and soap and washing powders. It was heated down under from outside. Once every week it was keeping us busy there.

The other place was the kitchen. Peeling potatoes and other vegetables and doing dishes. I certainly was not happy about this dirty work. Probably mistress had heard it and one time she said, "The best thing to overcome this unhappy feeling about dirty work is start loving it."

It reminded me when I was about fourteen years old and the oldest child in our family, Mama told me to wash the floors, even in the bathroom. I was not happy. So when Papa came from work about 5:00 p.m., I showed him my wet hands and he saw that I had been working. He smiled and said, "Don't worry about your hands, when they're dirty, you will eat white bread."

Although these experiences with dirty work and hands did trouble me, I was satisfied with the place where we were living. The war was ending. We were supposed to be more on our own. There was another family of Latvians, mother, child, a small boy, and grandmother. We needed some groceries, potatoes, cabbage, and such. The little store in the village had none. The boy's mother and I found out that we could take the train and go to Schwerin and shop there. That's what we did, and found a small grocery store in the old part of the city that looked like old Riga in a basement, where we found all that we needed. After that we walked with our purchases to the railroad station and got off in Pokrent. From there we had to walk the long road to home. All was good and our families were happy to see us back.

Then we learned that there was a dairy and one could buy skimmed milk and sometimes buttermilk, but it was as far away from the village as Pokrent, only the opposite direction. So we borrowed milk cans from our neighbors and got other containers and went to that dairy. It was a long walk. On both sides of this road was planted apple trees, about seven to eight years old, behind them were wheat fields; it was definitely farming land. All the way to the dairy there was not a sight of a house or farm for miles and miles.

Finally we reached the dairy. It was large and very clean. We got enough skim milk and some buttermilk for our families. We were so happy. The sun was shining and it was not cold so the miles on the road did not seem so long. The families were so happy. They had not seen or tasted milk for a long, long time.

With warmer weather the Klitzinger family was getting ready for a change in their home. So we had to move to a new place. The village elder (I have forgotten his name) had in his house an attic apartment, two rooms and a kitchen/bathroom. It was right in the village. I liked the view from the windows, the grocery across the street on the right corner and church about 150 feet on the left from the corner and the cemetery. Every Saturday at 5:00 p.m. and on Sunday morning we could hear the bells ringing.

Now Papa had his own room with a bed and all that he needed. Mama, Maija, and I had a room with two beds and one small child's bed. It had two windows with lots of light and we could see all that happened in the village. The kitchen had a little stove and in the corner was a real bathtub. So now we could heat the water, have a bath, and do our laundry.

On the other end of the attic were two rooms and a kitchen apartment. There lived the Latvian family—mother, daughter, and a little boy. This is the woman with whom I was going to the dairy and to Schwerin shopping.

I remember one time we were out of groceries and I had to go to Schwerin alone. So I went and purchased all that we needed. The day was very cold. Everything was frozen again after the thaw, and being still January, daylight was short. Still being wartime, the trains did not run regularly, so after shopping I had to wait for it a long time. When it came it was nighttime and it was very dark, and the same at the station Pokrent. The station was not lighted because of the war. And I did not see anybody. I was tired and had not eaten all day but I was not hungry either. I picked up my potatoes and other purchases and started walking as fast as I could homeward. At first it was not so bad, but the frozen ruts on the road were sharp and slippery, which made walking hard. It seemed that I would not reach home. Then my hands became numb. After awhile I started to slip and felt like giving up. I slipped and fell down. As I got up I saw across the road a light, then it vanished and was all dark again, then there was a light like a door opening, a long light on the ground, again closing and opening.

I don't know where all of a sudden I had the strength but I walked to that on again/off again light and saw that it was the door to the big, dark log house we saw when we first arrived in Pokrent. Now the woman said, "Come in, come in, it is so cold," and she let me into the house. The warmth of the house and the light on the long kitchen table took me in. The woman said, "Come to the table, have a seat." I took the seat at the end of the table.

She asked if I would like to eat something, but I refused saying that I was not hungry but if they had something warm to drink it would help. In that room was standing a man who looked like a farmer. He was saying something about milk to her. I was not listening, as I was tired. In the next minute she put a pitcher with hot milk in front of me and poured some in the cup. As I drank the milk she continued to refill the cup. Then she asked where I lived and I told her about Klitzingers and about shopping in Schwerin.

I thanked them for the milk and their kindness letting me in their home and then left for home. Somehow it was not hard to walk anymore. God and the milk helped me to get home.

Later I found that the farm belonged to a brother and two sisters. I have never forgotten the warmth and the loving hospitality of this family when it was so needed.

Yes, there was a war and all kinds of people, but the German people I met all through Germany were good people.

Herr Elder, in whose house we were living, got both families together and said that a Lutheran minister from another village came to see him. They have a lady with about a four-year-old boy sent to them but they have no place for them. So he wanted to ask us if we would take them in our attic. He said that the woman's husband was an officer in the army and they too were Latvians.

So the grandmother with her daughter and boy decided that their two-and-a-half rooms were a bit larger than ours and they would welcome the newcomers in the room they were not using.

The next day the Latvian Lutheran minister with the elder of the other village brought the lady with the boy and they moved in the attic vacant rooms. We who already lived there welcomed them.

The neighbor family grandma, child, and mother were getting along fine with the newcomers. The two boys now played together. The lady and grandmother liked to talk with each other.

After a while the lady's boy became sick. They called a doctor. I do not remember what he said but the boy died. I was sorry about it. He was a small, blond, intelligent boy. We all were sad. The funeral was in the cemetery near the church. Some Latvian refugees came from nearby villages as well as the Latvian minister. My father and I went to the cemetery.

I do not remember what the ceremony was about, but when the Lutheran minister said, "From dust you came, to dust you go back," I did not like to hear that.

The stupidity of this expression for that young, beautiful child as if he was nothing. Where did these stupid ministers get these stupid verdicts? The Bible I have read many times, but never found that God had ever created death or dust. I found myself in front of the house we were living in. After that I never went to any funeral.

Here and there Papa was working on the farms, splitting wood for the farmers. Pay for eight hours of work was a small piece of bacon. It did not cover the palm of the hand and was not as thick as the small finger of the hand. We thanked the farmer. One time they gave Papa two salt herrings. Mama soaked them in cold water. Then she took the meat off and we had it with boiled potatoes for dinner, but the head and fish bones she put aside and the next day she made soup with water, potatoes, carrots and onions and it was good. I never thought that from two fish bones one could make such good soup.

It was April and springtime. One day in the middle of the morning came a group of soldiers. They had no hats on and uniforms were not German. They had no weapons on them or any military insignia on their military coats. Maybe they were British or Latvians. They went through the village without stopping, but turning heads as to say, "Where are they?"

The next day another group of military came into the village. Their uniforms were again different, but they had arm bands around them and hats. They settled right next to the house of burgomaster. They were coming and going, cooking and eating a lot. After a few days they were gone, all of them.

Papa went out for a walk. When he came back, in his arms he carried American food cans about eight inches high, "Come here and see," he said, putting them down on the table carefully.

I did not want to look, but he insisted, "Look, I think here is something we can use!" Then I looked. The cans were opened, probably with a can opener. One can was orange marmalade. Inside on the sides and the bottom lots of it was left, still clean. We took it all out into a bowl. Then another can was from peanut butter. We scraped that out. Then Papa went out to look if there was something more and he brought two more. It was so unexpected and a big help to our nil food supply. That was really our lifesaver.

When these soldiers were here and saw the little village children they gave them small chocolate bars. My little three-year-old daughter Maija, being near German children, was also given one. Though all the children were given chocolate, none of them opened the "present." Maybe because the givers were strangers. Maija was so surprised too. Nobody had given her anything before.

Maija had the bar in her hand and seeing me standing by the house door she said, "Mama, the man in uniform opened one just like this and put it in his mouth, but the children did not."

It was an American chocolate bar. I opened the wrapper and gave it to her, "You can eat it." So she did bite it and her face had a happy expression.

"It is good, it is very good!" she was repeating.

These soldiers left and after awhile another group came and settled in the same place as the ones before. They had the same uniforms.

Before long Maija was coming from outdoors. She looked busy and excited and seeing me said, "Mama, Mama there are the same soldiers, but they had the chocolate all over them. On their hands, their faces, and I think over their heads too."

I had to explain to her that there was another reason why their hands and faces were dark. That there is a place, Africa, where sunshine is all the time, everyday. It is so warm that they get this suntan. It is called South. Where we lived was North. We had long winters, with snow and cold and the sun was not warm. Summer is only three months and it's not so warm as in Africa. But we had lots of snow in the winter. "Remember, not long ago we had lots of snow?"

"I don't like that snow, because you don't let me out," said Maija.

"We don't have warm clothes and shoes for you."

After a while she said, "I still like dark people because the sun likes them and puts the chocolate on them!"

"Yes, sun loves them and God created them too, as us all." So we had for a while one group coming, then going.

Then the Latvians from the other village came to see us. It was a couple and the Latvian Lutheran minister. The German Lutheran minister brought them in his car. The news was that we could leave Pokrent, this village, and move to Lubeck; that other Latvians from different places were going there. Maybe we would be able to return to our home. We decided that where we were living we had no work, no income, or a chance for something better, that if they could get transportation and are willing to take us with them, we will go to Lubeck. In a few days a truck stopped by our place and we boarded with our things and left with other Latvian refugees.

The roads we traveled were mostly empty. All the way to Lubeck I don't remember seeing more than one or two vehicles, but they were going in the opposite direction. We reached Lubeck in the afternoon and stopped at a two-story high school. We parked in the back in a big schoolyard. Already there were many people sitting and standing around. Somebody was counting and registered us. In the classrooms bunks were set up. There was very little space left for motion.

Maija and I were assigned a small corner in a classroom on the second floor, two bunks, away from light and windows. In no time the room was full of people. Mostly they were young men, most had on old, over-used clothes. The war was over. Probably they were soldiers who had dropped their worn-out uniforms. I felt sad for them. Some of them were very young. They had no families, no home, no money, and no place to go.

Somebody came in the room asking us to come along and bring a mattress for our bunks. No barracks, no soldiers, no need for a mattress.

I got two for Maija and me, took our sheet and blanket and covered our sleeping place. Then we went looking for my mother and father. It took us some time to find Papa. He was busy with the people, but said, "In about two hours we will have soup and bread, and the children will get milk and something."

When I asked where Mama was, he said to go to the office on the first floor. We both went and found her. She explained that Papa was put to work.

"This is his office and this end of the room I am standing in is our living quarters," she said. Opening a suitcase she took out blankets and pillows and placed them on the bunks in the corner of the room.

"How can you live here?" I asked. "This is an office, the people will be coming and going, in and out. You will have no peace. You will have to stay in this corner?"

After a while it was getting quiet. People were settling in their new places. Then later we heard the bell and went to have our meal.

The next day Maija and I went outdoors. The weather was warm, but after so many people, trucks, and cars, the whole place was trampled under foot and crushed. Here and there you could see a small green place where one or two could sit for a while.

In the sandy soil I picked up pebbles, round and smooth, cleaned a smooth square, divided our pebbles between us, and explained to her that we would play a game. She liked the idea. The larger pebbles were sheep; the small ones were the lambs. You stand outside the square and drop in the square a couple of sheep. Then one at a time you drop a lamb so it lands on the sheep or very close. So we will play jump and catch. After a while you will play sheep and I the lambs.

We were doing just fine, but later Mama came. Maija right away started to teach her grandmother how to play this game. So we played like this for a while. Then people were coming out in the fresh air.

Inside, Papa and other people started to organize more and more. They decided that the children looked so pale and something should be done about that. I think we had a young Latvian doctor, too, so he volunteered to go to the German Health Department and ask if they could help our children. He went and came back with a solution.

They have cod liver oil. They organized a program so that in the morning, I think it was twice a week, about 10 o'clock the children had to go downstairs to the dining room with a soup spoon and cup, stay in line and one by one go to the table where a nurse would give each child in his/her spoon the oil from a bottle. The child swallowed that oil and then the next child took his place.

Usually Maija was back very soon. The first time of taking the oil, I went with her, but since all was well organized I did not continue to go with her. Then she started to stay longer and longer. When it seemed so long and she still was not back, I went downstairs. The children were still there. The nurse and the cod liver oil bottle were still there, but not my daughter. I went around looking for her. She was so little between the larger children and I continued looking. Finally there she was behind a very thin, tall boy, still holding the spoon and cup in her hand.

"Where have you been so long? Have you had your spoon of oil?" I asked.

"Mama, Mama, I have to tell you something, but come here, here." She was pulling me away from the children.

"I had one spoon as soon as I came, but some children don't like it. So I wait and when no one goes I get another spoon."

"How can you do that?" I asked. "What do the other children say? You know one has to stay in line and wait."

"Yes, Mama, after I get the first one, I go to the end of the line and follow the others to get a second. But that tall boy doesn't like the oil, not even one spoon. I told him that the oil is very good. He said he would help me to get one more spoon."

"Not today," I said, "we better see our doctor. We have not seen him for a while. So today is the day."

We went to see the doctor. He asked some questions and examined her.

He found nothing wrong, but said, "Two spoons of oil a day will be enough."

Papa in the refugee office had all kinds of visitors. Some were high-ranking English military officers. He told us that after the war some would be stationed in Lubeck, occupying large houses in the best part of the city that belonged to the police chief or to the top government man in Lubeck. He said they were looking for good, trustworthy people who could speak English. They needed a cook and housekeepers, definitely people who knew the work. They did not want the Germans.

Then one day the same English colonel visited Papa again. He told him that they got a lady cook, but that they needed a hostess and housekeeper, too, and they had to be Latvians because the cook is Latvian. With him in the house lived two or three other officers. Sometimes they had visitors. It is too much work for her alone. He said that on the third floor in the house they have several nicely furnished rooms and a bathroom. The cook stays in one room, but she wants a Latvian to live and work there too.

After that Papa said, "Would you like to do some work there?"

"I have to think. What about Maija?"

"Well," he said, "I shall ask Mother. She doesn't have much to do here, she could take care of Maija."

"Can you ask the colonel if I could go there myself to see the place? Then I will know what to do."

"Sure, I will do that," he said.

Next day Papa gave me the address and told me where to go. I asked Mama to take care of Maija and went. That was the nicest part of the city. I had no problem finding the place, and I was looking for the kitchen. The door was on the side of the house and was open a little. I knocked, and then asked, "Is somebody in?"

Inside I heard the voice, "Yes, yes, coming!" A woman came to the door. She had an apron on, "Come in, I am in the kitchen. You Latvian?"

"Ja," I said.

We found that we both had attended and finished the same home economics school in Riga, Latvia, on Voldemar Street, she a couple of years later than I.

She was preparing a lunch and asked me to sit at the table so that we could eat and talk. Her husband was living in the Latvian camp but not the same as where I was. She had a room upstairs, but her husband was not allowed. Weekends she went to the camp too and returned early Monday morning.

After lunch she took me floor by floor to the top. The first floor had a dining room, living room with an upright piano, opened doors (sliding) into a library with bookcases along the wall, a good-size hall, a lavatory and a coat closet. Everything was nicely furnished and carpeted. There were comfortable steps going upstairs to the second floor. There were four bedrooms. One was large with two windows to the street; others were medium size, also furnished. There was a hall and laundry room.

"The men are sleeping on this floor," said the cook.

"One thing is good," she said, "we don't have to do anything for bedrooms; only once a week vacuum clean the carpets. These military men do it themselves. One big Canadian don't like to do his room," she showed one in the middle, "but the colonel offered to do that for him twice a month if he pays him half of his pay check."

Then we went up to the next floor. At the end of the hall she opened a door. It was a room with a bed, some furniture, and a window facing the street.

"This is my bedroom," she said, "big enough for two to sleep. That's why I go weekends to the camp, to be with my husband."

She then opened yet another door. The room was about the same size with a bed smaller than hers and a large window facing the garden.

She opened another door. There was a bed like hers, but the window was small and in the roof. One could not reach it. The room was larger than the others but not so finished as the other two. There was a hall and a good size bathroom. I really liked all I saw.

"What about the food?" I asked.

"All that I ask for they deliver. You know," she continued, "I wish you would work here, you had the same school; you would be such a help to me."

I told her about my little daughter, that right now she was with my mother and father and that we live in the same camp.

As I was leaving she said that she would talk to the colonel. I agreed and said that I would talk with my family, and I left.

Then the colonel came to the camp and my father called me to the office to meet him. Everything that I saw about their place and the offer now I liked, but hesitated because of my child. The door to the office opened and Maija, with a serious face, walked in and came to me.

Colonel, looking at her, asked, "Who are you?" She smiled but, not understanding English, did not answer.

"She is my girl, Maija," I said.

"If you would like to take her too, why not," he said, "there are enough rooms upstairs."

I liked the idea. The food would be better and more plentiful. Since we left Latvia with 36 lats in my purse, I still had it, because in Germany it had no value. Maija's clothes were outgrown and worn out, and I had no money to buy something new. So we agreed that I would live and work in that house.

Next day Papa came along so he would know where we would be living. We also decided that we would keep the bunks and the corner of the room that were assigned to us by the camp.

Anna, the cook, let us in. Since nobody was at home, she offered to show the inside of the house to Papa. After seeing the place and the rooms upstairs he was satisfied.

"I will go back to camp and tell Mama what I saw here. She will not worry. This is better than the camp. That's what Maija and you need," he said and left us.

So we started our life in this house. Maija was used to living all refugee time with grown-ups. She did not look for playmates. As I was working about the house she worked with me or she was with Anna in the kitchen. Since she had no toys, nor knew such things existed, she never missed them.

I noticed in the camps that children are more patient about food or lack of it, and clothes, even if they are so worn out with holes or patched up. They still loved their parents and tried to please them. In every situation and place I have seen this trust and unlimited love towards parents or somebody who was taking care of them if they really cared and were loving providers.

Maija had only one dress left. The bottom part was from a used white hand towel. For the top I had to use her only sweater (wool), which was shrunk and too small. I ripped the yarn and knitted the top with a little collar, which I embroidered with colored thread. Then I knitted sleeves and sewed them in. Her stockings were dark, also knitted from my unraveled socks I used in my ski boots. She learned to be very careful with her things. She had a white flannelette baby jacket, which tied in the back, like usually we do on a baby. She had nothing else to wear. My only blouse that I had worn every day and washed every day went to pieces except the back. That gave me an idea to use the back of it and the top of the sleeves because that was still strong and with needle and thread to sew by hand (we had no sewing machine) sleeves for a jumper to wear on top of the baby jacket. The material had a light print and came out all right.

Next door, to the right of this British colonel's house was a similar size house. Some military men of officer's rank were staying there. Anna learned from the cook on that side that the officers were Danish. Sometimes when Maija was playing with her pebbles on the driveway on our side, some Danish neighbors would stop on their side and watch her just a short time, but I never saw them speak to her.

It was easy to work in the British Colonel's house where I could see and know where my child was. Then one day we had a large dinner party. I think three or four guests were coming. Anna needed my help in the kitchen and I had more work in the dining room as a hostess. I kept an eye on Maija outdoors. Then I became busier in the dining room on the second floor. After I returned to the kitchen and looked outside I could not see my girl.

As soon as I could I went outdoors on the street, then the garden, but she was not there. Then I went upstairs, but she was not there. I knew that I had to help Anna in the kitchen, but I wanted to look more for my child but had no success.

Finally we were finished in the kitchen. I was at the door by the driveway. There was a low fence with little bushes on the Danish side of the street. I saw something white moving behind the bushes and fence almost by the street, then turning into our driveway and coming toward me, holding something in her hand. Maija stopped, putting one foot forward on the pavement and one hand pointing to her foot she said, "See!" Another hand stretched to me holding something, "And this too!" putting in my hand a big chocolate bar.

On her feet were no more white shoes through which her toes had grown out, looking for more space. They were the ones my father, her grandfather, bought in Riga before we left home. We saw that she needed a larger size but she did not complain. We had no money, no hope, and no expectation.

Now she told us that this morning when she was playing the big man came to the fence and asked her to come to him, motioning with his hand. She went and he took off the old shoes and in the box he opened were these brown shoes! He put them on her feet and asked her to walk and she did. Then he gave her the chocolate and sent her home.

"Thank you Heavenly Father, all is well. She is back home." I wanted to thank that Danish officer the next day for the shoes, but couldn't do it until 11:00 a.m. I knocked and another officer opened the door. I explained that I wanted to talk with the other tall and round-faced officer.

He said that the colonel had left early in the morning. I asked when he would be back. The officer said the colonel went home to Denmark. He had finished his work here and was not coming back. His family in Denmark has been waiting for him.

"He has a family?" I asked.

"Yes," said the officer, "family with children. He has been looking at your girl when she was playing. He told us that he has one like her at home."

I thanked him for the information and said that I hoped he was having a nice trip home.

I felt sorry that I missed the departed Colonel and could not thank him for such a valuable present, the shoes, the thing that my child needed so much.

I understood the gift of shoes when realizing that the Colonel had at home a child like mine and had a gift for her, but seeing the dire need of this child here he gave that pair to Maija.

I hoped that Heavenly Father would bless him for that.

Life went on. Colonel hired another girl to help Anna and me with the housework. She was also Latvian. We thought that Rita, the new girl, would use the third bedroom on our floor facing the garden, but she refused. She liked the room but was afraid to sleep alone in there.

The door to my bedroom was open. Rita saw it and asked whose room this was and if she could see it. I let her come in. She liked it so well and had an idea. It being larger, one more bed could be placed in it.

"Look," she said, turning around in the middle of the room, "with one more bed we still could dance here."

It was my free afternoon and Maija and I left to visit my mother and father in the camp. When we returned, Anna, the cook, was in the kitchen.

"I have your dinner here and it is still warm, come and eat," she said.

While we were eating she was informing us that there were some changes in our room, but not much. Walking upstairs I was wondering what kind of change I would find.

The bed from the third bedroom had been transferred to my room and set along the side of the outside wall, almost under the roof-top window. I am sure she could count the stars in the sky and she would be in my sight from head to toe. So now there were three occupants sleeping in my room—Maija with me in one bed and Rita in hers.

When we were in bed all was peaceful and in no time we were asleep. At other times when Rita did not go to sleep so fast, she started to tell about herself. She did not talk about her family, her parents. She was about eighteen to twenty years old. She did not mention what schools she went to or which city she was living in before Germany.

I could not ask her anything about her life before she came here. She was just like a small child lost in the strange world. She needed kindness.

Sometimes she would stop talking and ask if her talk was bothering me or maybe I wished to sleep. Sometimes if her talking was too long I suggested, "You know we have to work tomorrow, better we start sleeping now." She never disagreed and in no time we were sound asleep.

One time she was talking about a law when the German military was in Riga. At 10:00 p.m. all the houses, apartment buildings, and businesses were closed. Nobody was allowed to be on the street. But if anybody was on the street, especially young women or girls, they were taken to the police and Germans (military) put them in the houses where men visited them and girls were supposed to do what the men ordered them to. Was it truth? We learned later that it was true. If they would not follow Hitler's order, the man was to mistreat until she would be destroyed.

Yes, in 1943 and 1944 we had so many young people, women and men lost or missing. In Brandenburg, Schwerin, I have been on the streets in the daytime and have seen through second floor windows young girls scantily dressed, watching the street. They did not look happy. Passing one of those streets one elderly German woman bypassing me whispered, "It's not a good street to be on."

I felt sad about all this life, the world. The children had not asked to be born in this world. The majority of people, men and women, were decent, reliable people who had their countries, their homes, their church, and now they had nothing.

I remembered the Pokrent.

Just like garbage, refuse. Just like my father in the village of Pokrent brought one loaf of black bread from the store, took the knife to cut a slice and said, "It must be only a quarter inch thick."

His hand trembling, he put the knife back on the table and said, "You cut the slices a quarter inch thick for each of us. One slice for a day or I know we will not make it."

"Papa, you always cut the bread and do all right."

"I cannot do it this time, you will have to cut."

He moved away from the table and left the room. All his life he lived an honest life. He had worked hard and helped anyone who needed help whether it was a friend or enemy or stranger. He took good care of us, his family. He paid for our schools and tuition so that we would have a good education. He paid his loans and taxes on time. He believed in democracy and in God. Now he had a quarter inch slice of bread for his family. But he never complained about anything, not even now.

Anna, the cook, Rita, and I were getting along just fine. Some changes were coming in the colonel's house; the Canadian colonel was going back to Canada. Still three officers would stay.

Now I had a little more time to play with Maija outside the garden or visit my parents in the camp. I found that the back part of our camp passage was separated. The next time I went to the camp I walked through the backyard, then entered the back door of the separated part of the building. On the second floor were many young men carelessly dressed. I also noticed some nurses.

As I was nearing a dividing place in the hall of the camp, I noticed a young man with blond curly hair sitting almost in the middle of the hall floor. He was so young and smiled with such a childlike smile at me and said, "Good morning, are you living here too?"

I looked at his face, the caring loving expression, then on to the floor. He had both legs missing. I don't remember what

I said, but I looked on his face and loved him, desiring to take him and care for him. I don't remember if I said anything.

My father was meeting me and said, "You know you are married. That is a hospital." Maybe he saw something in my face. It doesn't matter. I have never forgotten that boy and prayed that God would take care of him.

Yes, my husband Voldis who in the beginning of June 1944 by the order of German invaders in Riga, Latvia, with twenty other Latvian men was ordered away with no reason given and had not been seen or heard from by anybody. Now it was 1945 and August. At the house of the British colonel, where my child and we three Latvian women now were living and working, the apple trees had ripe apples.

I did not talk about my husband with anyone or to my child about her father and she never asked about him. My father, being with us all this time, expressed so much care and love to her; I think she did not miss hers. I thought, the past is gone. The future we have none. We have only now. Some soldiers from big countries not like our small Latvia, Estonia, or Lithuania, talked about their homes, the cities, their people and their returning back home. They were so sure that all would be there as it was before the war. We had nothing!! No place to go. Only today. Now!

There were changes going on. The refugee camp in the school had to close, as the educational institute was needed by city. Papa was telling about army barracks outside the city, and asked me to go there and see if we can have a place.

Another woman from the camp and I went there. We talked to the officer in charge regarding a place for my family but the answer was not very positive.

Then I asked if we just could see any of the apartments. The bookkeeper agreed and said for us to go to the second floor. He gave us the number of the apartment and said, "There are three men from the concentration camp, but they will not stay there long."

So we went up and entered the apartment. We were in the hall. There was a door on the left; we knocked and opened the door. Across the room two good-size windows were facing us.

The painted walls were clean, the wood floor was spotless; it looked like new. The room had no furniture. Against the right side wall on the floor were sitting three men propped up or supported by the wall; that's how it looked to me.

They had on black and white striped uniforms, the kind the people wore in the concentration camps. All three were Latvians. They had nothing with them, only the uniforms on them, not even a blanket.

I started to ask them who they were and from where. I told them that I was from Riga with my father, mother, and little girl. I told them that our camp was closing and we needed a place to live, and that the office sent us to see this place.

As we talked I learned that the young, tall, very thin man was a student from the University of Riga. His father was ambassador in Poland. The German military got him and demanded money. They had learned about his father being an ambassador in Poland. When he said he had none they insisted that he had money in Switzerland and demanded that he get it for them. He refused. Then they took him to the concentration camp, for no return. Even his parents didn't know. He was very sad.

"I don't know if my father and mother are alive or where they are. I have no money and know not what to do."

The second sitting man was sad. He, too, was from Riga. He had a family business, Vodka (brandy). The Germans insisted that he give up the factory to them and resign. He refused. They took him to the concentration camp. He had no knowledge about his family and had no money. He was pale and thin and said, "I was heavy and big, and am glad for that. Those reserves saved me. I would never be here today without them. I don't know if I have my family left, or where they are."

The third man was middle-size. The concentration camp uniform was loose on him. He was from Liepaja. It was a harbor city, really a seaport with big ships coming in. He lived there with his family and was a master craftsman with leather handmade goods. He was Jewish. When the Germans saw the goods he had made, they took him and his goods to the same concentration camp. There other military men saw his leatherwork and asked him if he could make more of his kind. He told them that if they had leather he could. So they kept him in the backrooms and he was making these articles for them.

"How about food?" I asked.

"The same that everyone got in the camp, but the one who ordered my work liked it so well he came often to see and sometimes before leaving he forgot some food on my work bench. When I reminded him he said to just throw it away."

"Did you throw away?" I asked.

"No," he said, "I thanked God for the blessing. I knew he kept me going."

"Where are you going from here?" I asked.

"Back to Liepaja. I hope my wife and family are still there," and his face expressed love and a mild smile.

I went back to the camp to tell Papa and to share my experience with him. I also told him that these young men might be there a short time, but since I told them about our family and that we would be happy to occupy the opposite wall, they told me it would be all right.

One of them even said, "It would be nice to be together with regular people not like us." The other two agreed.

Papa insisted on going there himself and said, "If you don't mind, come along with me. I would like it. When the men see you with me, they will trust us more."

So we both went, but he did not go to the apartment. He went first to the office. When he came out he had a satisfied look on his face.

We went upstairs where the three men were. Papa became acquainted with each of them. After talking with them for a while he said, "We need something in this room. How about bunks or mattresses!"

The men liked what he said, but the ambassador's son said, "We don't know where to go to get what we need. When we came they said for us to stay here, then they will let us know."

"I know," Papa said, "let us go and see what we can get. I hope you can help me."

The young men went with Papa. They came back with three bunks and left again and brought three army beds, and three mattresses. Then they left with Papa again and brought three or four army blankets.

Papa insisted that these men use the beds, mattresses, and the blankets. He told them that we have our blankets and we would use the bunks because they are wider. They thanked Papa for his help.

Papa and I left to return to the camp where Mama and Maija were waiting for us. I picked up my girl and we both went to the colonel's house to continue my work there.

I don't remember when my parents left the camp and moved to the army barracks, but when I visited them the three Latvians were getting ready to leave. The ambassador's son had contacted somebody in Switzerland. He had received a package from Zurich (I think) with clothes and some money. I hope that he reached his destination and found his family all alive and well.

Mr. Dze, the owner of the brandy factory, was out, probably taking care of his family business. Papa said that Mr. Dze was having a hard time because Riga and Latvia were still full of Russian occupants and army. "You know they are like cockroaches. Where they are in, they don't want to leave."

I don't remember the name of the master craftsman, only that he was Jewish. When I was visiting my parents he was out. Papa said that he was a good, industrious, and God loving man.

"You know," Papa said, "God loves his sons and daughters. He is always with them."

Later I met him and he mentioned that he had been talking with a sailor from Liepaja who knows of a ship that needs repairs, and he knows he can do it.

The years have passed, but I have not forgotten these three men. I see them as if I saw them yesterday. For what reason did they have to suffer so? Who had rights to ruin their lives? God did not do that! No, no!

This army ex-camp was filling with the people. All kinds of people, nationalities, ex-soldiers, ex-service men, young, old, well, sick, families, single women, single men.

The people who had some musical instruments or talents were coming together, singing and playing with whatever they had. Somebody had a wooden pipe, possibly homemade, but he sure knew how to play it. When the instruments were playing, here and there his pipe came in and that brought out even more the beauty of the other sounds.

Somebody found an old piano. People came together and fixed it. We had concerts! Beautiful! All of it was outdoors, so what! The weather was fine. People were coming from all around to listen.

Lubeck was in the English zone. Now, since the war was over, when the people who lived in the American zone heard about the concerts they were coming from their side, too, to listen. When asked how they came the answer was, "Look, those cars there, the trucks, too, behind the people," their hands pointed to show, and we saw. There were lots of them.

It was wonderful. The war was gone! Really gone? It will never come back? I hope so! I am sure that all people who were there listening to the concerts were thinking the same.

Living in this ex-army camp, Papa had met more acquaintances from the old times. Talking with them he said, "Our country will be free, then we will go home! And all other countries too. All, all!" I hoped, but was not so sure as he.

The Russians still were vagrant, roaming around. Yes, I felt sorry for them, seeing them as lost sheep without a shepherd, looking like humans but not acting human. Why? Why? I wanted to know.

The work in the English colonel's house was coming to an end. The colonel's work was finished there and he was going back to England, back to his family, his life, and that was good. The cook and Rita did not want to stay there just to serve two men. One was military intelligence and the other a military captain.

They said to us, "Maybe a week or two, then we will be gone. Probably back home."

We said goodbye to both gentlemen, received our pay, and left the colonel's house. The cook and Rita went to their camp and I with my girl went to the ex-military camp where my parents were living.

Maija liked this new place because there were more children she could play with.

In the room where my parents lived were three bunk beds and still two army beds. Those two I asked Papa to give to somebody who needed them. We did not need those.

People were coming and going, moving around from north to south, east to west. There was lots of talking. Papa was listening and talking with Mama. I was so glad that Mama was fourteen years younger than Papa. She was so patient, a good listener, and no complaints or judging came from her. If she couldn't take something anymore, she would leave and go for a long walk.

One afternoon walking outside I met a young medical doctor. I think his name was Lusis. The English colonel in the house where I worked had introduced us. His English was good. How and where colonel and the doctor met I don't know, but colonel's mention about our Latvian cook and Latvian kitchen was the reason for this visit, I thought.

As we talked, Dr. Lusis told me that many young people, especially men, war veterans, were planning to go to Australia. He said that he was also planning to go there.

"See," he said, "most of these young men were damaged in the war. Most of them had not finished their schools. They lost their families, country, and their health. I want to help them there. I have my medical license and Colonel told me that in Australia I could practice."

It was so good to hear a man talking about his fellow man and desire to help them. To care how important are their needs, not his own.

Papa decided to leave Lubeck and to move more south to Oldenburg near Bremerhaven. He said that there were several refugee camps. He was interested in one that was near but outside of the city. The people lived in the camp in the small barracks. The barracks were divided into separate rooms with doors from the hall. "There is a little land by the barracks. Maybe one could plant a tomato or a flower plant."

Also Oldenburg was a smaller city and had not been bombed or damaged by the war. Papa definitely felt that it was the right place for us. They took Maija with them too. There were several other families who also were leaving for Oldenburg.

I received a message from Papa that they were in Oldenburg, that all was well, and they had a place for me too. He said Maija was well and happy and asking for me and hoped to see me soon.

Then I found that a truck with people would go in two days to Oldenburg and they had one place on the truck available but it had no top cover and it might be windy. That did not worry me. I just wanted to leave this place. I had nothing here and wanted to be with my family.

Sitting in that opened truck I really was joyful. The view was wonderful. The road was advanced as the highways now in America. The cleanliness and neatness of the road opened the view on the right and left to the passing towns, cities, farms, and woods. That sure was an experience for me to see and remember. Very few cars and trucks were on the road.

The war was ended, I thought, and people just wanted to work, to stay home, and to be at peace.

We reached Oldenburg in the afternoon. Just outside the city was the camp. We drove in through the open gateway. On the right side was the office in a green barrack. The truck stop was there. I saw Papa and Maija coming down the road. She was running to me.

Papa came and, lifting my suitcase, said, "I took care of your coming with Mr. Adminis. He is responsible for this camp, but I think it would be right for you to see him and for him to meet the new arrival. I will wait for you at home."

Maija, holding my hand and leading me to the office said, "Mama, I know where the office is. Come! I will tell Mr. Adminis that you are my mother."

So we both went in and my daughter did her introduction.

I don't remember what we talked about, but my daughter said, "Now we go home. I know where it is and Babite (grandma's name) is waiting for us."

We left the office and joined Papa by the road. We talked as we walked towards the home, as Maija called the barrack.

"On the right side of this road Latvians live in all the barracks. On the left side of the road live Estonians. They have their own office, kitchen, dining room and everything that they need on their side. Most all of them are ex-soldiers, young and single.

"These buildings on the left side are heavy and larger. We have a bathhouse in the church. The entrance from the back as you can see is the firewood house. And there to the side is a garage. We get old junk cars, take them apart, make new parts, and make a new car. The truck on which you came we made here.

"Now," Papa said, "we are home. The last door in this barrack we go in, then the second on the left is our door."

Mama, Maija's babite, had heard Papa's voice and was opening the door and saying, "Come in, come in. So you found her after all."

"Yes, yes," he was smiling, "she is with us." So we were in the new home. Just one room, but it was home. There was one window at the end of the room facing other barracks. By the door was a stove with a brick wall about four feet high and one foot wide. It was for cooking and heating the room.

Near the window were a table and a couple of chairs. By the long wall were two double bunks. In the middle of the wall was a cabinet wardrobe.

On the bunks were sacks filled with straw or hay instead of mattresses. The walls were unpainted wood boards about one-inch thick that separated one room from another. That and each room having a door gave us privacy. With such thin walls we had to talk quietly.

"I have made the bed for you with sheet and blanket. I know you still have yours, but we have been given these from the Red Cross. They said they are army leftovers. I don't think these were used, but I still washed them by hand," Mama said.

"How about some food?" she said. "Here is some soup I saved from dinner. I told them in the kitchen that you were coming today. They gave me more of the bread, too."

She put the warm soup from the stove and black bread from the cabinet on the table. We took the places at the table. The soup plates, forks and knives were the ones she had put in her suitcases when we left home in Riga.

"Would you like to have some tea? I am warming water on the stove," said Papa, and he brought a small jar with sugar from the cabinet.

Then he brought a little milk and poured some into the cup. "Maija gets milk any time we have it. Children, all children, every day in the dining room, receive milk, two cups a day. The small ones get more."

As we were sitting at the table and talking, a thought was clinging in my head, two cups of milk a day?

"What is around outside of the camp?" I asked.

"The farms. There is a village with one street in the middle. Houses on both sides of the street. The farm land is in long strips around the village."

"In Latvia, Baltianava, Papa, I remember, where your sister Karolina was living in a village, the land was in strips. Some strips were so far away. What about other things?"

"Close to the village they have a Lutheran church and next to that a very nice cemetery," he said.

"The Lutheran church was very nice and the German minister and his parishioners offered our Lutheran ministers, we have two, the use of their church," Papa was telling.

In the morning Papa and Mama were up early. Papa was in charge of the firewood house. I was glad that he was engaged in something. He had a couple of men working with him.

Mama was called in to go to the kitchen. It was her day to peel potatoes. Later I found that everyone living on the camp was assigned work. Since in the camp there was not much to do, people willingly participated when asked.

After my girl was up and we both had breakfast, she was willing to show me the camp. First she took me to a green barrack-like building with high small windows. The latrine was just a round hole in the floor. By the windows along the wall was the water pipeline with cold water.

"Babite and other women come here and do their washing," my girl was telling.

The camp had no fence, but nearby was a very silent road on which were some houses and a church. I decided to have a walk that way. The day was sunny and warm and we were happy to be together.

"Grandpa go to this church. I go with him, too," Maija was telling, "but if he forgets me and I cannot find him, I know he must be in the church, then I go there by myself."

"You don't go by yourself? It is so far."

"Yes, I do. It is not far. That door is so big and heavy, but I push it, go in. I know where Grandpa is sitting and I go right to him."

Later Papa told me that indeed Maija would come by herself into church when all were sitting. She would come by the rows of benches right of the main walk and suddenly on his right side people stood up. He thought, What now? and then he saw they were getting up so she could come in where he was sitting.

The life in this camp seemed asleep, uneventful, but it was not so. The name of this camp was Ohmstadt. The name of it came (Ohm-stadt) from a physicist Greg Simon (1787-1854). After all, the people were living there and progress in life goes on, it can never be stopped.

Some good things were coming to the camp. Red Cross from America, clothes, shoes, things for children. Then American cigarettes. I think it was straight from American tobacco factories. I did not smoke, nor did my mother. My father did but since his cigarettes from Riga had been used up, he stopped smoking.

Still what we were given we saved. We found out that some people were selling them for money. We noticed that people from the camp would go for a walk and come back not with empty hands.

Once Papa said, "Let's go for a walk. I have some friends that I have not seen for a while. They have a big farm and a big house with other buildings and big hog pigsty, chickens, and other things." So we were talking and walking on the road towards the village but turned to the right on the smaller road before reaching the village. Then the road turned to the left and we saw the farm buildings just as Papa was telling me about. We were a short distance from the village.

Now we were in front of a big log house with big comfortable yard, surrounded with the buildings and barns just as Papa told. There were big fruit trees on the sides and at the back of the house. It sure looked very similar to a farm in Latvia.

As soon as we were there the farmer's wife came out to meet us, she recognized Papa and seemed glad to see him, especially when she realized that I could speak in German. It was so much easier to understand each other.

Papa wanted to know if we could buy some milk from them and how to pay. With cigarettes, money, or with something else?

I don't remember if we had to sell the cigarettes or give them to her. I think it was the latter. From them once a week I came home with the milk can full of good fresh farm milk so my girl had enough. She really liked milk and had no problems with it. It definitely improved her food.

Then we received a packet from Stockholm, Sweden, and a letter in Papa's name. The senders were Mr. and Mrs. Ratseps. We met these people in Latvia and again in Pokrent, before the war ended.

They were of Swedish origin and their oldest son was living there. Now we knew that in their old age they were where they should be and were with their son who could take care of them.

We opened the packet. There were a couple of things in it. I don't remember what one was, but the other was my father's favorite Melange coffee. Papa put it aside and said, "We better save it," and put it in the cabinet.

Then we heard that an excellent tailor from Riga who had learned that trade in London, England, and Vienna, Austria, was willing to teach this trade. As a young girl I liked to sew dresses for my doll. I signed on when we were told we could pay with cigarettes or money. Since Mr. Caune had customers, we could learn and work with him on the jobs he had in his tailor's shop. There were four or five ladies who wanted to learn.

The camp gave him a big room and several long tables in one of the barracks and Mr. Caune opened the shop. At that time we heard that there were possibilities to find work if one had a trade.

So people became busy. They began to learn how to repair cars and mend woodwork by repairing barracks or building something that was needed. Some used the land between barracks to plant vegetables.

We heard news that some countries like Canada, Australia, England, and America needed all kinds of workers.

We received a letter from my sister Nina. When the war was over she was still in Ventspils harbor in Latvia. She said there still were a couple of ships in the harbor being filled with wounded and the last soldiers ready to leave, and she decided to leave with them on the ship before the Russians entered Ventspils harbor.

There was such a rush, she wrote, people running everywhere trying to get out of the city, the harbor. German captains were very helpful to get everybody on the ships. Their ship arrived in Lubeck.

The English soldiers were meeting the German ships and their soldiers. Then the ambulances came, too, taking the wounded.

Then the civilians were taken to the same camp where for a while we were staying, the one that was close to the harbor. She mentioned that she had a chance to go to England and work. They needed workers in the hospitals. Maybe she would like it there. A Latvian girl about her age came on the ship and would like to go with her to England.

After reading Nina's letter with Papa and Mama, we were glad that she had the opportunity to leave Ventspils and was free and in Lubeck. She was now 22 and grown up.

"She is sensible and her desire to work is a practical, normal thing," said Papa. I like the idea that she won't travel there alone but with the girlfriend. I like also that this England work has a basic one year contract and after that if she doesn't want to continue she can return here to us."

"Yes, Papa. You are right. She is not a little child anymore. If we would try to restrict her or set time limits she may not like it. After all, we ourselves do not know where we will be."

After awhile we received a letter from England. Nina and her girlfriend were working in a hospital in the nursing department in Manchester. Both girls liked their work, the people, and living quarters with other nurses.

Then later they moved to London. After a year Nina's girlfriend stayed in England, but Nina returned to Lubeck, Germany.

We received a letter from her, telling us that she wanted to travel a little. Probably to the Netherlands, Belgium, and Paris, France.

I don't remember how long she was in Belgium but she was in France awhile. When she returned to Germany and to camp Ohmstadt in Oldenburg, we could see that she had been in Paris. She looked like someone stepping out from a fashion magazine. The coat, the hat, the shoes, even the beautiful leather pocketbook. She looked wonderful. Papa said now every man would be opening doors for her.

Papa, coming from his work in the woodshed, said that he had heard that Voldis, my husband, had been looking for us and had been told where we live.

I heard it, but was not excited. It had been such a long time that passed. Even our daughter did not ask about him. My Papa and her grandmother had cared for her and loved her when Voldis, her father, could not.

Working in criminal police, the hours were long, very long, with no regard for weekends, holy days, families, and children. When he was leaving in the morning, she was asleep. When he came home past midnight she was asleep. He worked for the government and it looked to me that it was what he cared about. I was glad that my parents lived so close to me.

Now I was working and learning sewing and tailoring. I liked this work and was doing fine. Mr. Caune was satisfied with my work and trusted more and more of his customer orders to me.

One day I worked with a customer's jacket and had it ready to be delivered in the morning. It was past closing time so I locked the door and left.

When I arrived at home, Voldis was sitting at the table with Mama and Papa. Maija was clinging to her grandpa. "Good day," I said, and took a seat on the edge of my bunk, "you finally found us. Where have you been so long?"

"I will answer all you want to know," Voldis said, "but will I not get a kiss first?" I knew I had to do it, but I really did not want to. So long we had been separated.

He got up and came to me and kissed me. We have been for so long estranged that I did not feel anything and I know he felt my estrangement too.

My Papa saw that I felt uncomfortable and said, "I hope we will have some dinner coming. I am very hungry. How about you people?"

"Yes," Mama said, going to the stove, "all is ready. We have vegetable soup, fried potatoes, and bread." We sat at the table and ate and we were quiet.

After the meal Voldis told us that in 1944 when he was ordered to meet with other men by the police main station in Riga, they were sent to the war lines to dig ditches for stopping Russian armored tanks. With that, they were backed into Lithuania and then into Germany. They slept in the woods, sometimes in the ditches they had just dug. The food situation was bad. In Germany they were sent to clean the cities that were bombed. After the war he was going from one refugee camp to another. He had no money left. His clothes were worn out. He finally was in an American zone and camp, trying to find us.

"Then with the war ending, the Americans and English needed car and truck transport drivers. They offered to teach us." So Voldis joined them. As long as there was work he would keep working. Most weekends they were free, but Saturday morning and Sunday he would like to come here, home.

"That is, if it is all right with you," he said.

"We may need a larger place. Nina is visiting with some friends today and tomorrow. I will ask Mr. Adminis, the camp director, if he has something for us," said Papa, and we agreed.

Since we had four bunks, I slept with Maija on the bottom and Voldis slept on the top bunk.

Monday we talked with the camp director. He said that there was one in the middle barrack, a middle room the same size as Papa's place, but it is very dirty and it needs a stove.

When we looked at the place, we saw that all four walls were dirty, but pinkish dirty, and it looked as if the paint was moving.

Adminis looking, said, "You better use first a wash, not paint, and a chemical wash, then let it dry good. This place is infested with bed bugs. The German paint stores have very effective cleaners."

I bought the necessary chemicals and brushed it on the walls and ceiling and left it to dry. The next day I brushed the walls and floor and in the middle of the room was a pile of dust. No!—it was more than a foot high of pinkish-gray bed bugs.

Then came the painting and cleaning. A mason from our camp came and built a heating stove. Voldis brought with him from the American zone a new bunk bed. Then came other necessary furniture pieces including a table and two chairs.

As usual every week, I went to the farm for milk. The farmer's wife was standing by the byre. I got my milk and paid her. She said, "Come, I want to show you something," and she walked to the pigsty.

I looked there and saw a big, long sow lying down and more than a dozen piglets running to get their meal. They were not even a foot long yet. They sure were busy.

She said, "Would you like to have one?"

"Yes," I quickly said, "but we have no shed for a piglet. Where would we keep it and feed it? They are so little, they need their mother."

"Well," she said, "we could help you some. Look, we have there some old boards. My husband talked about burning those, but they are not so bad yet. In a couple of weeks you could take it away from the mother."

She then asked, "Do you still have that real good coffee?"

"Yes, we still have the coffee, but I want to talk this over with my parents." We agreed that I would do just that, and I left with the milk.

When I told my family, Papa said, "I will think about it. It sounds very interesting." And he did think. All his lifetime he never had an enemy. People respected him, trusted him, and loved him, regardless if they were generals, ministers, factory workers, street sweepers, Jew or Gypsy, Polish, or German.

One day after work he came and said, "We have to get ready and prepare a living place for the piglet. There is a wood shed by the next barrack. There is an extended roof and under it two walls, that makes a corner. It needs two walls not too high, a door and a floor." So we went to look at the place. It was like he was telling. The next day he found a shorter shed door. On the weekend Voldis came home and, being a country builder's son, the pig house was ready by Sunday.

I learned that several other Latvians and Estonians had bought piglets and were raising them. I was told how to feed them using leftover foods and along the country road go pick grass, weeds, dandelions, then go to the mill and buy flour and mix it with the food.

One afternoon I found the mill. It was not far at all. I did not see any customers. When I asked the miller if he would sell me some flour, he asked what kind I needed. I answered, " Any kind. And how much?"

Then he said, "What do you need it for?"

"I need it for a pig, a small pig."

He looked at me and said, "I will not sell you any, but it's the end of the day. You could sweep the floor, then put it in your bag and take it. That would be enough for the pig."

So I did it and had as much as I could carry. I wanted to pay him, but he said, "No, you did the work. When you need more for your pig, come anytime and take it."

So once or twice a week I was going to the mill to sweep the floor and get the flour.

The pig we bought liked the place. It was about 4 x 5 feet. It was eating well and growing.

Then there was talk that people could emigrate to Argentina. There was information about that country and applications to complete. Papa was interested in it and wanted to participate. I did not want to rush, but try to find out about that country, the people, and the climate. Also Papa's health was giving him problems. He went to see a medical doctor.

Then the month of August came and the people were saying that this year lots of mushrooms were growing in the forests. They even mentioned a special forest and taking a train to go there. So I joined a group and in the middle of the week we took the train and in the afternoon returned with full baskets.

I thought that the next time my husband was home we both could go to that beautiful forest. I did not mention this idea to him ever. when the weekend came and he was home. Sunday he left, as usual, with other men for work in the American zone. The week passed and the weekend came, but the American truck with men did not arrive. The coming week the truck arrived Wednesday afternoon but not all the men were on the truck.

Maija was playing outside. Soon I heard the door was opening, and Maija was bringing her dad in.

"I found my daddy and bring him home!"

He explained that they worked the last weekend and this morning early at breakfast the captain said they had no work for all of them, so they could take a few days and go home, but Sunday night all should be back.

The next day was Thursday and a group of people was going again to the same forest. I wished to tell Voldis about the trip, but could not.

Papa, sitting at the table sipping his hot tea said, "Tomorrow is the mushroom day. Ida, you are going on that trip. Why, now you both can go. Those woods sure have good mushrooms. We can even pickle them for winter. Bring all you can carry. This is September, not much time left for mushrooms, the weather now is good."

Voldis looked at me and I smiled.

"That is a good idea," he said, " away from the city in the woods. Fresh clean air. I think it will be a wonderful day. What time does the train leave?"

I liked what he said.

"We will have an early breakfast and leave with the group at 8:00 a.m. We had better take some water and bread. There are no stores," I informed.

"You better stay here tonight so you don't oversleep," said Papa, "and you, Voldis, have a good sleep and rest in your bed. You will need it."

Voldis kissed me lightly and left for our barrack.

Mama was up early in the morning. Papa was up before her and started a fire in the stove and had the teapot on. He had been doing that for a long, long time. I prepared baskets and other things for the trip. Then I washed myself clean and dressed appropriately, clean and practical.

Voldis came on time to have breakfast. I said, "Good morning."

I set the cup and food in front of him on the table, smiled, and slowly caressed his hand lying on the table.

He smiled at me and said, "You feeling good this morning?"

"Yes," I said, "and you too?"

We picked up our things and baskets and left for our trip. When we arrived at the railway station destination, we got out and walked to the forest on the narrow field road. There were quite a few from our camp and from other Latvian camps, too. We were walking quickly to get in the woods and start gathering mushrooms so that before sunset we could be back at the station and take the train home.

Indeed there were a lot of mushrooms and everybody was busy. In no time, here and there between the trees, I saw people with full baskets moving out of the woods. Our baskets, too, were filling. Voldis, coming closer to me, said, "We don't have to hurry."

"You're right," I agreed, "if you are tired, we can rest now."

"Well we cannot go home with half-full baskets." I looked at his basket; it was full but mine was not.

"I never was a fast gatherer," I said.

"You sit and rest," he said, "I will help you."

He came to take my basket and said, "Look, this place looks so comfortable, you could sit there. The young trees are so thick, protecting." He left me with his full basket and took mine.

I was sitting on the hump and thinking that my desire to be with my husband in this forest is fulfilled. I was glad that after such long time we were together again. We have one child, our girl, and I was glad for that. I desired more than one child, but now being alone these years has left me unfulfilled. All the excuses were around me. No, not yet. Later.

In the Bible it is said, "The good productive thoughts come from God." I needed a child. Being alone I have met men who were interested in me, but I wanted the child with my husband.

We all are God's children. In this desire I wanted this conception to be right, with God's blessing and action.

Voldis came with a full basket and took a place close by me.

"Are you thirsty, would you like some bread?" I asked.

"I am not hungry, maybe some water," he said. I gave him the water and bag with the bread. He took a little.

"What would you like to do," he said, "go home or still rest?"

"I would like to stay here longer," I said hesitantly, leaning toward him.

"If you will, I am willing too, and we can rest and talk."

"I have been thinking about you while you were in the woods. I am so glad that you came back to me. I needed you and missed you, but denied it myself. I felt why should I have dreams anymore? Dreams vanish in the daytime."

"What would you like me to do for you?" he said, and pulled me down from the hump I was sitting on. "I will do whatever you desire," he said, with such warmth. It made me feel so good, so safe and I wiggled closer to him.

"I want to have a child," I whispered, "for a long, long time I have wanted."

"Are you sure?" he said, "We can do it, if that is what you want. We can talk more at home."

"No," I said, looking into his eyes. "Not, if you don't want. Not at home with so many people around us with thin walls. Here, Voldis, in this forest, all the people are long gone. Here." I pointed to a dent behind his back surrounded by close, young tree growth. "It is not too deep, but enough for me to lie full length and for you on top to come into me full length, sliding into me, with all your love and body. And me receiving you with expectation, love, and desire, taking all of you and all you can give me."

"Yes, my love. I will give you all I have." We prepared. He took off some bottom clothes and I did too.

I was comfortable on the bottom and he was on top coming slowly into me. I felt his warmth on my body and lifted myself to welcome him in. We were not in a hurry. We had all the time in the world. We were in God's country; we stopped and kissed. Then he said, "I always wanted you, but thought you would forget me. So many single men around you in the camps."

I felt like we both were melting, becoming completely one body. Just as the Bible says for the husband and wife to become one. I said, "Give me all you have, fill me."

"Yes, my love, I am giving you all and will give all you need."

I gave him a towel and he got dressed. For about fifteen minutes I reposed, then was up. We were sitting for a while and rested. I knew we both were satisfied.

Then we took all our things and started to walk out of the forest and then to the station, but the mushroom pickers were gone. We arrived in camp and gave the baskets to Mama. She offered us some food, but we were not hungry. We took our girl and left for our barrack, for our bed. It being wider than bunks we could sleep comfortably. That's what we wanted, to be side by side, feeling each other.

Our pig was growing. Voldis went to clean the pigsty and told us that in another month she would be six months and ready for the roast. She was very big.

"You're right," Papa said, "I talked with our Latvian butcher. He will take care of that. In Latvia he was a country butcher. He will do the salting and smoking."

Papa's health was not getting better. He went to see the doctor, who mentioned a blood transfusion. We were wondering how and where it could be done. How much it could cost? The doctor's nurse suggested a war veteran in a nursing home who lost both legs in the war. He was about in mid-forties and looked healthy. He did not want any pay. He said that his body produced blood. Anyway, we paid him, as Papa said, in gratitude for his kind help.

It was near the end of October. Some people from our camp received messages from Argentina. In the meantime I had seen and read newspapers and journals about Argentina and was losing interest. If the woman was working and was married she could never receive her earned salary, but it was given to her husband. When I explained that to my family, Papa and Voldis could not believe it and laughed. Mama and I did not like it at all. To me it was not funny. It was not a joke.

"In this time it cannot be true," Papa said. "But if the husband dies, what then? It would take time and years to change that law. No, it's not for me. Being South America, probably the majority of people are Catholics. No, that's not for me."

The end of October came. I told my family that I was pregnant. Voldis was at work. Papa became upset. "You must have an abortion. This is not the right time to have children."

"No, Papa. No abortion. I have been hoping for a child for a long time. Now is October, I expect the child in June." Papa did not say anything more about it.

When Voldis came from work I told him, "Well, we wanted the child and now we have."

Papa worried about our living situation. "This is Germany. They have their own refugees from East Germany and have to take care of them. We cannot go back to Latvia where Russians and communists dominate."

"They would probably send us to Serbia to destroy," I said. "I don't think I'm going back. Since I learned how to sew and Mama got for me a sewing machine, I am getting more customers, not only our people, but Germans too. I am glad that I know their language."

"When we were still in Latvia, Mr. Ozols from America often visited us at our employment place and said if there was war or something like that, just to write him and he would get us to America. Just anybody who wants, he would get us there," Voldis was telling.

"Really I am not worried about what will happen. We did not start this stupid war. We did not kill."

"I don't believe that God would want to destroy people who did no harm to anybody, but the war makers full of evil, greed, and self-righteousness are stupid and destroy people's lives. Still they have no permanent benefits."

"We have to take one day as it comes and trust in God. That's all we can do." Voldis agreed with that.

One day I went to see Mama in their barrack. She and Papa were sitting at the table and had a visitor sitting with them. At first I did not recognize the man. Papa noticed my reserve and said, "You do remember Mr. Bruveris? He took us to Kurzeme. Remember the beautiful farm in the middle of the forest, his relative? Remember we traveled in the Riga factory's truck?"

"Yes, yes," I said. "I am glad that you came to visit us. We did not know what happened to you or if you had enough time to get out."

I had so many questions to ask about his family and children, but Papa too had so many things to talk about, so I did not ask. Since he seemed satisfied, I hoped that his family was with him. He looked good, but was about ten years younger than Papa.

After Colonel Bruveris left, Papa's health was not getting better. He went again to see the doctor. I suggested that he change doctors, but he did not want to. I thought Mama would change his mind, but she said no.

He was using several medical "pills." One of them was "kartizon." The medical diagnosis was that Papa had a carcinoma. The explanation was that it was cancer. It was separating the food pipe from the stomach. I asked Mama if ever during their life he had problems with the stomach.

She said, "Not really, but he always was afraid of cancer. Since they were married he would point his finger into his stomach and say, 'There grows a Cancer.'"

When he was working in the army, being in a high-ranking position, every spring he had to go to the army hospital for a checkup. He stayed there three or four days. One time they said they noticed a white, round spot but it did not look dangerous. So they left it for next time.

Papa still was walking around but his legs were not stable, especially when he carried something. I was in his barrack; Mama was outdoors. He came in and took a seat.

"I am glad you are here. We can talk. You take the family to America, regardless of what anybody says. Do not go back. Without God there is no life and will never be. In America, people have church. Take my Bible with you. Do not lose it."

Soon Papa's legs were swollen very big and he was taken to the hospital. Mama went with him. Later she came back. In the morning she went again and was with him until late.

She told us that Papa lay in bed and did not complain, only that he was cold, although he had blankets. I don't remember how long Papa was there. I was pregnant and felt bad since my body was adjusting for its new duty, and I planned to visit him in a couple of days when I was feeling better. But Papa passed away before I could see him.

We buried him in Ohmstadt's cemetery by the village church in Oldenburg, 8 November 1946. He was 71 years old and in a strange country in a strange land. Why? The war.

The time was passing in the camp. Nina was living with Mama in the same barrack. She was working someplace or visiting some friends. Voldis planted tomatoes in a large space between the barracks. They grew well and were beautiful, but when we started to harvest them they were brown on the inside. We were told that our soil had lacked lime. The next year we planted them closer to our barrack, radish, carrots, cucumbers, and onions. They grew better.

June 10, 1947, our son David was born in the hospital of Oldenburg. He was perfect and thin. The birth was not hard. My mother came to visit me but my husband was still working in the American zone.

Mama told me that when Maija was told that she now has a baby brother, she was so happy that she saved all her cookies for her brother. In our camp cookies very seldom were given to children, and then only four. This five-year old child was saving her best for her brother. I was grateful to God for both of my children, and that she felt love for her brother and the need to give.

When we brought the baby home, Maija was meeting us at the door. Indeed she was so happy and said, "Mama, I saved all my cookies for David."

I thanked her for that for him and for me, "When he learns to speak then he will thank you himself."

"I will teach him how to speak," she said, with a happy face.

David was a peaceful child, just eating and sleeping. I nursed him. Before his first month ended it seemed that he was always hungry and needed more nursing. We did not have baby feeding bottles, or money to buy such. Then somebody brought us some fresh, ripe strawberries. An idea came to me. I squeezed out the juice and got a quarter of a cup. I didn't add anything and with a teaspoon fed it to him. He took it so nicely and went to sleep. After awhile we had to give him more of the juice and it went to a half-cup, then a three-quarter cup. By the end of the second month I was out of juice. I bought semolina (a fine wheat groats, manna) and with half water and half milk I cooked it to a medium consistency and fed him a quarter-cup with the spoon. As time went on, I increased the portion and thickness. I was also still nursing him with my milk.

I remember when he was six months old I had nursed him in the morning and now was the next feeding time. I picked him up to nurse, but he would not take it. I tried and tried but he would not. Still he was whimpering as though he was hungry. So I had no choice but to feed him semolina. Since six months he never took my breast.

He was doing just fine. I was glad about the extra milk I was buying from the farmer and additional food, too. Voldis built a small child's bed for David with the boards he found in a reject lumber pile.

We had a hard time with baby's diapers and clothes. What my girl had was worn to shreds. We had no money to buy more. Papa's underwear was left. It, too, was worn out. I found that his shirt backs were still holding together, the fronts and sleeves were worn out. I used what I could from Papa's underwear and shirts to make shirts and diapers for David.

We had only cold water to use for washing and we washed by hand. We had only one change. That is one shirt on his back, another washed and drying.

Then he started to walk and needed pants. I had nothing. I went through Mama and Papa's clothes, still nothing. I saw my winter coat. Then I had an idea. I lifted up the coat lining. It was thin and silky and still okay, but it would not do.

I lifted the lining and saw the interlining. It was gray, soft, woven like cheesecloth except a little thicker. It looked like I could make two pants. I took it out, washed, and made the pants. As my coat lining was old and showed it, so did the interlining, but I had no other choice. They were all right with elastic around the waist and the legs.

Then we heard that the American Red Cross had sent clothes to the refugee camps, ours included, and placed in our bathhouse, probably the cleanest place on the camp. I found what I needed and since we had had opportunity to learn dressmaking I redid the one I picked out and received many compliments.

David was growing and had a gentle, sunny disposition. Voldis still worked in the American zone with the other men from our camp and on the weekend arrived on the big truck full of men. They parked the truck by our neighbor's barrack and unloaded the men there. Very soon David noticed that his daddy was in that bunch too and since he was almost two years old and could run, now he was running to him as fast as he could with one hand lifted up and a smile as bright as sunshine.

The men from the bunch standing and watching this scene, shouted, "Hey, who is that?"

Somebody from the group answered, "That is Voldis's boy, his son!" There were other voices, then laughter.

"That his son? Impossible! He don't look like him."

"No way," other voices joined, "he could never have a son like that."

Voldis hung his head down toward me. His face suddenly looked very unhappy. David dropped his outstretched hand and looked sad, his head also hung down.

At the age of two David suddenly spoke in sentences. Even complicated words, which he heard the first time, he tried to say. I remember we were walking toward a lake. It was not close. He was getting tired but was not complaining. I lifted him up to carry. He never had a baby carriage or a children's handcart. Seeing a churchman passing us, "Perminder" (a worker), David said carefully, "penda-pinda." A long word for a beginner.

My mother who way back was a teacher in grammar school had a wealth of all kinds of stories to tell and children's books she had read. I did not know that she took some children's books when we left our home in Riga, and Maija was two-and-a-half years old. Now she started to read to David. She especially noticed David's uncanny attention when she was reading.

Since Maija was four years old, my mother, Babite as we called her, taught her to read, write, and do arithmetic. Within two months' time Maija could read anything and also write. In 1950 we arrived on the Strode farm in America. Mrs. Strode told us about the school, mentioning that at her age she should be in first grade. She even called the school for us. She took Maija there.

Within one week her teacher called to tell me that they transferred Maija to second grade, because in the first grade they had nothing to teach her. Even in the second grade it was the same except learning English. Maija was bright and always a good student in school.

One weekend Voldis came from work and was telling us that America was looking for workers, someplace south in the cotton fields, picking cotton. My sister Nina suggested that we get registered. I did not like that idea. Since I started sewing, my business was growing. My sister went and brought the forms to fill out saying, "After you fill in the forms and if you don't like what they have to offer you, refuse!"

Still I did not register but she did it for us in her handwriting. She told Voldis about these forms. "If you don't like where the job is, you don't take it." She said, "All necessary pictures and health checks of everybody can become very handy when the right job is available." Hearing all this, Voldis agreed. The forms were carefully completed and our health checked by the doctor.

Voldis said he had a feeling that soon we would hear from Mr. Ozols from New York.

"I think he will send us a visa, because he has asked me for information about us and I have sent it to him." Hearing all this, I was more at peace.

Mama heard all the talk, but did not say anything. I was knitting woolen pants and a sweater. I was glad that I still had my knitting needles. The cold weather was coming and I had nothing warm for David. Nina brought knitting wool from London.

"Mama," Nina said, "we both will stay here for a while. Then when they settle there I will help you to get there too."

I noticed that Mama smiled. She felt better knowing that we were not forgetting her. Nina was knitting a cardigan for Maija from angora wool she bought while working in England. We were sitting on the bench in front of our barrack near the entrance door. A neighbor from the next barrack passing by stopped and started to talk with us. He was a bachelor near my sister's age. He was telling us that he heard about our registration to go to America. Nina answered that we all will have to decide what to do. The Germans will not keep us free on the camp, except maybe very old people.

"Well," he said, "you're right, we all have to get busy. My parents were farmers and they were talking about Canada."

"I think," my sister said, "you all big strong, young men working and coming home weekends on that American truck, laughing and blabbering, should not carry on when little David runs to meet his daddy, so happy to see him. Who made you judge, did God give you license to say that Voldis is not David's father?"

"I am not with that bunch. Those men are only joking." He said, "They are afraid about tomorrow, where they will work when this ends soon."

"You think that acting ugly with stupid joking will benefit the jokers? You are Latvians; most of you are farmers. Have you forgotten the well-known proverb 'what you sow, so you shall reap'?" My sister was giving the Bible truth.

The young man insisted that she was right but that he did not participate with them.

"That is nice to hear," she said, "but your brother is a Catholic priest and you, God loving man, can close their mouths with the proverb to please our Father God."

The man said he would see what he could do, but that these men even at work often acted stupid.

I do not remember the name of the Catholic priest's family. I think it was Parzelis, father and mother, a strong couple. The oldest son was the priest, then there was a daughter in her early thirties. Anna and Andrew were twenty. They would make good farmers in Canada.

My father became a close friend with the priest. I think he was in his early forties. Since my father loved the Bible and knew it well they often were seen together. As I mentioned before, my father never left home without his Bible and just before he died he gave the Bible to me, to take to America and I still have it though with many pages are missing, especially Psalms. It was a valuable help for the family here in America and still is.

Papa had told that his friend said that Catholicism (Roman) is not what it seemed to be. Now since he knows what it is, he would not be a Catholic priest, but now he is over forty and thought it is too late to make a change.

His sister Anna and I became friendly. She was not married and told me that she had planned to marry somebody but her father did not like him and would not allow it. But the one her father selected for she did not want. I agreed with her that she had a right to make the choice with whom she would live her life.

Then she started telling me about the future of the world. She said that Roman Catholicism would be the only religion in the world. Then there would be peace. It would govern everything and everybody.

I asked, "Why does the Catholic church forbid their people to read and use the Bible but give them a little booklet half a finger thick?"

She said, "The little booklet is right for them. They are too ignorant to understand the Bible. The Pope knows what people need. God tells the Pope what to do."

"Why do your people have to go every week to confession?" I was asking.

"Because the priest has authority to forgive sins. Then the man knows that his transgressions are forgiven, and he has free way to heaven," she said.

"The priest is not God. When we pray to God, He only can forgive sins. God is the only creator of us and can forgive and is willing to forgive," I said.

"You're wrong," Anna said, "God has no time. That's why he makes the pope and priests."

I wanted to say that God had sent us His son Jesus Christ who brought Christianity not Roman Catholicism. He was healing and feeding people with love and truth and life. Not like Archbishop Albert who came to our country with sword and fire to give us Christianity, misusing and abusing our young, hard working people. When they asked him for some rest and food, the archbishop ordered that their tongues be cut out with the sword. Christ Jesus did not tell him to do that. Jesus never came with a sword like the Catholics.

I realized that Anna was speaking and thinking the way she was taught by the same kind of teachers as she was. They were not permitted to use the Bible, because by reading that book, God would change their thinking; that the pope, the archbishops, and the priest would not like that anybody interfere with their fancy lifestyle.

I did not think that I had the right to talk about her religion because it might interfere with her opinions. I did not avoid her in our daily life, but besides "good morning" or "it is a nice day" I was about my daily duties.

Later, when we were in America, I read in the Latvian newspaper that her brother, the priest, served in the Catholic church. I don't remember now in which city it was, only that it was in Canada. About other members from Parzelis family I never heard, but am sure that brother, the priest, took good care of the family.

The time was now moving on. Voldis got the lumber and was building a box for my sewing machine. It was big, with a foot pedal. When I learned to sew, Mama found somebody who had a good old machine and since we had bacon from the pig we raised, we now traded part of it for the machine. Several years I used it and both parties were satisfied.

I had no money, not even one dollar but with my work-tool I could sew anything and earn. And so it was in America my machine was earning for me. We were putting things together.

In the beginning of October we received a message to get ready and prepare to leave the camp for Bremerhaven. One group with bigger children left in October, but those with smaller children left the last day of October. They took us to a railroad station in the trucks and bus. I think it was in Oldenburg in the morning. We said goodbye to Mama and my sister in our barrack room. It was not with hugging, kissing, and crying. We just said we would write you when we can and left, walking to the parked truck. The thought came to me. We left. Left what?

At the railroad station there were many people and the passenger train continued to wait for

*Ida in 1949 before leaving the refugee camp*

more people. When the conductor made a signal and opened the door, Maija, holding my hand, and Voldis, holding our two-year-old son, stepped into train. To our surprise it was very full with mostly grown ups and men.

We got a seat at the end of a bench enough for Maija and me, and Voldis sat across from me and held David on his lap.

I have no idea who the people sitting on that bench were. They were not Latvians. They were well dressed. They whispered a little between themselves, except one tall, skinny man raised his voice and accused Latvians. I was surprised and looked on my husband's face. Without opening his mouth, his calm facial expression was telling me *don't say anything*.

Nobody else said anything and we continued peacefully to Bremerhaven. This man's sitting companion opened a small bag and took out a less than half-inch thick dark sweet/sour rye-bread sandwich of bread and butter, already cut in half and gave it to the skinny accuser. He ate one half, then the other and was quiet to the end of the trip.

When we reached Bremerhaven and left the train we walked not too far to a wide gate with gatekeepers in American uniforms.

It looked again like a camp inside. We went through the gate and were stopped. Men were told to turn to the right and women with children to the left. So we did. David, Maija and I were in a barrack with single bunks. They also told us that we would have three meals a day. When we heard the bell ring we had to go to the dining room. Our husbands would be there at the same time. The men had separate sleeping barracks.

So now we were walking outside with the children, eating our meals together in the dining room and resting on the bunks in our barracks. The time was going slow. Outside a radio was playing music or singing or information announcements.

When the radio was playing the national anthem, wherever one was at that moment he was to stop and stay still. If one still was walking, immediately a guard in uniform reminded us to stay still.

One day Voldis said to me that just before we left Ohmstadt he received a letter in the mail from his friend Ozols in New York with a Visa for all of our family. So, he said, we would not have to go pick cotton from the cotton fields some place in Alabama, Georgia, Texas, or Mississippi or wherever.

With the visa we would have to go to the state of Maine. His friend, a Latvian, had a farm. He was retired and was a boxer before he left that sport. He did not mention this to me before because we started for the cotton field but now he had a real personal Visa. He was in the office and showed this Visa and they said they would make the change to the Visa and Maine.

I felt so much better about this change. It seems that Mr. Ozols really cared for his friends and kept his promise. Now we were wondering what would be the next step. So far everything looked good.

That night sometime in our barrack, David, who was sleeping next to me on the bunk, felt more warm than usual, but he was not sweating. I was thinking about what to do. If I go to the office and ask for a doctor, he may delay our crossing the sea to America. What then? They may even send us back to Oldenburg and then what? Probably start this journey all over again. What would be gained? Whom can I trust? I knew that there was nobody I could trust.

I turned to God. God being the only Creator knows each and all of us. We all are His children. Jesus Christ tells us, "I will be with you at all times." I was thanking him all that night because he was our savior, our teacher, companion, our Master and was willing and able to heal all diseases and even from death.

All this praying I was doing in my mind, without sound, because this barrack, in fact a half barrack, was a room full of bunks so close together one hardly could get up and walk out. Every bunk was filled with somebody sleeping. And everyone deserved to have his sleep in a quiet place at night.

In the morning David felt almost normal. I don't remember if he ate anything, probably took some milk. That day he was a little bit slow.

The next night he slept peacefully and normal and did not get hot. The Heavenly Father took care of him.

Then one day we were assigned to meet the American Ambassador. Voldis and I and our children at the appointed time went to see him. I don't remember at that time seeing anybody else in the front room waiting, but thought maybe they were before us and left.

In a very short time the door to the ambassador's office was opened and we walked in. He was sitting at the large desk. He was black, very dark face, intelligent, kind. He asked a few things and we answered.

Then he got up and walked toward us on our side of his desk. He was tall and young and congratulated us on going to America. He stretched his hand to Voldis and he took it. David, seeing what his daddy was doing, stretched his hand right away to the Ambassador and with a step forward took his.

It was unusual to see a two-year-old acting with such calmness and dignity. There was nothing childish in that room. David acted and looked in that room as if he was as mature as these two mature men and knew the importance of this occasion. I caught the light smile and the expression on the ambassador's face as we were leaving, as if saying, "that young kid had the right manners!"

Now we were sure that we were leaving for America. So how did I feel about it? This was Europe. We have been in this country almost six years. These people were not bad to us. Yes, it was wartime and with that all kinds of hardships. Still all that I was in contact with were as helpful as they could be. My son David was born here in the hospital and the doctor who took care of us, David and me, all nine months was kind and good. I know I will remember this time in Oldenburg, but it still was not my country, Latvia. My father's last desire was to take my family to America. He knew the world, had lived in many corners of it, and always did the best for his family. Now he entrusted this duty to me.

I still had 36 lats, which I had in my purse when I left my home in Riga. He had said, "Bring up your children right, choose the right church. Back home you could not do that. The big neighbor was and is destructive."

I understood, no more looking back. I thought that my husband had made up his mind about it the same way. So better not to talk about it anymore. So quietly we returned to our barracks, he to his and I with our children to mine.

Before too long we were told to get ready, that we would be picked up to board the ship.

The ship we boarded was *General Sturgis*. It was an army ship built to take the army men to the war. It was really a big one.

They separated us. The women and children were given cabins but the men were sent downstairs. Voldis helped me with the children and carried all our belongings into the cabin. I was given three bunks and there were still two more bunks. After awhile they brought another mother with a boy. I am sure he was about David's age. With them came a man, her husband. He set the boy down and helped her with her things and bunks.

I did not pay attention what language this family was speaking but when my husband was ready to leave he stopped by the door and said, "See you later," in Latvian. The father of the other boy turned toward us and said in good Latvian, "You are Latvians, I am too; my wife is Polish." So we introduced ourselves.

Then he introduced his son, Uze, and we introduced our children David and Maija. Then both men left and I put my children on the bunks for a nap and I lay down for a nap too.

The young mother with her boy Uze left for the water closet, and then came back and both lay down to rest.

I heard people walking in the hall and talking but not too loud. We all were tired and fell asleep. I don't remember how long we were sleeping, but then I heard some noise. It was quiet in the halls. Uze and his mother were still asleep, so were David and Maija.

Eventually we heard the bell. It was the call to come to supper. So we got up and went to the hall looking for the dining room. Now people were coming out from their cabins, their doors opening. The passageway in the hall was very narrow. It was hard to pass somebody in the hall.

Since we were going in one direction, we moved slowly. We didn't know the layout of the ship nor dining room or anything. So we didn't know when or where to turn to the left or to the right. This was not a fabulous excursion tourist ship, but a war ship, built strong and practical for army needs.

Finally, we walked in the dining room. Long tables were stretched from one end to the other, with chairs around. There was more than one table. We were coming and taking seats at the table till there were no empty seats left. There were so many children sitting between grown ups. I always loved children and think that they are the most beautiful and interesting people in this world.

As soon as we all were sitting, plates with food were brought and put in front of each person. Then the drinks came, like milk, tea, and water. When all had a meal in front of them, somebody in charge of the dining room said to us, "Now we can eat!" and we did. I think we all were hungry. The forks and spoons were very busy removing the food from plates to where it should go till they were empty. Then somebody took them away and brought us ice cream and cookies.

For a while we stayed there in that room and talked with our daddies and husbands. Not one of them complained about sleeping down below. They said it was easy to go up to deck and see all around and what was happening.

The next morning we were asked to come on deck where we had to put on life jackets and other lifesaving gear. Then we were instructed how to walk and what to do if the ship and sea, weather wise, gave us problems.

Most of the time the weather was not too bad except one or two nights, but it was December and we were told that the sea in that month is rougher. Then one morning we woke up and in our cabin water was on the floor and rising higher. There were a couple of other families who had the same problem in their cabins. Somebody was at our door and told us to get dressed and leave the cabin. So we did and with our children went upstairs. Some children were upset. My David and Uze were not afraid, but Maija was.

When my husband saw that our girl still was worried he asked her about it and she said that she would not sleep in that room because the water could come again at night. She would rather sleep here in the dining room on the chair. We asked the ship's people who were serving us and they told us the ship was being repaired, that it was a strong ship and the repairers know the job and do it very well.

"In about one more hour the work will be done, and your room will be clean and nice and the beds will have clean sheets and blankets," they said.

Then my husband had an idea. He said that he sleeps downstairs and next to his bed is a vacant one, and asked if he could take his girl with him there tonight. They asked our daughter if she would rather go to sleep where her father sleeps. She sounded happy and said yes. The rest of us returned back to our cabins and had a peaceful night.

One time we had a big storm. It was at dinnertime when we all were sitting at the table. When the ship was bending one way all of our plates were sliding down as fast as they could. As soon as the ship bent the opposite way, the plates slid too. No food was spilled on the table when it finally stopped, and hoping that each one now had his plate, we continued our dinner. It was so funny that everybody was laughing even after the dinner.

At Christmas time we were still on the ship. There were no Christmas trees any place, but we had little trimmings on the tables in the dining room and on the radio or something, we had some Christmas music. It somehow did not touch our feelings. We just only felt that we existed.

I don't remember exactly what day we reached the New York harbor. It was dark and we saw harbor lights. We slept that night on the ship. We were served a good supper, but many people were so excited they could not eat. Sleeping that night was good since the ship was standing in one place.

We had our breakfast very early, mostly for the children. That morning my David had a big appetite. He ate his in no time. The girl next to him did not touch hers. He was still hungry and was looking at her plate but not touching it. Her mother, sitting next to her, said, "Take it and eat, she is not hungry." So David did eat and still looking on other plates left with food, was given a dish with ice cream. We walked up and stepped on the boards of the ship. It was the end of December 1949.

I saw the Statue of Liberty. It was so perfect and beautiful. It was so breath taking! It made me speechless. All I could do was look at it. Then I noticed that all the people on the ship were speechless too.

The statue expressed strength, beauty, and welcome to us all. It looked as if our Heavenly Father had put himself there and was saying, "Welcome children, welcome all to me." I felt such peace of mind. It felt like a heavy burden fell off my shoulders.

Then it was time for us to leave the ship. When we were in the harbor, we were separated in groups and taken care of by some organization. It was so organized. Before somebody would ask, we were led from one place to another, and then we found ourselves in the main station of New York. It was so big.

Somebody who brought us to the station gave us the tickets to the state of Maine. He said we would have to change trains in Portland to another station and then a long ride to a small station at our destination. I cannot remember the name of it anymore. We were told that Mr. Grasis would meet us there and take us to his farm. He said that now we have to wait many hours for our train. Then he said goodbye and left us alone in the Grand Central Station.

Voldis and I were sitting on the benches with our things, but Maija and David walked around. Not many people were in the station. Now and then they asked for a drink. I had my cup with me and Voldis would bring us some water. After awhile I wished that the children would lie down on the bench and sleep, but they would not.

I don't remember if we ate anything while in that station. We had no money to spend; but there was nothing in the station for sale anyway, and we had no food with us. We did not talk between us. I knew I was not hungry. The big change in our lives was in my thoughts and my husband's, too.

The refugee children, that I noticed these past 6 years were hungry. If they were young they cried, but then they would beg with their eyes. Then they didn't cry anymore; they just gave up.

In Grand Central Station Maija did not ask for food. She was seven years old, but I could not tell if David was hungry.

I was glad that he had a big appetite on the ship and I let him eat all he wanted. Now, after so many hours in the station, he was groggy. So Voldis took his son in his arms and was walking with him. He fell asleep and slept a long time till our train was ready to receive us for the next trip.

We were in Portland a short time before another train picked us up and we continued the trip to our last station where Mr. Grasis was waiting for us. He was a big man in his sixties or seventies, kind and friendly. He had a big car too, but I don't remember the make.

At his home we were met by his niece, Milda, his sister's daughter, her husband, and two children. We learned that they had arrived from a German refugee camp about three weeks before. Milda welcomed us and said that she had prepared a room for us. She showed us our room and the location of the bathroom.

"I know you are hungry, and dinner is ready. So you may clean up and come back to the kitchen," she said, and gave us two towels.

We did what she asked us to do and set our things by the beds, and then went to the kitchen.

The table was set. The big bowl of steaming vegetable soup and home baked bread, still warm, was a welcome sight. For a sweet finish there was apple pastry, milk, coffee, and tea. After more than a day without food this was just the right meal, I said, thanking our host for her thoughtfulness.

"About three weeks ago when we arrived in the Grand Central we had the same problem. So our experience taught me when we arrive, that first we needed a warm soup," Milda was telling. We talked about our experiences on the ship and in the harbor. It sounded very much alike, but the need for sleep was sending us to our beds. With a "good night" to all we left for our room.

The beds were prepared and we retired for the night. The next morning they allowed us to sleep as long as we wished. Voldis and the children did sleep later, but I had so many things on my mind that I woke up when I heard somebody walking in the kitchen. Quietly I got dressed and slipped into the kitchen.

Milda was in the kitchen doing something with clothes, mostly her children's. They had a girl about eleven and a boy nine.

"I thought you would sleep a long time this morning," she said.

"I have a lot on my mind," I said. "Is there someplace here for me to wash our clothes, maybe in the barn? We were in the Bremen harbor camp more than a month and about two weeks on the ship. I have no change left. I am not afraid of work and can do your laundry and mine too."

"Thank you for offering to help with my wash, but it is not so complicated. My grandpa, that's what we call Mr. Grasis, just two weeks ago got a washer and it is connected with electricity. We put our laundry in and turn on the water and it washes. Come," she said, "it's in the hall next to the bathroom. When the clothes are washed we run them through the rollers to press the water out, then we hang them out on the line. Today is a sunny day; the clothes will be dry in no time."

She showed me how it worked. I was ready to learn. We put her laundry in and started the wash. It was easy and I went to our room to get my things to be washed after Milda finished hers. It was a surprise to me, the washer doing our washing. In Latvia and Germany, at least in the camps, we did the washing by hand. So I did the washing and hung the clothes out to dry.

We bathed our children and ourselves and it was a wonderful feeling to put on clean clothes. We were very thankful for this opportunity to take care of the children and ourselves in a necessary way.

After talking with Mr. Grasis, Milda, and her husband, we knew we had a lot to learn about this place. This village was very small. There was a small Calvin Protestant Church and a Roman Catholic Church. All around there were farms and forests. We wanted to find work but it was now January and winter! We didn't see any possibility. Milda's husband was also looking for work.

Like we did for six years, they too had lived in the refugee camps in Germany, bringing up two children with no income.

Mr. Grasis thought that it would be a good idea to visit the Calvin Church pastor because he knew everybody and could have some suggestions about work. He meets all kinds of people.

Soon Mr. Grasis took us to see that church minister. He received us in his office. He asked some questions and said that he would ask people from his congregation about work opportunities. Very soon we heard from a local M.D. that he needed a housekeeper. His wife was a teacher and they needed somebody to take care of the house. It would be at least five days a week.

That meant the work would be for me. What would happen with the children? Who would take care of them? Who would feed them, clean them? Voldis could do nothing as far as taking care of them. He cannot cook and take care of himself. I decided not to take this work.

Soon we had another offer on a nearby farm. They showed us a two-room house, but they had no work for us, but they said that they had plenty of pork and beans. So we would not be hungry and the house would be free.

Because of the way we were taught in the old country we could not understand this generous offer. To be fed and maintained without doing work did not seem right at all. We really appreciated their generous offer, but we could not accept.

So now what? Mr. Grasis had another suggestion, the Catholic priest. He explained that he knew the priest well. His late wife was Catholic, a devoted woman, and he himself had given donations to the priest when there was a need and the priest had asked.

So why not visit the priest. He said he would make an appointment if the priest had time to see us. The next day or so Mr. Grasis called the priest and made the appointment for the following week. Mr. Grasis took us there saying, "Well, it is time for me to see my friend." The priest let us in and asked us to take the seats. He was kind and a fatherly-looking man and asked what he could do for us.

"This is the family you mentioned to me on the telephone?" the priest asked Mr. Grasis. "What so far has been done about the work?"

Since Voldis did not speak English, Mr. Grasis told of our unsuccessful attempts.

"Well, that is true, this is not the right season for work in our corner, but do you really want to work here or another place?" the priest asked us.

Mr. Grasis was translating his question to Voldis in Latvian and he answered, "It doesn't matter which state so long as there is work to be found."

Then Voldis mentioned that his father was a carpenter-builder in the old country houses.

"How about Virginia? They are always building something and the climate is good. Winters are short, and there's not so much snow, cold, and ice as we have here. For that reason it is always easier to get work." Then he said he would call Richmond in Virginia and let us know what to do next. So we thanked the priest and left. Mr. Grasis stayed behind for a while, but not long.

We walked to his car and waited. Soon he came, too, and looked satisfied.

When we were in the car, Mr. Grasis said that the priest wanted to know a little more about us in case the Richmond office should ask him.

Within three days the priest asked us to come back to see him. Mr. Grasis took us to his office. There he told us that he spoke with the Catholic priest in Richmond, Virginia, about us, and was informed to let us know to take the train to New York's Grand Central and there change to the Washington, DC train. There we had to wait for the Richmond train. He said that in Richmond somebody from the church would meet us and take us to the guesthouse. There we could stay and decide where we would work and live.

He gave us the schedule for all the trains we would ride. As I remember we had to leave Maine on Monday morning.

Mr. Grasis, as planned, took us Monday to the railroad station after a good breakfast. Milda had prepared for us a bag with sandwiches and apples, so much that when we arrived in Richmond we still had some left. Mr. Grasis gave us the train tickets. We asked if we owed him or somebody else money for them. He did not say, but said, "God be with you and be thankful for His care." At the station he gave us some money for the road. We thanked him and said that we shall repay him. He said not to worry. When the time comes we will see. After a year or so I mailed Mr. Grasis the money, but he returned it all, thanking us, and wrote that he would be happier if we used it for our needs.

We said goodbye to Mr. Grasis and got on the train. We reached New York and didn't have to wait too long for the Washington, DC train. On the train the children were hungry so we fed them a sandwich and apples that Milda had given us. There were not many people on this train. It was a good day and the children were looking through the windows at sights passing by. It was a beautiful vista. It was early evening when we arrived in Washington, DC and we had to wait for the Richmond train a long time. We were prepared for this waiting, but it was hard for the children.

Still with all that they had good manners. It was dark when we got on the Richmond train, and the children were tired from the long day. David lay down on the seat. Maija was sitting for a while next to her daddy, leaning on his side, and went to sleep.

When we arrived in Richmond, Virginia, it was still dark. I don't remember the time, and it did not matter anymore. I was tired. We walked into the station. Voldis carried sleeping David. Maija was walking with me. We stopped in the station. Then a man came to us and asked if we were Mr. and Mrs. Mednicks. He introduced himself and said the priest from the church in the state of Maine called their church in Richmond and he was selected to meet us at the station and to take us to the guesthouse. He took us there. It was dark. It was a two story building in the city. We were given one good size room with three regular size beds and one small child's bed. Everything necessary was in that room. The bathroom and our room were on the second floor. Since it was so very early in the morning we put the children to bed and went to bed ourselves. It was very quiet in the house as if nobody lived there.

The bathroom was clean and had hot and cold water and a tub. It was rusty and not very clean. I thought that probably we would use it. Then I went downstairs looking for a kitchen. There was a nice one. It had a table, several chairs, a gas range, and a medium-size icebox. It was clean, but there was no ice and no food. I left the kitchen and was walking to go upstairs when I saw an elderly woman just coming in through the front door. I said good morning to her.

"Oh, are you the new residents who came last night?" she asked.

"Yes, we are. We were so tired that we went to bed and fell asleep. Only now have I woke up."

"It's all right. You can use the kitchen. Seldom anybody uses it," she said.

"Do you live here? Or do you just come here to take care of this place?" I asked her.

"I live here," she said, "two rooms, a kitchenette, and bathroom. At the end of the hall, that is my place."

"I will go up to take care of my children and see if my husband is up and get something to eat," I said, leaving kitchen.

"Wait," she stopped me, "I will show some things in the kitchen and how to use that stove. After using it, just keep everything here clean. You all can even eat in the kitchen."

Upstairs Voldis was up and getting dressed. The children were awake too. I took care of them. We still had food in the bag Milda had given us. I opened it on the table. Everything was good. She had baked Latvian sweet-sour black bread and there was a piece of ham, some apples, and a small bag with oatmeal for porridge, and sugar. In the oatmeal bag were six fresh chicken eggs.

"We are going downstairs," I said, "in the kitchen we can cook the oatmeal, eggs, ham, and tea." I sent Voldis to the store around the corner for milk, as Mrs. Shurp just had told me. In no time Voldis was back and we had our meal.

It was January. The date I don't remember. We ate and took care of the kitchen. Voldis was telling us that it was warm outside. I could not believe it because in Maine it was so cold. But this was not Maine; it was Virginia. So we all went outdoors for a walk.

We were looking at the houses and the nice landscapes around some of them. Then walking back I saw in a store window a notice that they needed a dressmaker. I said to my husband that I could do this work, possibly this is a dressmaker's shop. I will have to come here tomorrow. He liked the idea and it was only two blocks from the place we were staying.

That evening after we came back from the walk we had to decide what we would do about our supper. Maija said that we should go to a restaurant, but David, Voldis, and I did not want to go anyplace. So we decided to use our today's leftovers and then we would tell the stories of "Once upon a time." Our children loved those.

We were listening and telling. Voldis was brought up on the farm and his stories were very interesting. There were rivers and they liked to fish, forests where they picked berries and mushrooms, and on their homestead, which they acquired, his father decided first to build a good size two-room bathhouse because he was a builder-carpenter. Every child in the family had to help him with building. Voldis had to carry stones and water because he was the oldest child.

The next morning I decided to go to that place where in the store window was the notice for a dressmaker. As I went in the store, a well-dressed dark man met me. I told him that we had just come from Europe and that I could do that kind of work, that I have a family, two children, and my husband.

Farther in the back was sitting a black woman by a sewing table. The man asked a few questions about where we were staying and I told him in the Catholic Church visitor's house. He thought a little then said, "I don't think this would be a right place for you to work." Then he turned away and went to the woman sitting by the table. I left to go back to my family.

I did not know why he did not give me the job. Only later, much later, I was told that this is America, I had white skin and he had black. I could not understand, because we used to live by the Black Sea in Odessa, Istanbul. There were living many very dark people like Palestinians, Gypsies, Turks, and Africans. Everybody got along fine. The children played together. Well, what could I say, this was America.

Later that day we went to a small restaurant to have dinner. The prices were reasonable, but when they brought hot steaming, good looking soup it was very salty, so salty it was dangerous for young children. Then they brought us potatoes and meat and that also was too salty. After this experience we just bought some food in a store and prepared it in the visitor's house kitchen.

A day after the restaurant dinner David was not well. I was awake all night with him. The woman in charge of this visitor's center noticed that something was not right with the child. I did not complain to her, but later came the same man who picked us from the railroad station and she said to him that our son was not well.

He said that he wanted to see us and asked how we were doing. When he saw David he insisted that we have to take him to a doctor. I did not like that at all, but he insisted that maybe David had measles and if so he would pass it to the other people. It seemed we had no choice. He took my child and me to the Richmond hospital.

We went to a waiting room. Then he went after a nurse who came with him. She said that a doctor would come to see us if it was all right with me. She left and a man in a white coat came in and gave his name. The doctor checked David, then opened the door and three or four young men with white coats came in, then four more, then six, looking and touching David, the little two-and-a-half year old. It looked like a cattle market. Then I understood it was a medical student class.

Then they said that David had to stay in the hospital. They carried him out from the waiting room. I asked if I could see him. The answer was no. "How long does he have to be there?" Their answer: "We don't know."

The same man who brought me to the hospital took me back and gave me a telephone number, saying to call this number if we needed some help.

He also said that there is something about a job he would tell us both and hoped that my husband was at home. I told him I was sure that Voldis was at home because our seven-year-old daughter was there. He told us that there was a church that needed a caretaker, janitor in the Presbyterian Church. If we would like to see that place and talk with them he would call them and give them our address.

"Would tomorrow be okay for us to see that place?" he asked.

I looked at my husband after I translated all that was said and he said "fine".

Our visitor departed.

"What do you think about that kind of work? Voldis asked me, and what about David? What did they say in the hospital?"

I told him what I knew about David what was said about the work I could not tell, but that we definitely had to see it. We needed work. For the children's sake alone we needed a normal life, a normal place for us.

The next day a couple, a lady and a man, came looking for us. We introduced ourselves. They were from the Presbyterian Church and invited us to come with them to see the church and the work to be done keeping the inside and outside clean.

Since we could not leave our child alone in the guesthouse, with these peoples' permission, we took her with us.

The church was very large and beautiful, and on the outside there were flowerbeds, shrubs, trees, green grass squares, and stone footpaths. Downstairs there were big Sunday school rooms and some offices.

The pay for all that would be a house to live in and a monthly wage. They did not offer to show us the house at that time. Then my husband said to me, "If you are willing to do the part of your work," with his arm and hand showing all places inside the church building, as saying all the inside cleaning and polishing, "I will do my work easy."

Hearing that, I realized that he, as a man, considered cleaning was strictly woman's work. His part outside was man's work and that he could do it easy. Could I do the work inside the church and the same at home, plus taking care of the children, cooking, and shopping? I knew that I could not.

We thanked the church members for their offers and said we would like to go back to the guesthouse to decide this. They took us back as we asked and before leaving they asked us to give them an answer soon.

After they left I knew my answer but did not say it to Voldis. I wanted him to reason out by himself his work, my work, and my responsibility to the family, the time, and my strength.

The next morning he said that what I decided would be the answer. I did not question him. We never talked about the church. I called the church and said that we could not do a good job in such a large place, that we have two children and have to give some time to them too.

It had been two days since our son was admitted to the hospital. I called there to find out about David, but still got no information. Nobody knew even if he was alive. I did not like it and called the same man who brought us to the visitor's house. He promised to call the hospital and then call me. Much later that evening he called telling me that the hospital had nothing to say good or bad, but that David would not eat, did not even touch the food.

When I heard that, I said, "Please, tomorrow, take me to that hospital. I have to take him out from that place and bring him here. Will you please do that for us? I want my child still alive."

In the hospital they sent me to the second floor. Still they did not give me the room number. I went to the nurse's station and she said for me to wait. I wanted to see his room where he was these three days, but she said no, to stay where I was at that minute.

So she went; I think after him. One door opened in the wall and my child walked out. His head was hanging down and he was looking down on the floor. His face was sad, no smile, as if he had given up at two-and-a-half years. I could not wait anymore. Nobody was around us. In a few steps I was by him. "David, my dear David, we are going home to Maija and your daddy. You will not have to come here anymore."

I picked him up in my arms. He felt as if he had no life in him anymore. I walked outside. The man who brought me was by his car. Seeing me with the child, he opened the door of the car to let us get in. I held onto David after I got in the car.

We reached the visitor's house and the car stopped. I flew out of the car, saying "thank you" and without looking back at the driver I vanished into the house. Finally, we were upstairs in our room.

"Thank you Heavenly Father, we are home and our David is home with us too. Thank you! Thank you!"

Voldis and Maija were looking at me, still holding David in my arms. Voldis came to me and lifting him out from my hold set him on the floor and said, "We have to see how tall you are now, how much you have grown. You know we have to eat apples and milk and bread, then we will be tall. Do you want to be like me?"

David listened, then looked at his daddy and lifted up his head and moved it as if to say, "Yes, I want to be tall too."

His sister slowly came to him, holding a cup with some milk she was drinking and gave him the cup.

"Drink, David, it is good. I will bring you more and some cookies that I have been saving for you."

Maija was feeding David, and little by little he was eating. I was worried if now so much food at once would be a problem, but my husband suggested that we let the child eat as much as he wanted. He was sure the boy would stop himself. Soon he did and pushed his sister's hand with the cookie aside and said, "Enough!"

One word, "enough." We heard it and were so happy and knew that our son was well and would live.

We felt so good again. The family was all together. Day by day David was getting stronger as he was before going to the hospital.

Then Sunday we all went to the Lutheran church. I think it was in Richmond and the minister was Mooney. I am not sure if my spelling is right. Since I wished to hear all of the service our family was sitting in the front. I liked the service and could understand the minister very well. After the service, as we were going out, somebody stopped us, introduced themselves and asked us to wait with them for minister Mooney, as he wanted to meet us. It was not long before the minister came. He introduced himself to us and asked our name.

From his questions I felt that he already knew something about us. He asked if we were looking for work. We said that we were looking for work.

"I would like to speak with you about that," he said, "tell me your address."

"In the Catholic visitor's house," I said.

"You are still at that place? Would you like to have dinner in my home with my wife and me tomorrow and we can talk about it?" asked the minister. "I will come for you at one o'clock."

Then he said to the couple that introduced us to him, "Take them to where they live."

The next day minister Mooney came after us at the set time and took us to his home. Mrs. Mooney had the dinner ready on the table. I don't remember what was served as the first course, but for dessert was sliced bananas with sugar and milk. It was good, easy for the children to eat and they liked it. We thanked them for the meal.

After dinner minister Mooney and his wife took us to the living room where he said we could talk. He said he wanted to tell us something about a very nice place in the center of Virginia belonging to a widow lady. "She is teaching at the woman's college. Her home is on a farm in Amherst. She lives alone and needs somebody to help her around the place. She has a vacant house, two rooms, large kitchen and a bathroom with a tub. It is an old brick house but in good order and livable."

It sounded good to me. Since Voldis's English was very limited I was sharing this with him in Latvian. When he understood the offer he liked it. He wanted to know if we could make enough from the work that we could pay for our daily needs. Could we meet that lady? He would like to see the place if it's possible.

"Would you like to go there?" minister Mooney asked us.

"Yes," Voldis said, "if it's possible, that would be good."

"The place is in Amherst, Virginia. I will ask Mrs. Strode."

Two days later, as I remember, the minister called to tell us that Mrs. Strode is expecting us all in Amherst and to bring all our things with us. If we did not like, she has many friends who are farmers and some that are not farmers and she would find a place for us.

We liked what he was telling us. Then he asked, "When would you like to go and when could you be ready?" Then we asked when was the best day for him. And he said, "Tomorrow!" And we agreed. He gave us the time when he would come for us.

Next morning we had all our things down by the door. I put the leftover food and bread in a bag. It could be handy on the road. I cleaned the room and the kitchen we used while in Richmond. The minister arrived at the time as he said. We put our things in his car and were ready to travel.

Which road we were on, 29 or 60 West, I don't know. Maybe some others, but it was beautiful, passing by forests, farms, fields, crossing rivers and streams. It was January and still winter. The trees were not green, except evergreens. But I could see it was big, beautiful country.

We reached Amherst on the south side, not entering the city and turned to the left. The area was mountainous, thus the road went up and down. Finally, we reached the end of the road. The gate was open and the almost level field allowed us a view of a beautiful red brick house with large tall columns in front.

About seventy feet from that place on the right was a two-story small, old brick house. Minister Mooney stopped his car by this house and said to us, "This is it. We have reached the right destination. Here we will take out all your things." We did as he said and put down our things near the door.

Then the minister said, "We will go to the big house to see Mrs. Strode to let her know that you are now here."

As we were approaching her house Mrs. Strode came out to greet us. She unlocked the door of the small house to let us in. There was a comfortable size kitchen with a big, black stove, a table by the backside window, a wood box by the wall and a couple of shelves on the wall for plates and dishes. Then she led us to a room next to the kitchen. It was small and narrow, with a window and sofa and stairs leading to the second floor. There was a bedroom with a double bed, a small bed and a baby's bed. In the center was a potbelly stove. There was a bathroom with a tub.

Mrs. Strode said, "I hope you will like this place. We will talk about it tomorrow. Minister Mooney is tired and hungry. Dinner is ready. Could Mr. Mednicks come with me? He could bring your dinner for you here while it is still warm."

"Yes, he will go with you, Mrs. Strode, and bring it for us," I said, and my husband left with her.

I was very glad for her warm and ready dinner offer and right here in our new place. It was considerate of her. We will get along with her just fine, I was thinking.

We had to unpack. It was cold and we had to put some wood in the stove to get warm. I checked the beds upstairs. The top covers were on, but what was under that? The baby's bed and Maija's bed would probably need more blankets. We needed to check the water in the bathroom to see if it was hot and cold, and in the kitchen, too. There had been a fire in the stove that day. It had wood and coal left over. I lifted the cover from the wood box next to the stove and saw some wood.

Voldis came in with the food on a tray. He placed it on the table, and put some wood in the stove and it started to burn. He checked the teapot on the stove. It had some warm water in.

We took the seats at the table. The food was good. We were hungry and ate well, but I don't recollect what we ate.

Voldis put some wood in the potbelly stove in our bedroom and started it to warm up the room before we went to bed. We were very tired. I put the children to bed. The fire in the potbelly made the bedroom warm. The bedroom had one big window with thin glass panes. I looked at the children; they both were asleep. I put extra covers on their beds. Voldis went to the bathroom. He said something about a bath, but I did not hear water running and fell asleep. I don't remember when my husband came to bed.

The next morning when I woke up the sun was looking in the window. The children were still asleep and they had still all their covers on them. When I got out of bed the room was chilly. I got into my clothes in a hurry and went to the bathroom. When I tried to wash my face and hands there was only cold water.

Then I understood that we would have to heat the water in the kitchen in the teapot, kettle, pots and pans and carry it upstairs when we needed to wash or to have a bath. So what! I said. We have a roof over our heads and a room to live in. That is very good. Voldis was waking up. I made a sign to come down and not to wake the children. Voldis came and started a fire in the stove and filled the teakettle.

Very quietly we talked about the heat and water problem and agreed not to talk about it with Mrs. Strode, at least not yet. I cleaned up the supper dishes. There was left a half jar of milk.

"No milk for us for tea or coffee, only for the children till it will be settled," he agreed.

I heard the children upstairs waking up.

"Now," I whispered, "let's go upstairs to help them get dressed in that cold room, so they don't get cold. We have to be fast and bring them down."

We dressed them very quickly and then had breakfast. They had oatmeal with milk and sugar and some bread with cheese. Voldis and I had leftovers from yesterday.

I put Mrs. Strode's dishes on the tray and gave it to Voldis to carry back to her.

When I looked out the window, I saw both of them coming to our place. They came in. I offered her the chair in the kitchen because it was warm. She sat down near the table and we talked.

The road from her house to the main road had to be redone. Voldis said he could do that. Then she needed some work done on the farm. He said that he could do that, too. She said that every morning her farm worker would bring a bottle of milk and put it on the table by the back door. We would not have to buy milk. Then she said that in the barn was dry cured pork and she wanted me to use some of it. Sometimes she would like to take her dinner with us. I don't remember how much she said she would pay Voldis for his work, but about cooking and me she did not mention. Since we were living in her house with all accommodations, I did not feel like asking.

Then she offered to take us to the town of Amherst. "Then you will know where the post office, the store, the church, and the school are. I think your girl will go to school there, she is that age."

As we were driving on the main street we stopped at the post office, then she went to the gasoline station, stopped there and filled her car. Then she showed us where her bank was and where a church was. Then she stopped by a store. That place looked very busy outside and inside. It was a big store and the shelves were full of products.

She went to the grocer and introduced him to us, telling him that now we are living on her farm. She asked us if we would like to get something today. I did not know.

She asked what we would like to have for dinner? I had no answer. Then she asked, "Could you make a meat loaf for dinner?"

"Yes," I said.

"What would you need for it?" And I started to tell her meat, onions, some bread, a couple of eggs, a little salt, and if we have potatoes, peel the skin and put around the meatloaf and bake it in the oven until they are brown. This would be good in meatloaf gravy.

"That's it?" Mrs. Strode, smiling and turning to the grocer, said, "Give her everything she needs for our dinner."

He, turning to me, asked, "How much ground meat?" I hesitated, then he said, "Two pounds or more?" I said, "Two, then..." and he was getting all that we needed to prepare dinner.

As we were driving home she said, pointing to a small, white, two-story house, "This is our doctor's home. He is a good man. He has been here a long time. He helps in all kinds of sickness."

"And there," she pointed to another house on the other side of the street, "is where our dentist lives."

Then she turned onto her farm road and stopped by our house to let us out and take in the groceries. The children were hungry. So I made sandwiches with butter and cheese and gave them some milk.

Voldis went out to look at the road he would start working on the next day. And I started to work on the meatloaf and other foods for the meal. I found a bag with potatoes and jars of home canned goods, like green beans and corn.

At the right time the meatloaf was in the oven and half of the potatoes surrounded it. The rest of the meal was coming together with the vegetables. I found a jar with apple butter and decided to use it, too, hoping that at least the children would like it.

When the suppertime came, Mrs. Strode came to take her dinner to her place. I told her to take as much as she wished and she did. Later she came back and thanked me again. We ate our meal in the kitchen and we all were satisfied.

The next morning Voldis went to the barn for the necessary tools to do the roadwork. Mrs. Strode introduced a colored man who lived and worked on her land telling Voldis if he needed some help to work with that man. It was a sunny day and the children were playing outside. I had some washing to do as I had no time and place in Richmond. In the bathroom, I put the sheets and other things in the tub, turned on a slow tap and went to the kitchen to get pots and pans filled with cold water to put on the stove to heat. Then I went back upstairs. I was surprised. The water in the tub was red. It was clay and it covered all the laundry. What now? I took out the laundry, washed the tub and ran water until it was clear, put the laundry back in the tub and rinsed until all the red was out. Then I brought the hot water from the kitchen and did the laundry by hand in the tub and hung it outdoors.

I spent so much time with the wash that what now with the dinner? Voldis came from work. He was tired, and then I remembered yesterday's leftovers. The stove was very warm and in no time we had our dinner.

Later Mrs. Strode came to tell about the school for Maija. The next morning she would take her to school. She asked me her age and if she had been in school in Germany. I said, "No." Mrs. Strode asked, "She is seven years old and not in school?"

"We were living in the refugee camp and there was no school for children. At least not for our children," I said.

The next morning she took Maija to school and said she would ask the teacher to put her on the school bus to return home and would tell the bus driver where she needed to get off.

I observed the time of the bus coming and David and I met her at the bus stop in the afternoon. When the bus stopped and Maija got off, David saw her and was calling, "Sister, sister." He ran toward her, taking her hand and said, "Come home!"

Now every morning our girl was taking the school bus at the same place at the end of Mrs. Strode's farm road. At the end of the school day she came back by the same bus.

At the end of the week on Friday her teacher called to tell me that Maija was removed from first grade and put in the second grade. They did not know that she could read and write and knew arithmetic. She had nothing to do in the first grade. In the second grade she can at least learn English. "Where did she get this learning?" the teacher asked.

I explained to her that my mother used to be a teacher. In Germany in the camp children had nothing to do so she started a game with words, reading, and writing. Maija liked it. In a couple of months she could read and write. The arithmetic was another easy subject for her.

Her teacher said that Maija would bring her reading book home if I could help her with the English word meanings. I agreed. Within a month she was doing fine in the English language in reading and speaking.

Seeing how fast Maija was progressing in language I decided that with David at home we would speak between us in Latvian. I was sure that with time he would acquire English too.

It was February. Voldis was working on the same road. It was changed noticeably on the parts where he had worked. He was getting compliments.

We still had problems with keeping the house warm. One morning I found David's small aluminum cup with a quarter cup of milk frozen while sitting on the potbelly stove that was heated with wood before we went to bed.

I decided to do a good floor cleaning in the kitchen and hall/living room. I found in that room a chest in front of the only window. I put my hand under the chest legs and realized that my hand was outside the house wall. I had in my hand grass and dirt. The wall was not connected with the floor; there was about a six-inch space above the floor! So that's why it was cold!

I had to prepare our supper. I went to the shed where the salted meat was hanging. Mrs. Strode told me to use it. I took a piece from the jaw. It had green mold and was hard as a stone.

I had to wait until my husband came to cut it up. I scraped the mold and the salt, washed and soaked it, but there was no meat, just skin and fat and still very salty. I prepared it for dinner after soaking twenty-four hours, but I still could not give it to the children. Voldis was not used to any meat. He had potatoes and vegetables in the camps. I took most of it to Mrs. Strode and she told us it was good!

The next time I met Mrs. Strode she thanked me for the meal then said she meant for us to use that meat. She herself didn't care for it.

As was promised in the beginning, every morning in the room outside the living room door was a quart-size bottle of milk, not full, but I was happy with that. After awhile, one morning the bottle was not there. I did not say anything and managed with the milk that was from the day before. Then the next day there was a bottle. The next morning we were in the kitchen at the table by the window. I saw Mrs. Strode passing by the window and heard her entering the storage room where the milk was brought to us. Then I saw her passing our window back to her place and she had in her hand the bottle with milk.

After that there was no more milk for us. She never said anything to us and I never asked. I went to the store in the town and ordered a bottle of milk to be delivered every second day by the mail box (hers). We paid the bill to the grocer.

Since we had no food except potatoes from her, I had to go to the grocer, but he was more than three miles away. It was not an easy road. Up hill, down hill and a little level in the town. David was only two-and-a-half years old and it was hard to carry him and the groceries. I had to do something so the next time I put David in his crib at twelve o'clock to sleep and I left for the store. I rushed to the store for what we would need for a week, and then rushed back with purchases in my arms. When I reached home I was out of breath. David was still asleep in the crib. When I lifted him he seemed heavy, but he was not.

One week when I was shopping I noticed some fresh pork chops. I bought eight so it would make supper for us for three days. That afternoon I cooked all eight. Three were for our supper that day, two for my husband and me and one to be halved for the children. The five left, the large ones carefully divided would be enough for us for two more days.

At six o'clock, we were sitting at the table having our dinner. There came a knock at the door. I opened it and Mrs. Strode, smiling, came in. She said that something smelled good from our house and that she wanted her dinner now.

I was surprised. She did not give me any groceries except those potatoes. Now she asked for her dinner. I looked at Voldis. He did not say anything. So I put on the plate one pork chop and some potatoes and whatever else I had. Then she said to put another one on a second plate. I did as she said and she left. So our three-day meal was gone. We were sitting at the table and wondering what to do.

We almost had finished our meal when there was a knock at the door. Mrs. Strode came in smiling and saying, "It was so good, so good. Minister Mooney is visiting and liked it so well, he just has to have another pork chop."

I was so glad that I had removed the other three pork chops so they would not dry out and said, "I have nothing more to give."

She looked around, did not see anything, and left.

One day we received a letter from my sister Nina from the camp Ohmstadt in Oldenburg. She wrote that our mother would soon leave the camp for Bremerhaven and would be in America in March. We were so glad.

Mrs. Strode took us to an Episcopal church in town. It was strange for me. After that I said that I was Lutheran and would like to go to the Lutheran church. She said that it was in Lynchburg. The minister there was the son of Richmond's minister Mooney. So one day the young minister Mooney and two other people from his church came to visit us. They wanted to see the place where we were living, the work we were doing, and the children. They looked at my husband's work on the road and farm. Mr. Mooney asked if we would like to live in the city? They asked if my husband would like to work in a lumber mill? He said, "Yes" and that he was finished with the roadwork here.

Then I mentioned that in March my mother was coming from Germany and we didn't know how we would bring her here. One of the men heard me telling about it and said, "But you have here only one small bedroom, four people sleeping, the small hall and the kitchen. There is no place for another bed."

Minister Mooney said, "No problem, we can find the right thing to do."

Then they were leaving and told us they would be in touch with us and not to worry, everything would come out right.

In about two weeks Mr. Burruss from Lynchburg came to see us. He was the lumber mill owner. He talked with my husband and asked questions about the lumber. Voldis told him that his father was a builder and as a youngster he was working with his father. Mr. Burruss liked what he heard and said that he could work in his business. He said he would talk with somebody from the Lutheran church about lodging and then we would see.

Then March came. I don't remember how it happened, but one day Mama was brought to our place. I think it was the Lutheran church's doings and she said that the trip was easy. She had met some very nice people on the ship and everywhere. Mrs. Strode gave us a very narrow cot. We put it at the top of the staircase. Between that cot and the stairs there was barely two feet of space. I was afraid for her sleeping there. The steps from there were steep down to the hall.

Then again somebody from the Lutheran church came to see us, asking if we were ready to leave this place? They had found a little house for us to rent on Thomas Road in Lynchburg. It was on the city bus line; the house had two bedrooms, bathroom, living room and eat-in kitchen. It had gas heat and hot and cold water. The church would pay the first month's rent, after that we would have to pay.

They gave us the letter from Mr. Burruss to come to work Monday. It said that somebody from our church would pick him up that day and explain everything and take him to his lumberyard. After work somebody would bring him back home.

I was surprised at hearing all of that. So much to take in! So many questions.

"Do you have some furniture?" somebody asked us.

We had no furniture, only luggage, two travel baskets and a wooden box.

Then somebody said not to worry about furniture because they had some pieces from church members. They had two double beds, a sofa, a couple of chairs and tables and something more.

"How about Saturday at 10:00 a.m. we come here after you in a pick-up and take you to that house?" We agreed and the man left.

Saturday they came as promised. The driver insisted that my mother, with David on her lap, and Maija sitting next to her, share the driver's seat with him. He said, "Now my friends you can see through these windows the city you will be living in."

Voldis and I were riding in another car. We arrived at the Thomas Road section by the Baptist church and turned to the right on the street and then to the left and stopped by one of the white cottages. The whole place was filled with the same kind of little white houses.

The man from the church opened the door to the house. It was so clean and some furniture was in it. We looked in the bedrooms where we saw that beds had been placed. On the beds were used mattresses, but we were happy, very happy for them. Each bedroom had a closet. There was a sofa in the living room. In the kitchen was a table and chairs. We could sit at that table. The bathroom had hot and cold water. The kitchen had an electric stove and refrigerator.

In the kitchen were a couple of boxes. There were dishes, pots, a frying pan, teapot, and so much more, spoons, forks, knives.

There was even a basket with food for us. I could not believe it. It did not seem real. Then the church people were leaving.

It was time to put things in order. We made up Mama's bed. She and Maija would sleep together in that double bed.

In our bedroom we had to take David. It was not too good. Then we decided we could use the sofa in the living room as David's bed. Voldis decided to get lumber pieces and make a crib safe for him to sleep in and it would be in our bedroom. For now he had to sleep on the sofa.

I was glad we still had a couple of pillows and blankets, those that kept us warm all those six years.

Now we were hungry. With the basket of food left for us and the leftovers from the farm, we had enough food for a couple of days. That was good too. We did not know where the store was. The place around us was only residential.

Sunday morning Voldis took a bath. He said there was plenty of hot water. Since we knew that somebody would come after us to take us to the church, we had to be ready for that.

Mama felt too tired this morning to go with us. We had breakfast but Mama did not feel like eating. The church people came and took us to church. The children went to Sunday school and we also went to the service. After that we were introduced to some people in the congregation. Someone took us after church to the grocery, and told us how and where to use the bus. We went into one store. It was very big. I got a loaf of bread.

They showed us where Voldis would catch the bus to go to work, where to transfer to another bus, and how to get back.

When we came back Mama was better. She had put the kitchen in order and peeled some potatoes for our meal. David was busy telling her that he was in the school, not church. There were other children, too, and the teacher was talking, but he could not understand. I was sure that in the school he would learn to talk like the other children.

Our living on Stratford Road in the little white house was becoming settled. Voldis went to work at the Burruss Lumber Company. Maija went to school in the second grade and was doing fine. I started to work in alterations at The Vogue, a fine dress shop. I don't remember how much I was paid. The shop was on Main Street downtown. Mama and David were at home.

David was nearing his third year. Mama started to teach him reading and writing. Sure, it was in Latvian. We subscribed to Latvian *Laiks*. In a couple of months David could slowly read and write. He liked it very much.

Some people at the church thought that it was wrong to teach a child so young. My mother, being a schoolteacher, said that it depends on the child. For David this was right. He liked it. He never had toys. This was like a play toy; he enjoyed it.

So it was learning, reading books, study and later music was David's life foundation. It was never too hard or too much. He loved to do that.

The weeks passed with the work. At that time on Saturdays we did not work, but we had an opportunity to do our shopping for groceries for the week and other things. One Saturday, I took the children to Dr. Davis on Memorial Avenue. He was a children's doctor. The waiting room was full of children and parents. He had snow-white hair and was bent in the shoulders. He was probably seventy years old; his wife appeared younger, near sixty.

I was wondering about so many children, as if there was no other doctor in Lynchburg. One mother said, "He is the best doctor. Many bring their children here from other towns."

That first summer in Virginia was very hot, especially July and August. We went downtown. Voldis wanted to buy a hat for David since the sun was so strong and he was playing outside. That day we had our boy with us. We took him to a nice department store, Leggett's. Voldis picked some hats that he wanted to put on David's head. David would not let him. Then his father said, "You pick one out if you like." But the boy would not touch anything, insisting that the hat was not his.

I took him aside, "David, you are right, these hats are not yours. We will pay here in the store for the hat that you would like. After we pay, then that hat will be yours."

When he chose a hat, I took him by the hand and in my other hand I had the hat and we went to pay. I put the money in his hand and said that if he wanted to pay for the hat he could give the money and he did. "Now this hat is yours," I said, and he took it.

All his lifetime David was honest. When he borrowed something he would give the date when it would be returned. If he could not return it on time, he would say so and why, asking to extend and setting another date. Then on the dot he took care of it. He was three years old.

Voldis bought a couple of carpenter tools and the lumber for David's bed and was measuring and cutting. He was working so neat and easy as if it was just child's play. I did not know he had that kind of knowledge. Then he painted it light gray. It was a beautiful bed. David liked it too. He could easily get himself in and out of the bed. Still it was very safe. We put it in the corner of our bedroom so that we could see him from our bed.

Being a war refugee child, he had no toys. In one of the boxes of gifts from the church my mother found a "toy" 38 size original pistol. She did not tell about it to anybody, not even me, but hid it in her bed. When the garbage collectors came on Monday she brought the toy pistol out from her room wrapped in paper, she opened it and I saw the pistol. "Now it goes to the garbage!" she said, and went out and dropped it there. "Can you imagine that a toy?"

I could not believe my eyes. Church people who are supposed to be God loving bringing such a gift to a little boy who had to come here because his home was lost in the horror of war weapons and pistols included. Jesus Christ, as he was going around, did not pass out pistols or swords.

So we continued to live on Stratford Road. We had a lot to learn. Like one day somebody came from City Hall and asked why we did not cut our grass, that the neighbors had called them complaining. We did not know that there was such a law and where could we get the necessary tools. So it was now explained to us and we started to do it.

In the back of the house was some land. Voldis bought a spade and a rake. He dug it up, removed some stones and planted tomatoes, radishes, and some other vegetables. At least on the weekends he had something to do.

He started to correspond with some Latvian friends who were living in Washington, DC and some in Canada. It seemed some were doing better there, working in construction business. Voldis and his brother Peter were used to helping their father in that kind of work. Voldis's specialty was carpenter-trimmer. He started to talk about going for a visit to Washington. About a month later he did, taking the trip by Greyhound on a weekend and staying two more days.

He returned home telling us that he was glad he made this trip. There were many Latvians. He met many friends who are carpenters and working on the buildings, but to rent one room to live in cost very much. Financially at this time he could not do it.

Working at the dress shop I was not earning much. It was an off and on seasonal job. The people I worked for were nice, but our needs were big.

When reading in the paper advertisements I noticed a dressmaking factory needed seamstresses. It was on Main Street where my present work was, but at the other end of the street. The work would be five days and eight hours a day. So I went there and got a job.

I found that on the same street was a big grocery store, with a good choice of food and it stayed open long hours. So now after my work I could go in and buy what we needed for home and not have to go on Saturday. That way I saved a day and a bus fare.

I found on the same street a fabric (textile) store where short cuts (one yard or less) of material were at a reduced price and at home my sewing machine was all put together, ready to be used. I had French patterns with me; now I could use them. First I made new outfits for Maija and David, then for the rest of the family.

When Sunday came and we were at the church, people were asking about the clothes. I told them that in the camp I learned to do this work. Then I was asked if I could do some sewing for them, too, if they would bring me the material, and I said that I could.

Working in the factory and on weekends doing some sewing for my customers, I could put some money aside. On Main Street was a big solid bank. I think its name was Lynchburg National Bank. I had an idea and wanted to talk about it with my husband. First he looked as if he was preoccupied. Sometime later I tried again. Not very willing he said, "What do you have on your mind?"

I said, "You are working and I am, too. We could now put some money aside. There is a bank on the Main Street, Lynchburg National Bank. It will bring a little interest."

"How do you think we should do it?" he asked.

"We could open an account in both of our names. Then when somebody needs we both can take it if there is a need," I said.

"I already have done it," Voldis said, looking away.

"Did you put it in your and my name?" I asked.

"No," he said, "I put it in my name." Then looking uncomfortable, with eyes down, he continued. "If you need, go to the bank, it's in my name and they will give you money." I was stunned. He had not mentioned this idea to me before. He was my husband. Why did he not tell me his idea? He just went and did it. When he left Riga in June 1944 under German order, he did not give me any money. All I had in my purse was 39 lats in coins. All those six years in the camps I did not use it because it had no value. Before leaving camp in Oldenburg my mother gave him money. Does he not trust me, my family? Why?

I decided since he was my husband and this thing had been done I would not say anything more about it and I would continue to put the biggest part of my income for deposit in the bank.

So we lived on without arguments. One Saturday we had to go downtown to the main post office on Church Street. It was beautiful warm weather, hardly anybody on the street. Then from the post office a white-haired man came out and seeing us smiled, saying, "Good morning." Then I recognized our children's Dr. Davis from Memorial Avenue. He passed by without stopping.

Voldis, suddenly grabbing my arm above the elbow, asked angrily, "Who is your lover?"

I told him that this was our children's doctor. Voldis did not speak English. He never came along with the children and never met the doctor. It seemed he was satisfied with my explanation. We went about our business.

Sunday was a nice day. Like always we went to church. At home we had a very nice lunch. My mother did not come to church, she could not understand English and she was a member of the Orthodox Church. That was 1950. I don't remember if at that time such a church was in Lynchburg.

That Sunday night we went to bed at our regular time. At about 1:00 or so Voldis was waking me up, "Who is your lover, the one we met by the post office?"

I was still asleep. He persisted with this question. Then I awakened and said, "Why are you waking me up? You know I have to go to work in the morning."

Then he said, "I think when you are partially asleep you will tell me the truth who is your lover."

I had nothing to say. I already told him and had nothing else to tell. I turned on the other side and tried to go back to sleep, but it was not easy.

About a month later, a similar thing happened. One Saturday we were shopping at the grocery store on Main Street. About finished, I pushed the full cart with the purchases to the checkout counter. There were very few people in the store and no one was in front of me or behind.

I had never seen the cashier at the checkout before. He was young, probably in his twenties. He smiled and said something; I smiled too and answered. I speak English with an accent. I don't like it but cannot get free from it.

So he asked me where I was from. To make this talk short, I just said from across the ocean. Then he asked how long I had been here and I said less than a year. That's it. He did his work and put my groceries in the bags. I paid him and was leaving. My husband was there too. Since he didn't speak English, he had nothing to say. So we both picked up our bags and left for the bus and home.

In the bus Voldis asked who was that man in the store with whom I was smiling and talking. I said, "I have never seen him before. Not in the store or any place."

"You were smiling at each other. He is your lover."

I had nothing to say. In the middle of the night he woke me up insisting that now being so sleepy I would tell the truth.

I hoped that he would stop these accusations and we would be able to have a normal, peaceful life, but he did not. I remembered back home he was jealous, but his working hours were so long we hardly saw each other. It was the same when our baby was born and then the war came and there was separation for several years. What shall we do?

Then one day Voldis, coming from work, came through the front door. David, our three-year-old, was standing in the middle of the living room floor; the space all around him was open. Voldis suddenly very angrily raised his voice, "Why does he have to stay in the middle of the room and not to the side?"

I said, "This room has only one sofa, two chairs, and a small table by the wall. You have free space all around."

Then I remembered the Oldenburg camp when Voldis and the other men arrived from work and they made the "joke" seeing David running to meet his daddy, that this definitely was not his son. That "joke" was doing so much harm now.

How can I live with this man? Now the child is in his way because of his jealousy. How can that boy grow up being pushed in the shadow? What can I do? Kill myself? Who will take care of the children? Not Voldis. No, no! I was losing desire for my husband as a man.

I decided to pray to our Heavenly Father and trust him completely and expect and wait for his solution.

Voldis continued working at the lumberyard and I worked at the Dale Garment Co. We went to church on Sunday, but shopping we did separately. Anything else was the same. No unnecessary visiting or talking.

The winter was gone and spring was in. Voldis was still corresponding with his friends in Washington, DC. What about? I did not ask. Then one day, saying nothing about it, he took his briefcase and left, I assumed for Washington. I don't remember if he told when he would be back. He just left without saying goodbye to the children or me.

The end of the month came and we had to pay rent for the house in advance. I had my paycheck but it was not enough to cover all the rent. The bank that held our savings account was three blocks from my work place. During the lunch, I could go there and take out enough money, then Saturday go to our real estate company and pay the rent.

At lunchtime I went to the bank and said that I needed the money from my husband's and my account. The teller listened and after I gave my husband's full name and address he said there was no money in the account. I did not believe him. I repeated the name and address to the teller, but he insisted there was no money. I said, "Every month I gave my check to my husband to deposit and he said that he did. I need now to pay the rent or we will be put on the street."

Then the teller said, "Wait just a minute," and left through a door. Then came an elderly tall, gray-haired man who said, "Mrs. Mednicks, your husband came here a month ago and took out all the money."

I was stunned. I could not understand. All year I trusted him, gave him my earned money to deposit. It should be about six or seven hundred dollars. Why did he do it?

I was returning back to my work and thinking that the lunchtime probably would soon be over. Tears were running down my face. Bitter tears. He did not care for our children. Why? Now the real estate people will put us on the street. Where will we go? Tomorrow I have to go and tell them that I cannot pay the rent.

The next day I went downtown. On Church Street was Acree & Peck Real Estate Company. I was so ashamed that I did not have enough for the rent.

In the office were three ladies working that morning. No men. I was so glad about it. They were so kind to me, asking what happened. I had to explain but tried to tell them as little as possible. Then one of the ladies said not to worry about it, to pay when I could.

I had to find another place for us to live. If we stay in the house my income will leave six dollars a month for food. It was not enough. Since I had to bring up two children I could not drop the work in the factory and the weekend job selling cemetery lots. I needed money so we would have a place to live, to buy food and provide an education for my children.

I found an apartment in a house on the second floor with three rooms, kitchen, and bathroom. The price was forty dollars with heat and electricity included. I also found another job of the same kind within walking distance from that apartment. No need for the bus expense. My girl's school was in the next block so close to our new apartment. Since this apartment was vacant the landlady let us occupy it within one week.

When I told our minister that we were moving to a new place he asked why, and I told him that Mr. Mednicks found work in Washington, DC and left. Then he asked if we too would leave for Washington; I said that I didn't think so.

Just a couple of days before leaving the little white house on Stratford Road, Voldis arrived from Washington. It was afternoon. We were eating dinner in the kitchen. He came to the table. He did not say anything; neither did I. Then he went to our bedroom. He was gathering all his things and tools together. Then I asked, "Why did you take all the money from the bank and not tell me?"

He answered, "Because I needed the money."

"There was my money, too, and I had to pay the rent. I did not have enough," I said. He did not answer.

After cleaning up the dishes, I was sitting on the sofa in the living room. Then David was coming. My mother saw him and said, "Where are you going?"

He said that he had something to say to me. He came close to me and said, "Mama, Daddy has a big bed in his room. Go there. It is big," and he left me and went to his bedroom. I did not follow David like I usually do to check up and cover him.

I took my topcoat from the closet and slept on the sofa. In the morning my husband left.

Before he reached the edge of the street he stopped, turned toward the house and me standing in the doorway, and said, "If you come to Washington you could work in one of the hotel kitchens. They pay eighteen dollars an hour. Then I will build you a house."

I heard the words, but it did not mean anything. I felt as if we were strangers. I was not angry about what was happening or what I would do next.

Then some men from the Lutheran church came and took our things to Monroe Street, our new apartment. We lived there a couple of years. Then our landlady, who had been a widow for some time decided to marry and she moved to her husband's place. She rented her apartment downstairs to a young couple with a girl about seven years old. For a while it was all right but later they were very noisy.

I told them that I was a working woman and asked if they could stop being so noisy so late in the night. The man laughed and said, "If you don't like you can leave the apartment."

I talked with my mother and we decided to look for another place and we found one on Diamond Hill. It was a two-story house with two apartments. I took the one on the first floor. The second floor was rented to a young German couple with two children, six and two years old. Their English was minimal. They were nice, clean people, hard working, and studious learning the English language. Two years later the German couple left for Maryland. They had improved their English and had an opportunity in Maryland for better work with higher income.

Reading the Latvian newspaper *Laiks*, I saw an advertisement by the Chicago Technical College regarding enrolling to study drawing in architecture and mechanical design. I always felt good with a pencil in my hand. The price of this school was fair. Because the college had only dormitories for men, a suggestion to the college was not to make dormitories for women but mail that course as correspondence to their homes. It worked fine after they accepted this idea.

I continued working daily at the garment company and at home and weekends on the correspondence college course. I had top grades. In a two-year time I received my diploma.

I got a job as a draftswoman. I left the garment company and the $23.00 a week pay for $50.00 a week for drawing work.

While employed at the garment company, a worker, E. Harris, was working in the same department, cutting, and also as a mechanic. He was a bachelor and said that he would always be a bachelor. I liked that. I felt safe, because I had no interest to ever marry again. I have two children, a wonderful mother, so helpful and reliable, and peace always at home.

Harris had a car. Sometimes when I was walking home and he was passing me on the street he would stop and offer a ride. Usually I refused because I liked to walk home after work, but on a rainy day I accepted a ride. Still even then I tried to avoid him by changing the streets. He was asking me why I needed to get home so soon and I was avoiding telling him about the college. I said that my mother's age make me rush home.

I also changed apartments to a cheaper one. It was closer to school for the children. It was an attic apartment with two rooms, bath, and kitchen. It was right under the roof. I had my drawing board in my bedroom/living room. When hot months came, all the windows upstairs were opened. I had a wet towel on my back and sometimes even my feet in a bucket with water. Still my schoolwork was being done and mailed to Chicago.

In the meantime Mr. Harris and David were becoming acquainted. They were talking about horses, dogs, fishing, and other sports. One time Mr. Harris asked David if he would like to go fishing. David answered that he had no tools for that.

I started to think, that's true, he had no toys, only books. The library here in the city had books. Both my children liked to read.

Mr. Harris said to David, "I have several fishing rods and hooks, too. If you would like, next Saturday we could drive to the lake, if your mother would agree."

Now David turned to me about the lake, fishing, and the trip. "Do you really want to?" I asked him. His answer and desire I could see and I said, "O.K., but he has to be home before supper."

So David and Mr. Harris's friendship was developing. Mr. Harris even told David when he was sixteen he would teach him how to drive a car and show him how to repair it if the car should have a problem on the road.

Then Harris invited us to a picnic, even my mother, to his parent's home on Old Forest Road. They had a new home, with some land and woods around it. It was a midsummer, beautiful sunny day. He came after us in his car. His father was a retired railroad man. All their children were grown up and married except Eugene Harris, Jr.

They were country people of the Baptist faith. Next to their property on the right side was a new large Baptist church built not long ago on the Harris donated property.

We were introduced to the family including Eugene's brother Clifton and his wife Betty. They all received us kindly. We had a nice picnic meal. Later Mr. Harris took us home to our attic apartment.

After living in America four years I decided to apply for American citizenship for the children and myself. That was 1954 and I received it.

I did not like changing our living place so often. For the children's sake we needed our own home and for my mother's sake, too. There was no one I would trust the children with more than her. I had been saving for a down payment on a house and prayed that now very soon I would have enough for the right one.

Looking for a house was not easy because of working every day, then college and taking care of my family. Harris noticed my difficulties to go and see the offered properties because my only transportation was the city bus and that only ran on the main lines, so he insisted that he take me in his car. I did not like to burden him, using his car and his time, but I really had no other choice.

Then he said, "If I did not have time, I would tell you. I like to see those properties myself. I just enjoy knowing what is new on the market. I may see one that I like and would like to buy." So we started looking together.

We also agreed when we found one that I really liked we would bring the children and my mother to show it and then only decide what to do. Finally we found a house that I liked. It was a brick building with two bathrooms, and several bedrooms. Eugene, Jr. liked it too.

The present owners were moving to North Carolina and had kept this place in good condition. It was time to bring my family to see this place for themselves and let them tell us if they really would like to live in this house.

The price seemed to be decent and with my income as a draftswoman I could afford monthly payments. In my savings account I also had enough to make a down payment.

I told the family what I found. Then I described a little about the house and asked if they would like to see it and only if they think that they may like to live there would I purchase it.

On Saturday Eugene came after us and took us all to that house. In the car David asked Eugene if he had seen the house and if he liked it. He answered, "Yes," that he had seen it, but about liking he would not say because David's mother is buying the house and they have to look carefully at everything and then decide if he likes and if he would want to live there. O.K. was David's answer.

We reached the house and drove into the driveway. Eugene stopped the car and said, "This is the house and by the door is a real estate salesman who has the key and will let us in so we all can see."

So we went in and were busy walking from room to room, looking at the basement, and the rooms and the bath upstairs. The place had an oil furnace so we had no need to chop wood to keep the house warm. There was a fireplace in the living room. Maija looking at it said, "Where will we get the wood to burn and the Christmas tree?"

"We will have wood for the fireplace and a Christmas tree if you would like. There are plenty on my father's place," Eugene said.

"There is a school nearby. Just in walking distance. I will drive you there and show you the shortest way," he said to David, "and for Maija the school bus stops right there," he was showing across the street corner.

Now we had to decide whether to buy or not. Both children liked this place. I had to return to the real estate agent to make the purchase. Talking with my mother about the house, she said that it seemed to be good, that she liked everything about it; it looked just right for our family's needs.

"If you can afford the payments do not delay," she said. I went to the bank to withdraw funds for the down payment and then purchased that property.

Soon we moved in with Harris's help. David expressed an interest in music. He wanted to learn to play. I talked about it with a retired friend who was a concert piano teacher. She wanted to see him and talk. She liked his answers and said that the best would be piano. What now?

We had a neighbor who was a piano tuner. I talked to him and he suggested buying a used one, older but a good make. He gave us the address where there was a good selection. We found a Wurlitzer. Its cost was $200.00 but we could pay $15.00 each month. The retired piano teacher agreed to teach him. David liked to practice and gladly followed her instructions.

Maija was selected at her school to learn to play the violin. The school even gave her one and she attended her lessons regularly with other children. Later it was so nice when my children and some of their friends came together with instruments and played concerts in our home.

We did not have many children in our neighborhood. There were some girls, and a few more boys. All were about the same age. Sometimes a boy or two attacked David. I did not see any reason for this since he was standing on our property. He backed up more and more but never attacked. One time I asked him why not and he calmly said, "Mother, if the boy is smaller, I would beat him up, but if the boy is bigger he will beat me up. What will be gained with that?" he asked me. "When they try to touch me I say, "We will fight, catch me!" and I run. "Soon I look back and see they had given up the running." Then he continued to the Black Water creek as it meanders. When he had enough, he turned back. He felt good after the run and by then the boys were gone, too.

So he was growing up with friends without fights. He subscribed to *Science* magazine and he often went to the city library for books, he played tennis, and he enjoyed running and walking.

Voldis, living in Washington, one year sent a Christmas card to the children and one time $15.00. Now David was in school. It seemed to me that Voldis did not care for them or me. I was paying for the house. It was my property. My mother was living with us. She was healthy and took care of all our needs at home. I decided to get a divorce, especially for the reason that all I had, the house and property, and savings were mine and my children's and so that nobody could appear and take everything because "somebody else needs it."

Sundays as usual we went to church. The children went to Sunday school. To get there we had to take the bus and cross the city. I remember one time it was cold, windy, and icy. The bus stop was one block away from us on the corner where we had to stay and wait. I did not want to go, but David had come to me and said, "Mama, we have to go to church. This is God's day. I know he wants us to be there."

We went!

One time we were sitting in the living room and Maija looked disappointed. She was about twelve, David seven. It was Saturday, about lunchtime. I asked her why she was sad. For a while she did not answer, then she said, "Why is my father not here? He should be here."

"You know from the Bible who is the creator?" I asked.

Then David said, "I know that is God!"

"That's right, David. Heavenly Father is the only creator of the world and all people, all of us. Only He knows where each of us should live and work."

"I don't like it, I don't like it!" Maija repeated.

"If you don't like it, write a letter to God, but put on the right address and stamp," I said.

Then David stood up, came a step closer to her and said, "No, you're not! You don't write the letter!"

His voice, his expression, though young, had changed. It was grave and mature. A voice one must obey.

Maija's face now had changed too, the sadness was gone and she had nothing to say then and never later as the years passed by.

The friendship with David and Harris was continuing. He acquired a horse and a cow that he was milking himself and bringing us milk, saying, "It's good for their health." The horse was for David to teach him how to ride. These animals were housed on the Harris' place outside the city.

Then one time David said to me that he would like to have a daddy, someone like a friend that one can always talk to and learn from, somebody to be with us.

I did not ask if these two friends had been talking about that among themselves. Then sometime later on a beautiful sunny day Eugene took me for a ride to the park by the river. We talked. It seemed that we were getting along fine—the family and he. He asked me to marry him and gave me an engagement diamond. When at home we told the children and my mother about the engagement. They wanted to see the ring at once and were very happy.

We were married in the Baptist church in Lynchburg and afterwards had a dinner party at my home for his family and mine. The next day was Monday and we both had to work. About two weeks later Gene decided to take his new family on a honeymoon trip.

The children and my mother took the back seat in his car and we were in front. We had a good breakfast at home, then traveled to the Blue Ridge Parkway. Sometimes we stopped to enjoy the royal beauty of the mountains. We stopped in a small town and had a snack, then continued to the caverns. Some of them were deep underground and had rivers and lakes with the water so clear. For dinner we had our meal in a fine restaurant. Everybody was happy. We were offered dessert and it looked good, but we were so full. Gene looked at us with a question in his eyes.

David said, "I cannot, but could we take it with us?"

Maija smiled as if she, too, liked that idea.

Gene asked the waitress if we could take some of it along, that we would stop by the lake on top of the mountain and finish our dessert there. The waitress said we could do that.

Gene asked us to choose what we wanted. David and Maija did and Gene too, saying, "just for company's sake," after Mama and I refused.

The waitress brought us a box with desserts. Gene paid the bill and we left. When the sun was setting that evening and we were driving along, David said, "Mama, I love the honeymoon. Now I want you to marry every month and have the honeymoons." I was so surprised and I wished to vanish in the air.

The next day was ordinary. Gene and I went to work and the children to school. Mama was up early and made breakfast for us. Gene was thankful to her. One day when I came home after work Mama was sitting in an easy chair in the living room and looking at the TV across from her. I asked where this came from. She said that Gene came and put it there and told her to sit and watch and then he left. Mama's English was very limited.

Later he told us that Mama was by herself all day. We are all gone. She needed some companionship and she cooked his breakfast. He wanted to give her a gift. He hoped that she would like it and it would help her not to feel so alone.

Mama did like it and used it. She thanked him for being so considerate.

So everything was nice. The children were growing. David took the grass-cutting job from Gene, his daddy, and earned a dollar, which he was saving.

At Christmas time we had a fir tree with lights on, trimmings, and presents. Christmas eve after work Gene came home and told the children to get ready, that we would drive to Williamsburg. He had made reservations for us and tomorrow we would have an old fashion Christmas dinner there.

We already had our baths. It did not take us long to pack what we needed. Mama decided to stay at home. When we were in the car Gene said that we would pick up two youngsters and said, "They come to Cleitons filling station to do any kind of work they can get. They are teenagers, but good workers. They said today that they never had any Christmas celebration, that their parents could not afford it. So I invited them to come with us to Williamsburg if their parents would let them."

I thought, that is Gene, always ready to help somebody if there is a need. Then he was nearing the run down part of Lynchburg and stopped by a house that was "crying" for repair. He went to the door and waited. An elderly woman opened the door. They talked and she asked him to come inside. He did not, but pointing to our car he came back, took his seat and soon the boys came out and Gene let them in the back seat. Then he decided that Maija would sit with us in the front and David and the boys would be more comfortable in the back seat.

We arrived in Williamsburg late and tired. We slept in the Inn. The place was reserved for us. We slept quite long. In the morning Gene took us for a ride. Someplace we had a small snack. About 1 or 2 p.m. we went to dinner at the Inn. Gene had reserved a separate dining room for us. It was like a family size dining room with a large single dining table decorated with tablecloth and napkins and a festive table setting. There was lots of food beautifully prepared. The waiters serving us were historically dressed in white fitted pants, red embroidered jackets with white trimming at the neck, and three corner black hats. They brought a brown aromatic turkey and set it on the table.

Then the waiter was helping the men put on big napkins to cover their fronts and tied up in the back so that food would not dribble on their clothes. David did not like it, wanted to take it off and said, "I am not a baby. I don't drip food."

The waiter explained, "It was custom here that all men, including generals and presidents, always used these covers and even General Robert E. Lee." That impressed David very much. He was very fond of General Lee and his history. So he let the waiter put the cover on him.

Now the waiter was serving us. It was wonderful as if we really were in the old times. Everything was delicious. After this meal Gene decided that we would go home.

All was wonderful, but returning home was even better. Mama was happy seeing us back and well. After Christmas the children often were telling their grandma about the Williamsburg dinner and everything about the place.

I was very grateful that my mother was living with us, since I had to work. When the children came home she waited on them. She had cookies and milk waiting for them. She helped them with schoolwork. In her lifetime she had been through so much. Born in Ukraine, she married my father and they went to Latvia, then World War II came and they went to Germany. Since she too had moved from camp to camp for six years, then came to America, she really had much to tell the children about the world.

Life went on and Gene changed jobs several times. Sometimes it was better, sometimes not. He loved cars and changed very often. I thought if our bed were larger we would have the car sleeping between us.

One summer Maija was invited by my sister to spend the summer with her family in Montreal, Canada. Her two boys were three and six. Maija was about twelve years old. She liked the offer to be with them. We put her on the Greyhound bus and she had to transfer in New York to the Canada line, and was met by them in Montreal. She did that trip by herself. Then next time David did the same trip with me. He was very happy and helpful on the trip. Children are naturally good, loving, and helpful when parents love and appreciate them. After one week's visit we returned home.

When Maija was sixteen Gene taught her to drive the car. After a one-hour lesson they came home happy. Gene was telling me how easy it was teaching her. He had explained to her how and what to do. She listened and then took over. She did not make any mistakes. Later they went downtown on a workday and she got her driver's license.

Then came David's turn. Gene taught him at sixteen, too, but there was a difference. "Since David is a boy," said Gene, "he needs to know more about the car. If when driving the car stops and no one is around, maybe it's just a little thing you have to do to be able to fix it." David also felt that was a good thing to know. They both were serious about it. Then came the driving lessons until David and Gene were sure he could pass the test.

Later David had more opportunity to be thankful to "his daddy" Gene to use this car fixing knowledge, especially when on the road and no help was around.

Then the time came for David's junior year in high school. His schoolteachers suggested that he continue his education. I asked him how was the test. For a while with his head down he did not answer, still thinking. Then he said sadly, "I got only 169. Not so good. I hoped for more." Only later I found from his school that his IQ was very high.

Thinking about college David told me that he would go to Washington, DC to see his birth father. He said he already had called him and would meet with him after school Friday in

*David Mednicks*

Washington's Greyhound bus terminal. Sunday evening he would be back and he asked me if I could meet him here at the local bus terminal and bring him home.

I agreed to do as he was asking. But I asked him to do something for me too. "Since your father is married, be kind and thankful to his wife and have good manners. If you would feel that you want to return home sooner, keep some coins in your pocket, find a telephone outside their place, and call me. Tell me what time you will take the bus there and when it will be here in our city and I will meet you."

As planned, on Friday he left for Washington right after school.

Saturday about 4:00 p.m., I heard the telephone. I picked it and heard David's voice, "Mom, can you pick me up?"

"Where are you?" I asked, thinking that he was still in Washington.

"I am here in Lynchburg," he said.

I never thought that his visit would be so short and I left for the bus terminal. When we were driving home I asked him how the visit was. For a while he was silent, then he said, "I don't want talk about it."

When we were stepping out from the car and walking to the house, he said, "A biological fact don't make man a father yet! He is not my father!"

Sometime later he told me that when he arrived there, his father was waiting for his bus and took him to his apartment and introduced him to his wife Mary. She was serving dinner. She did not talk and nobody talked. When it was finished she got up. Then she opened the refrigerator and David saw there a cake with one slice out.

"And she did not even offer!" he said. My father pointed to the sofa in the living room and said, "You will sleep here." And he went into their bedroom where Mary already had gone and closed the door. "I wanted to talk with him and hoped he would come out, but he did not," said David sadly.

"The next morning my father said, 'Now we will have breakfast, then I will show you the place where I work.' "

"After breakfast was over, a small brown sandwich bag was left on the table. Father took that and walking to the door he said, 'Take your lunch bag, too.' But there was none on the table. 'I don't have any,' I said. Then Father told Mary to make one for me too, and she did. And we left.

"We went to a construction place. He was walking and talking about his work, his life, and his hardships and not asking me about my life. Then I said to him, 'I want to talk with you about school, about college.' He interrupted me and said that his earnings were small, that he didn't have much money and on and on."

David realized that he would not talk with him and said to his father that he just remembered something he had to do at home in Lynchburg and was walking away. His father called, "Where are you going?" and was running after him." Stop, stop, we will talk, we will talk."

David stopped; his father came and said, "When you are in college, I will send you $15.00 a month. That is all I can do."

He did not even ask how much the college would cost and David did not volunteer to tell him the price of $2,000 and $250 for books and that we just did not have that money.

"You said that you have to go back home, I will take you to the bus," Father said.

"You don't have to take me," David answered.

"Come, I will take you there, I have to go that way myself."

The next spring David graduated from high school and immediately got a job with a road-building contractor on Rt. 460. Work was 6:00 a.m. until 9:00 p.m. five days a week, Saturdays until 5:00 p.m. The pay was ninety cents an hour plus overtime pay. He earned $1,000 dollars. I managed by January to give him $1,000. Yes, his father sent $15.00 a month. David attended Hampden-Sydney College.

At age fifteen, Maija decided to go to Washington where her father lived and take a two-weeks long confirmation class in the Latvian Lutheran Church. She lived with my father's (her grandfather) friend, Colonel Graps. Every morning she went to the church to the classes. After two weeks her confirmation was in that church. My sister Nina with her husband and sons Peter and Andris came from Chicago to the confir-

mation service. They were staying in a hotel, since Graps' apartment had only three rooms. We had dinner at Graps' apartment. It was a beautiful day. I still have pictures from that day.

After graduation from high school Maija went to Lynchburg College. At the same time she had a job at the J.C. Murphy store. Mostly it was after school time. She was doing fine. The people in charge of the store were very satisfied with her work, and her grades were good at school.

Since she lived at home and was a day student at school, the tuition fee was not large and her father offered to pay it. He was not married at that time to the woman called Mary or any other. Here and there she dated some students from school only on weekends. At springtime the local paper selected six or seven students for a fashion show. All the girls were pretty, but my daughter stood out more in the picture. I received compliments even from strangers.

When the cherry blossom festival was in Washington, her father, being in charge of the war veterans' organization, invited her to the dance ball in their club. He insisted that she participate. She was first runner up.

One day while reading the newspaper *Laiks*, I saw an inquiry by our relatives about our family and that our brother who was lost since 1943 was back in Riga and was looking for us.

I was so happy about the news. He had been looking for us for 18 years. Immediately I told Mama and the family. Mama was very happy too.

"I don't believe," she said, "it has been so long, so long. It cannot be true, Misha is back and alive."

Since we left Germany she expressed doubts about her son. I could not agree with her. Never! Because he was always so good, so helpful to all, so forgiving and honest. He trusted our Heavenly Father, had never done anything bad to anyone, but helped people even if it would not benefit himself. All these years I trusted that God would protect him regardless of where he was and in what situation. Christ, as he promised in the Bible "to be with us all the time, even to the end," will bring him home.

Immediately I wrote a letter to him that we were very happy about the news in the paper that he was back home, and that we were waiting to hear more from him. I also told him about our family here in Virginia.

It was not long before we received a letter from him. It was such a loving letter, more love expressed to his mother. How all these years he was praying and thinking about his mother. Grateful for her love and care she had given him when he was growing up. That when he was in the war and in danger thinking about her love helped him to endure, even when he was wounded (his left side torn out) her love and feeling for him saved him.

Then he wrote that he was married and his wife was Jewish, from Ke-yev (Kiev) where he was badly wounded. When he came home he did not find us. He had no money and not even a bread crust. She helped him. He had to sell his accordion that still was in the apartment. He was still missing it.

Mother listened but I could see she did not like something. I did not ask her, knowing that she probably later would tell me.

"I don't like that he married a Jewish woman," she said. "Why, why he could have married anybody else. You are not going to write him any more. We are not going to send him anything."

I listened and thought how one being a mother receiving such a loving letter from a long lost son could say such things. Not knowing the woman. Not being in her son's places and in the war. He was a grownup man, not a little child. Why pass such judgment? He has not even asked her for anything yet.

It did hurt me. He was my brother. Would I obey her? We have to obey our parents! No, I cannot! I did not discuss with her what she had said. It's not for me to teach her, nor to judge her. She lived her life as best as she knew and it was not easy. Now she was old and that is all I could say.

I continued correspondence with Misha. In 1978 I had an opportunity to travel with a group of other Latvians to Latvia after so many years and met with my brother Misha.

We had corresponded for several years. I knew his desire for his accordion that he bought at his age of 20 with his savings and in 1944 October came back from Russia, but we had already left Papa's apartment. He had no money and had to sell the accordion.

Now I just had to get one for him and take it with me to Riga. It was not easy to get the kind he wished at the right price. And the packing had to be just right or it would not pass customs inspection.

From Lynchburg we left for New York, the group's meeting place. About 11:00 p.m., all had arrived and we boarded a Finnish plane for Helsinki. The flight was at night. In Helsinki we had a long wait for a Russian plane to go to Leningrad (Saint Petersburg) in Soviet Russia.

It was a short flight, and we were in the airport of Leningrad. It was daytime with light, north, pale sunshine. The airport field was empty. No other planes but the one on which we came. A hundred feet away I saw a forgotten tree with not much leafage and few branches. It looked so sad. No buildings, nothing around.

The bus came and took us to a big, new hotel in the city of Leningrad. We were there two or three days. I shared a room with a Latvian lady from North Carolina. Everything was clean and simple. As tourists we saw the city, which was old but well taken care of. We also saw the king's palaces and several art museums.

Then we were to go to Riga, Latvia, in a Russian plane. We had to wait a long time in the Leningrad airport. Finally a plane came. It was small and old. When we boarded we could see the age of the plane. There were not enough seats as some had been removed. The plane was clunky and noisy, but we were happy when we started to see the view of our country Latvia through the windows and missing floorboards of the plane.

It was a cold day near the end of September 1978 when I arrived in Riga. Misha left Riga in 1943. Now it was 35 years later. The airport waiting room was not large. People were waiting, meeting, and leaving; I did not see him. Then there were but a few left. When the crowd had thinned out, I noticed a small, thin man and a small woman passing by, going to the end of the room, looking, then turning and going out toward the door.

The profile of the man's nose seemed familiar. Very quietly, in a whisper, I said, "Misha." He stopped and looked at me. He did not recognize me. Then they both were at my side. It was Misha, my brother, giving me carnations. He introduced the woman, Rose. "She is my wife, my friend, and my companion, my lover." I liked her from that moment. She definitely did not look Jewish. After 35 years I was reunited with my brother Misha. It was wonderful to see him again.

We all left for the hotel Riga in the tourist bus. On the fourth floor, in the room I was given, I gave Misha the accordion that I bought for him.

He opened the box where it was packed and was so surprised. They both were happy. I also had some presents for both of them.

Then we took a cab and went to Misha's home. He thought that I should stay with them and eat at his home, the apartment where I grew up, to keep our father's old tradition, but the Communist government at that time did not permit it. Still we had more freedom than other tourists before us.

The apartment was very clean, the floors painted. The walls had cracks. The park across the street was all grown and well kept up. Our Papa's old apartment was now scantily furnished. Meeting me, Misha had on a blue suit, hat, and gray coat. Later I saw that he had one set of working clothes, and one winter coat, the same he had before World War II when he was 21 years old. That's all that was in the closet. Rosa had the same. One coat, one blouse, one skirt, one dress.

The one she had on had patches, even at the underarms. After a very light supper, tea, and a slice of cake, Misha took me back to the hotel.

Sunday after breakfast we took a bus to Sigulda. It had grown. It looked strange. We went to see our summer home. Papa sold it about a year before we left Riga. The main house was changed and finished and the log cabin too. We wanted to see the house inside, but the owner would not let us in. It was sad to see that place. The apple orchard trees left uncared for had left only trunks and some branches dry and dead. The garden where we had lots of strawberries had not been cared for and now was dead.

We went to have lunch at "Senite" (Mushroom). We had smoked chicken, fresh tomato/vegetable salad with fresh sour cream and red whortleberry (bruklenes) lemonade. Very tasty. Then we had fish soup, roast with potatoes and gray peas with browned bacon and onions. We finished with fruit and whip cream dessert.

It was a wonderful meal with my dear brother and his loving wife in the most beautiful place, encircled by trees, meadows, and some smaller forests, with the blue and white clouds here and there, sky blessing the view with peacefulness, serenity.

We returned to the Riga hotel. The next day I was visiting my relatives. It is very hard for me to write about the change in the city. Russians were walking endlessly on the streets, in the stores and markets, overcrowding everything.

The time came for me to leave Riga. We were flying to Leningrad. There we waited because of customs regulations and had to pay duty if we bought anything in Latvia. For some reason, I don't know why, the customs did not check my very full bag. Then we left for Stockholm.

When we arrived there the sun was just setting against the north sky, painting an unusual pink color over the large aerodrome and all its buildings. Different world! Beautiful! Not like Riga.

Yes, a different world. We were taken to the Sheraton hotel. The room was comfortable with a wonderful bathroom and soft, white towels and two pieces of soap. In the Riga hotel there was no soap, no towels.

I thoroughly enjoyed the bath in this hotel and rubbing two times with soap. I was red and looked like a cooked lobster. It felt so good.

Supper was at 8:00 p.m. in the Royal Blue Room. First they served shrimp salad in half-pound bowls, then roast with vegetables and fantastic dessert.

In Stockholm we went sightseeing in the old city and the new city. Then we went to Upsala, and had our dinner in a beautiful old cabin built from large logs. The food and service was wonderful. In the middle of the dining room was a large table. On one side was hot food; on the other was cold food. At the end of the table were two stacks of clean plates, small and large. As soon as one got up from the table to go for more food, a beautiful Swedish girl immediately removed the used plate and we had to take a clean plate. There was a variety of seafood and meats, fruits, and vegetables.

One time we had a supper by the Palace Square on the fourth floor in the basement and later listened to a beautiful concert. We also visited Sigtuna, another old city. We went shopping for presents to bring home. Sweden has many beautiful things and rock crystal.

The next day we left for Copenhagen in Denmark. There we would change planes for New York and Washington, DC.

My husband, Gene, had again changed jobs. The Greyhound Bus Company here in our city was expanding and planned a restaurant in the station. They offered him the job. He liked the offer and took it. He had to start it from beginning and he did well, but it kept him so busy that he had hardly any time left for home, the children, and me.

Maija was in her second year at Lynchburg College. Her boyfriend graduated in the spring from that college and on the first of July he left for Pensacola, Florida, for Navy officers' school. In November, on Thanksgiving Day, she left school and went to Pensacola, too. Her boyfriend Wayne finished the courses and received the "wings" in October. He came home. They met. He had some time off and bought a car. At the beginning of December Maija called us from Pensacola to say that she and Wayne were getting married. She needed our permission because she was not twenty-one; she was twenty. Gene and I went to a notary public and sent the permission.

A chaplain married them in the chapel. They celebrated in the officers' club prepared for them by fellow officers. There were seven couples married that day.

They came home to me for the Christmas holidays. Not to his mother. That was fine. Maija's bedroom with her furniture and her double bed was in order.

I was told that Wayne's mother was not happy that her only son married a refugee girl and communist. In fact, Maija's birth country was Latvia and had a border with the communist country of Russia. If this neighboring country had not forced itself into Latvia (and two others, Estonia and Lithuania) sanctioned by other big countries in the conference of Yalta, we all would still be in Latvia and his mother would be happy. She did not permit Maija to visit her place.

*Maija and Wayne*

After Christmas they left for Florida and looked very happy.

Then Gene was transferred to the Charlottesville Greyhound bus station to open their restaurant. I visited a couple of times. Then David's graduation from high school was coming; and my mother fell and broke her leg.

I was working at the State Highway Department as a draftswoman and taking care of my mother and David. I could not visit with my husband.

I was worried and could not sleep, nor eat. Thirty days later my clothes were hanging loosely on me. I started to wear Maija's clothes, size 6. I was not hungry. One or two bites of a sandwich was enough.

At night, when I could not sleep I read the Bible, but it did not answer my questions.

I just had to ask somebody who knew the Bible well. I went to see our minister at the Lutheran church. Our first minister had left. The new minister was older. I liked it; he had lived a long time and would know the answers.

"When we die, what happens?" I asked.

"That we don't know," he said, "maybe after we are buried we will find out." Then I went to see another minister in the Presbyterian Church. This church was just one block away from our home. David found it, liked it, and since high school went regularly and was active. He played bells in the orchestra.

This minister was in his mid-forties. I asked the same question as the one in the Lutheran church and received the same answer. I left thinking, I don't know about God, but neither does he.

Then it was the last Friday in September 1962. I think it was the twenty-seventh, a sunny day and payday. Usually at lunch everybody left to cash checks and have a bite to eat. I was sitting on my high bench. I did not want to go anyplace and I was not hungry. Then I heard a mature man's deep voice say, ;"Christian Science." I looked around the room, but there was nobody. What does it mean? I knew the word "Christian" was about church, but "Science?" That belongs to mechanics, inventions. What is it about? Where did that voice come from? Nobody was in the room but me.

I decided that since I didn't eat and didn't sleep I was losing my mind. The next day being Saturday I will go to ask my children's doctor to put me in the colony before I do something bad to somebody.

Then suddenly in the same "man's" voice I heard "yellow pages." What does that have to do with the "Christian Science?" Now I know I have lost my mind. Thinking about the yellow pages I got up from the high bench and walked out of the room to the hall, "telephone" was in my thought. But I remembered that all telephones at lunchtime were switched from offices to the guardhouse. So what now? I am in the hall. All doors to separate offices are closed. But then, at the end of the hall, one door was completely opened. This office belonged to Engineer Ansty from the Delvin district. He owned the key to this office.

It was always locked, but now the door was open. He came only once a month.

I went into the office. It was in perfect order. The desk, too, was in perfect order. Next to it was a small table with a telephone and telephone book on it. I lifted it up. It opened in my hand and my eyes saw Christian Science Reading Room tel xxxx. I dialed the number, a woman answered, "Christian Science reading room. What can I do for you?"

I asked, "May I speak to your minister?" She said, "We don't have a minister."

I did not understand. No minister? What now? I thought! And suddenly I asked, "What do you do if you have a problem?"

"We have practitioners," she said. "We have two here. Both have been in practice a long time. One is a widow lady; the other has been married a long time. I will give you the names, you pray to the Father, and he will show the right one for you."

I thought, How will I know? Which? She said, "One is Mrs. Young, the other is Mrs. Fitzgerald."

When I heard the name "Young" I wanted to stop her, because I just knew that name was right for me.

The Reading Room lady gave me Mrs. Young's address and telephone number. Later I called her and made an appointment to see her. I drove to the given address and parked my car several blocks away from Mrs. Young's house number. I was not familiar with that part of city, and walked along, reading the house numbers as I went.

I found the house. It was a four-story apartment house. She lived on the fourth floor. I walked up. She opened the door and let me in. She looked young, forties, perfect complexion, no wrinkles, and no make-up. I wondered about what I had heard from the Reading Room "a widow, long time in practice." Later I heard that she was seventy.

She offered me a seat and started to ask me what I thought about God. I said that I feel he is Father. She asked me many questions. We talked about two hours. Then she said, "You are ready for Christian Science. You start reading the book and I will pray for you."

I bought the book from her. She gave me some Sentinels and a couple of Christian Science Journals and with that I left her place. I walked down the steps and out to the street. It was sunny, the same as when I was coming. But now everything had changed. The sky was bluer, and I could smell the aroma of roses and bread baking. I must be near a bakery. It looked like the air all around me was vibrating. I walked to my car and drove home.

As I was reading the book and the journals it made me calm. The reading was interesting and comforting, I felt at peace. My life was changing.

My husband Gene was transferred to Philadelphia in Pennsylvania to continue the same work with the Greyhound station, opening a restaurant. I went one time to visit him, but found it was too busy.

Having my books and starting now to understand the Bible, I enjoyed being alone. David was in college at Hampden-Sydney in Farmville. He seldom came home. He could only come when a student from this area who had a car came home.

I started to go to the Christian Science Church. I liked the simplicity. It was not like in the Evangelical church, only preaching, then accused that we are sinners. I have never found in the Bible that God ever created sin or death, sickness, or disease. In the First Book of Moses, Genesis, Chapter I, "He created all, in the verse 31, …God saw everything… and, behold it was very good."

In this church are shown the works, how to heal. James 2: 14: "What doth it profit, my brethren, though a man say he hath faith, and have not works? Can faith save him? 2:17: Even so faith, if it hath not works, is dead, being alone." (From the Bible) I saw "the works" are important.

Then Gene wanted to see me, but since we both were too busy, we used the telephone. He told me that he wanted a divorce, that a young woman eighteen years old was pregnant with his child.

I told him that I had no intention of interfering with his newfound happiness. I don't need a divorce. If he needed one, then he could get it. I would not even go to court.

Then his friend, a lawyer, came to talk to me. He kept insisting that I should keep the house we were living in. Gene said that we had lived together ten years and he had nothing to show from this marriage. The lawyer said that my banker told him that the deposit on the house was made from my savings account as well as all monthly payments. The house belonged to me.

I came to America with two small children with not even one dollar in my pocket and a coat with a big hole on its front. Yes, I saved because the children needed a home. I will never fight anybody for money. The man left saying, "You should have kept the house."

I needed a place to live and soon bought a house on Diamond Hill in the city. It was very old, built by slaves. The first owners had coalmines in West Virginia, but did not care to live there. This house on Diamond Hill had a magnificent view down to the James River and across the countryside.

It had big windows and high ceilings. It had no need for an air-cooler. Open windows would bring a pleasant breeze.

The inside of the house was in very bad condition. It needed restoration. The furnace and the rest of central heating were gone. I wanted to study architecture in my old country but World War II took it away. Now I had my chance to use my ideas in this house.

The first step was to remove all that was old and used up, and then select the right replacements. Even some windows had to be replaced. The carpenters, electricians, wall paper hangers, all professionals were working with me, until it was done right.

Sometime later a reputable builder from the city came knocking at my door asking for one of my neighbors, who was away. He noticed the change and said, "This is the Judge Moor's estate! You restored it? May I see it? Just this floor." I let him. He looked in a couple of rooms.

"If this house were out of city, not here, you would get big money for it. You did wonderful work with it," he said. That was some compliment for me.

When David came home from college in the middle of the second semester, I knew something was not right, but I did not ask, letting him choose the time to talk.

The next day he told me that he had misbehaved in school, and now was being punished by being sent home. I was unpleasantly surprised and I did not ask for how long he was sent home. Too many troubles had come my way.

Then I thought that David also had his share of troubles. His birth father left us early in his age, and now his selected father whom he loved and trusted divorced me after being with us ten years. I said, "Think and tell me what you now want to do." He was almost twenty. It's time for him to learn to make decisions for himself.

He said, "I know I can find work, then return to college. Or, I can enlist in the army and after three years I can get my college paid."

I heard but did not like it. The thought came to me. Army? Vietnam war? No, no! I did not want that. I will not let him go.

I just had to get out. I gave him the choice, now will I take it away? I walked fast on the streets to get peace of mind. I prayed to God that nothing bad would happen and I knew as long as I live I would pray.

My daughter and her husband lived in Norfolk, Virginia. He was with the Navy. I visited them there. Darren, their son was four years old and in kindergarten. Parents were telling me that the teacher thought the boy was not bright enough for the next grade. He was in kindergarten two years. It seemed that he had not heard what his parents told him.

When the parents left the room for the kitchen Darren left what he was doing, came to me and asked, "Grandma, do you have a kid at home?" I said, "No." Then he said, "Could you use me?"

I wished to take him and leave. I learned there are no stupid kids, but some grown ups. He understood negative judgment.

Then he opened the door and went outdoors. They lived in the first floor apartment. A bunch of children were standing outside. He said, "Now come in one at a time. There (he showed with a hand) is my grandmother (I was sitting on sofa); then go to that door and to the kitchen, then out," then the next child and . . . he repeated until all went in a single line. When some slowed he repeated, "Yes, she is my grandmother, now go in line and out that kitchen door."

When his father came back to the living room, Darren said, "Daddy, I will join the Boy Scouts and go away and not come home."

I don't think the parents understood how much they hurt the child's feelings by talking about stupid teachers' estimates.

When I returned home from Norfolk, I wanted to learn more about Christian Science and started to look for a good teacher, using Sentinel and Christian Science Journals. There were recorded wonderful healings and its practices.

David enlisted in the army for three years. It was his choice to join the army because he felt it was his duty to the country and it would give him the possibility to continue his college education. He left home for boot camp in New York State and then Germany, first in Heidelberg to improve on his German language. Then to Stuttgart, then Frankfurt. In November I received a letter from the government. It was congratulations that my son passed all requirements and now was a lieutenant in the army!

He told me that after he became a lieutenant they had special exercises where one group in the "war" was meeting the other group, "the enemy," and he would have to order his men to shoot. He knew that he could not do it. "I cannot and do not hate anybody so much as to kill and I would endanger my men," he said. "So I said to my officers that I misled them. I deserve to be punished. What you choose I will accept." For thirty days he had guard duty outside and in the kitchen he was peeling potatoes. No sleep for thirty days. He took it and with no complaints.

Now I understand his uncommon way of sleeping and eating. I am sure that because David loved and trusted God he survived punishment.

His sister's little three-year-old girl Whitney loved her uncle David so much that every night she prayed to God that no bullets would touch him. After three years he came home in one piece and she and we too were very happy.

I went to the Mother church in Boston, Massachusetts. I had an appointment to see a practitioner, Mrs. Helen Wood Bauman, CSB teacher. I had read an article in the Sentinel about the birth of a child in the hospital without a rib cage. There were questions about what to do now; medicine had no solution. The mother of the child turned to a Christian Science practitioner for help to pray in the Christian Science way. On the second or third day the nurse went to take care of the baby and found the child well and complete with rib cage.

So I met Mrs. Bauman and we talked about finding the right teacher. The talk was beneficial for me. Before I left she said, "So often we pray only for self. When you pray, then pray for all, because God doesn't answer selfish prayer."

I found the teacher when C.P. from the Mother church visited our church in the spring and gave a speech. It was to be one hour, but when he stopped he said, "Good afternoon!"

He just started, I thought. How that one hour did vanish. I wished that he would not ever stop.

When later I found that he was selected by the Mother church to be the teacher, I just hoped that I could study in his class.

I was accepted to his class and took a two-week course in 1968 in Richmond, Virginia, by H. Dickerson Rathbun, C.S.B. I paid $100.00 for the course. It was the best investment in my lifetime. It opened the life for me. The health, the right housing, the right employment and income, and harmony. I used to wonder why I am here, now I knew—to receive our Father's blessing, in America. The best Science in the world to live in.

Before I left for Richmond to take the class, I employed a retired nurse living on the same street to be with my mother most of the time. Mama often was forgetful. When I returned home Mama was fine. The nurse had done her work well.

Maija with her family came to visit us. As soon as they were in the house, Whitney asked where was Grandmother Baba. At that time she was in her room. Whitney went to her door and knocked, then went in, carefully closing the door behind her. She stayed in for some time. When she came out her daddy asked, "What did you do there?"

She said, "Talking, Daddy."

"What did you talk about?" he asked.

"Girl talk, Daddy," she said.

Later Mama would tell me how wonderful that girl is, and I could see how happy my mother was having Whitney's visit with her.

In March 1970, my daughter called me from Virginia Beach where they just had built their home and she found that she was pregnant. They had not finished furnishing the new house. She said now they have two children and they are happy with that. If she had $1,000.00 she would get an abortion, she said.

I listened. It was a big surprise to me. Then she continued that just last month she gave away all her baby things. Everything!! She had nothing left for a baby!

Her husband is not with the Navy any more, and the hospital and doctors would cost so much. How can they pay the bills?

"It will all be provided in time, the right time. God knows what we need and supplies everything," I said.

"I have been on the pill all these years so I would not get pregnant and just dropped them thirty days ago. I was on it more than eight years, was full of it," she said.

I listened and was thinking. Dear Heavenly Father, what should I say to her? Abortion! They are such a loving couple. Good to their beautiful children. But all this eight years of medicine in her body? Destructive medicine? I thought they were perfect to have and to bring up another child. God is the only creator, as it reads in the Bible, and provides everything to cover the needs.

The more I thought, I saw their education, health, ability and desire to work and no need for an abortion. The body belongs *only* to her. She has rights to decide what to do.

Then I thought about my David in the Army and Maija having her family. Mama and I were living alone in this house. I called Maija to tell her that I had a suggestion. "You carry the child full time. Then I will give you $1,000.00 to do as you wish and I will take the child, bring it to my home and my mother and I will raise the child."

As time went on there were some calls from her, telling me why they should not have the child. Now they could travel any place with their children, as they are now big, or waking up at night when the child is crying, needing a change or a bottle of milk.

I repeated my suggestion lovingly and patiently. "After the child is born I will give you the check, pick up the child and you will be free to go and do what you wish."

Then I started to pray for the mother and the child as I am taught in Christian Science. Her complaints stopped and she started feeling good. She even got a job on the weekends while her husband stayed home with the children.

Late in September on a Saturday morning I was led to call her. Usually she was working, but now she was at home and told me that at night she was spotting. I asked if she talked with her doctor and if she takes medicine. She said, "no" and he would see her on Monday if it had not stopped, but for now she would stay in bed. She had been pregnant almost ten months.

Immediately I started to pray. The only creator is God. Controlled by divine Mind. His ideal man is perfect and harmonious. The timing of His creation belongs to God. Science & Health 476 man is the idea of God. My 239-19 Man as the idea or image of God.

Monday came and all was very good. The birth was January 8, 1971. My grandson, Patrick, was born in a half hour after Maija arrived at the hospital, and all was perfect. Even the doctor rejoiced that all was so good and easy. No pain, no suffering to mother and none to the child. With Christian Science there is no suffering.

After five years of Navy duty in the Vietnam War as a flight-commander, Wayne left the Navy, but continued on with reserve duty. It meant that every weekend, Friday to Sunday, he went to work in the Navy. Once a year they came together for maneuvers for a short time. This year he was sent to Hawaii for two weeks. This made him earn much more. It paid the hospital bills and everything that a child needs. He stayed with the reserves for twenty-one years.

After a while I went to see my newest grandson and my daughter to settle our business. I had saved a couple of days. Patrick was beautiful and healthy. He went to sleep at 9:00 p.m. and at 7:00 a.m. was awake, but did not make a sound until 9:00 a.m., and then he called for his breakfast.

I took a seat on the sofa where Maija was sitting and took out my checkbook. "Now I will give you the check for $1,000.00 as I promised and other expenses I will add to it. Tell me how much. If you want to give me some clothes for him while on the road, you can, but if not that's okay, I can buy some."

Maija looked at me and said with surprise, "Mother! You don't think that we will give him away? What would Wayne say? He is so absorbed with this child. All he talks about is him."

So I left without the child. I drove home alone, thinking about this beautiful child. My mother at home asked, "Where is the child?"

I said, "They did not give him to me."

"I thought that they would not," said Mama.

The time was approaching for David to return home from the service in the Army. He was stationed in Germany. His three years were up. I hoped for some message from him but so far nothing. I would drive my car to meet him and bring him home. Still I had no idea if it would be by airplane or the bus.

The next day, about lunchtime, I heard somebody quietly by the door. It was David. It was so wonderful to have my son back home.

"Are you hungry?" I asked.

"Yes, if you have something ready in the refrigerator. I need a bath even more."

I took out a fried chicken and wanted to warm it, but David would not let me. "Mom, your fried chicken always is good, it doesn't need heating," he took a seat at the table and had lunch. Then he went upstairs to his room for a bath. After that he slept two or three days, waking up a few times to go to the kitchen to have a glass of juice and slice of bread and to go to the bathroom.

After he was rested and started to feel more comfortable at home he shared experiences of life in Germany. Because of his work he had often flown to London, England. Danish pilots flew him in Danish airplanes.

He had the opportunity to attend wonderful concerts, theaters, museums, and restaurants.

Once walking in the business section on a London Street, he noticed a small door and a sign at the top of the door, "St. Anthony." He went in and it was a large room. The floor was covered with a carpet. Deeper on the left side were shelves with cloth materials. He looked at them; they were of good quality. On the right side of the room was a big desk and a man was sitting behind it. Seeing David standing by the shelves, he came to him and introduced himself as "Anthony," asking if he could be of some help.

David's hands were resting on a brown-gray piece of material and he said, "A nice color for a suit."

Mr. Anthony, looking at David and the cloth said, "Your complexion being ruddy it would not benefit you, but" he said, placing his hand on the silver-gray material, "this would suit you perfectly."

David, seeing the color and perfection of material, asked Mr. Anthony if he could make him a suit. So they agreed, and a month later, after five fittings, he received the suit. It was the most elegant he ever had seen. Here at home later when he took the suit just to be pressed, he selected the best cleaners who told me that they had not seen that kind here in our city for ages.

David told me how wonderful it was when he received twenty-pound packages from Maija, his sister, filled with goodies, cookies, cakes and more, all eatables. He was keeping it under his bed.

"As you told, Mother, don't just hide but share and I did as it came. Sometimes I came from work so hungry, pulled out the box, but nothing was inside. Not even a piece of popcorn."

When mailing boxes to him, Maija used popcorn as packing material. So all the things arrived undamaged and useful.

David shared goodies his sister sent to him even when it was not sufficient for himself. It is inexcusable to send army men to Germany, or any place and then to starve them. At the same time the officers made for themselves parties using food supplies from their army kitchen.

I noticed one morning as David was going down the steps from his room to breakfast in the kitchen that he stopped in the living room and went to his piano. In no time, beautiful music was filling the house.

He could not pass a piano. His heart was in it. His breakfast was on the kitchen table for more than two hours before he ate.

He listens to music like an "Alley cat," then goes to the piano and tries to play, then again. When he plays, one can see the picture—the alley, dark sky, and the cat gently walking so as not to disturb the beauty of the night. One could do nothing but listen and live it.

It was in June when a telephone call came. A mature man's voice was asking for David. He sounded serious, so I said, "David is not at home. I am his mother, if you have a message for him tell me, I will give it to him."

The man said, "I am Roberts, from Roberts Piano Store. David came last week into store. Did he tell you anything?" Mr. Roberts asked me.

"He did not," I said.

Then he continued, "David is interested in a grand piano, and I offered for him to try out any in the store and so he did. It was a warm day. The store door was opened. David played so beautifully and the people from the street started to come in—the cab drivers, students, ladies and men from the street, and from stores. My store never was so full, not even at Christmas. They were standing so still, so silent. Something like that I never had in my store. Please tell David to come any time and play any piano or any instrument he wants."

I was surprised that not only I loved David's music, but other people, too. All kinds of people, people of all ages.

What I heard made me happy and I promised Mr. Roberts to give the message to David and I did. I am sure he went to Roberts many times.

Now he was looking for employment. He told me that his two friends who attended local colleges could not find work, and even though their fathers had top lucrative jobs in their business they could not help them.

Living with Christian Science I felt that an unexpected stone was thrown in my lap. It did not seem right that young men graduated from good schools who desire to work, are prepared to work, and are not able to find a job. No! That is not right.

Our Heavenly Father, the only real Creator of man, knows what he is doing. All men are his children. For each one is prepared a right occupation.

"Divine Life, Truth, Love is the basic Principle of all Science, it solves the problem of being," by M.B. Eddy in Miscellany 348-29.

Then I heard the door opening. David was back. I looked at the clock. He was away only two hours.

"David," I said, "you were away only two hours. Did you get anything?"

"Yes," he said, "I got four jobs."

"Are they any good?" I had doubts. "What will you do now?"

"One is with the newspaper. I will take the one I like best, where I don't have to sit all the time by the table and the other three I will pass on to my friends. So they can go and take those."

Since he was away three years in Europe and had traveled often to London, Paris, Switzerland, and many other places, I thought he might get tired of my home cooking. I asked him how was the food in the army. He did not answer, as if he had not heard me. Then I asked, "David, what did you have Sunday mornings for breakfast?"

"Pork and beans," he said.

"What did you have for dinner?"

"Pork and beans," he said.

"What did you have for supper?"

"Pork and beans," he repeated.

"Did you have some bread with it?" I continued.

"No," he said, "if we wanted bread, we had to go and look for it."

"What did you drink with your food?" I asked.

"Nothing. We had to go and look for something in the kitchen."

Then he continued that the cook was a country boy. He did not know how to cook. They had to drink what they found in the kitchen and with the bread the same.

"We were hungry all the time," he said. "One time a big plate full of pork ribs was placed on the table. We were so happy. We thought now we will eat. But it was only bones covered with ketchup. Our cook, Duncan the "dangerous," told us that the officers ordered him to remove all the meat from the bones and serve to them, but give the bones to the soldiers. 'They had a big laugh about it,' " Duncan told us.

"I remember," said David, "we all heard them laughing and eating."

"How did you manage still to live?" I asked.

"My music, flute and piano, and some other boys had their instruments. We started to play together. There were parties, we were asked to play together. Our officers, too, had parties in their homes. At the parties food was served. So we had some food there, if there were leftovers."

Mama was very happy that her grandson, David, was back from the army. Here and there we heard her saying, "It is so good that David is finished with the army."

They had a bond between them. She taught him to read, to write, and arithmetic before he was three-years old. Since he learned to play the music she was listening, sitting on the chair in a quiet corner. David loved the stories grandma told. Some were funny, some historical about the old country and some were new.

She told him, "If you have a problem go to the library and look for the subject you are interested in. Read as much as you wish. It will help you make the right decision."

Then David was offered work in a juvenile delinquent home. He liked it. He liked the children. When I asked him what's the matter with the children that they are delinquent, he said, "Nothing! They are all good children. The parents are the delinquents. They consider them as toys. They get tired of them, they have no use for them."

Once he told me about a seven-year-old boy. His mother was never at home. There was no food at home. The refrigerator was empty; the home was empty. Naturally the kid had no money to buy food. He left home, was stealing in the stores, here and there, and was brought to this place. The man in charge put him in a room, ordered them to take out the bed, and everything. Here was this kid, hungry and scared, locked in, lying on a cement floor with not even a blanket.

"Who did that?" I asked.

"The Baptist minister," said David, "I don't understand how anyone can be so heartless. Instead of loving and feeding the child, he mistreats him."

"Christ Jesus never mistreated a child or anybody like that!" I was dissatisfied with the inhumane treatment.

David loved those kids. Sometimes he brought home the little things the children were making in crafts class.

Mama's health was not good. She wished to see a medical doctor. I took her to one she chose. He gave her medicine for blood pressure. She took it for a while, but she felt worse. I asked what she wanted to do. She said that she would not take the medicine any more. Then she had a problem with her legs. Once she was sitting for a while, it was very painful to get up. It is called joint rheumatism. There is no medicine for that problem.

One afternoon we were sitting in our living room. She was on the sofa watching television. I was sitting in a chair across from her. It was a sunny day. I noticed that several times she tried to get up, but could not and gave up. I started to think about her. All her life she took care of our family. When anybody was sick she would not sleep, but did for us all that was needed. She taught us from an early age about God and the Bible. She told us stories from the Bible.

I thought now about God's ever presence, as I learned in Christian Science, who created my mother and all men, perfect and well, and keeps her well.

I prayed for his love never ending with Mama and us all, being our divine Father, and his perfect creation.

I did not tell Mama about my praying. I did it in my mind, knowing the divine love would embrace her like armor.

For a while she was still sitting. Then she got up and walking straight, left the living room. After that she never had problems with her legs, but walked up and down steps or got in or out of the car with no difficulties, just as any young woman. She was eighty. She was healed. There were no traces left of the so-called arthritis.

David renewed his friendships with some of his schoolmates. One of them was Rodger. He had a car. They were going here and there together. Then David bought a car. He made a down payment and in three months paid it off.

Then he met a young woman and dated her. They even went to California. After awhile they returned and I met her. Her name was Daphne. Her family consisted of her father, who was a retired marine captain, her mother, and two sisters. The oldest sister was in college, the youngest, Stephany, just a twelve-year-old kid. They invited David to their home.

Daphne told me that her mother had health problems. Our church was giving a free Christian Science lecture for this community. I sent her mother and father an invitation. I never met the lady, but later she called me to say that she liked the lecture and it made her feel better.

David was progressing in work. Now he was employed by a big company rebuilding the 495 beltway around Washington, DC. Weekends he usually came home to Lynchburg, Virginia. He still planned to continue college and his music.

Mama's health was failing. She was getting forgetful. One time I came from work about 5:00 o'clock and she was not at home. I went around, asking our neighbors, but nobody had seen her. I called the police, but they said it's too early to do anything, just to wait. Next day, after praying all night I went out and on the first street to the left I saw my mother coming towards our home. Slowly and calmly I asked her where she had been. Mama calmly answered me that she had found a room for herself. I asked if she was hungry and would like something to eat. She said that now she was going home to eat.

"Good," I said, "then we both can go home to eat."

I let her walk a few steps ahead of me, just to see where she would go. She opened the gate, continued to the house, then down to the kitchen and took a seat at the table. After she finished we went upstairs and to her room.

I went to the house from where I saw her coming. A lady opened the door. I told her about seeing my mother coming out of these doors and not being at home last night and asked if she could tell me what happened. She explained that this woman (my mother) came and asked to rent a room. She showed one small room upstairs. Mother looked, saw the bed and said she would take it. So my mother slept there all night.

I asked the lady if she paid. "No," the lady said, that she did not ask and would not take any money now.

I thanked her for her kindness and promised to look out for mother more so that she would not get lost when going for a walk.

Since I had to work I prepared her breakfast and lunch and brought it upstairs to her room. I put it on her table and explained which is which. The breakfast in front, farther back was the lunch. The door from my bedroom led to a small hall, bathroom and her bedroom. That corner was on the second floor and had the necessary conveniences, but she could not get outdoors. I told her that I had to go now, but I would be back soon, then we both could watch television. Then I left for work and locked my door to her part.

When my lunchtime came I took my sandwich with me and went home to check on her.

It took ten minutes from my work to my house on the highway, ten minutes to check on mother, then ten minutes back to work. Often by the time I arrived she had eaten all of her food. When I asked if she ate, mostly she said, "no," that she's had nothing to eat today, nor for a long time. Even when the chicken bones left on the plate were smiling at us! If I had a few minutes I ran to the kitchen and brought more food, then left for work. When I was home I never locked her in, she was free to walk around.

After a while Mama had another problem. She became incontinent. We had to use diapers. I had to change her at night and in the daytime. She was worried about it more than I, because all her life she was used to taking care of us. But now she was helpless. That made her unhappy. I had no knowledge about nursing.

I changed her almost every hour and washed diapers by hand. Our washing machine was worn out. It went like that for a long time. Mother refused medical help. Finally I could not take care of her. I called her doctor whom she had seen some time before. He came to our home, checked on her, and called the ambulance to take her to the hospital to intensive care. She had a bowel tumor, but it could not be operated on. It was Saturday; I visited her on Sunday. Monday I went to work, but after 7:00 p.m. I went to the hospital to visit her. There I met her doctor. He was so kind to her, so helpful. Seeing him I stopped and said that I was coming to visit with mother. He said, "She is unconscious, she cannot hear you."

When I still asked him if I may see her, he said, "Yes, but she will not hear you, she cannot."

I went to Mama because I knew that she could and would hear me. She was not dead. She lay on the bed. I took her hand and said, "Mama, I will never, never be angry at you anymore."

She smiled. I said, "I love you, Mama!" She smiled again. Then I left and went home.

I knew since God never created death, we couldn't lose hearing. In *Science and Health* by Mary Baker Eddy it is explained and easy to understand.

Early Tuesday morning, Mrs. Fitzgerald, C.S. practitioner, called to tell me that my mother had passed away during the night.

The funeral home picked her body up and a few days later was the funeral. Maija and her husband invited a Greek Orthodox minister from North Carolina to do the service in the funeral home and in the cemetery.

The service was nice and peaceful. A few of my coworkers and members from my church came. I was glad that David came home from the army before Mama passed away. I noticed Daphne, David's girlfriend, sitting alone way back in the funeral home.

After the funeral when we returned home and were getting ready to have our meal, David did not come. So I went looking for him, asking if he would eat with us, but he did not answer. Then I noticed how pale he was. I could see now how much he was missing his grandmother. Maija cried bitterly in the cemetery. When I tried to calm her she said to me, "Mother, you don't understand how we feel about her. She brought us up. She took care of us. She was always with us, for us. We miss her."

She was right. I had to work; I had no choice. David did not eat, but left the house. He came back home late in the night, tired. I asked him, "Where have you been?"

He said, "I just was walking and walking. I am tired. I will lie down," and he went upstairs to his room.

The day was ended. The house was quiet and I knew that my mother was walking to her creator, to our dearest Heavenly Father, to continue to live.

Maija and Wayne with the children left for their home the next morning.

My mother, Helena Verhovska Kesse, passed on June 22, 1971, and was buried in the Fort Hill Memorial Park, Lynchburg, Virginia.

David left for work in Washington, DC. He continued dating the same girl. I did not know why she left her parents' home and rented a room near Lynchburg College.

David and Daphne continued seeing each other and were considering marriage. Then came the day David went to see Daphne's parents to ask her hand in marriage. Later, when he came home he did not seem to be happy. I did not ask him anything, leaving him to sort out his thoughts. I don't remember how long it took him to tell me about the meeting with her parents.

The girl's mother did not ask David about his and Daphne's plans or desires, but spoke about her personal desires.

You have to be married in the Catholic Church. Your children must be Catholics. We will be at your place in Richmond all weekends.

Since she had no sons, but daughters, she had made the choice that Daphne's husband would be her son-in-law where she would live and spend her retirement. "The oldest daughter is bright and is in college. She has good grades, but she doesn't have good looks. The youngest girl is too young to be considered," her mother told him. Then she expected David to accept her demands and requests.

David answered that he thought if his wife wished to go to the Catholic Church he would respect her wish. About the children, they would decide which church they would attend. After they are twenty-years old, then they can make their own choice.

The girl's mother told him if he didn't agree with her requests he had to stop seeing her daughter and there would be no marriage. David tried to meet with Daphne and her mother so they could talk, but with no success. Then he went to see the Catholic priest to see if he could help them reason together with her parents.

When he came home he was worried. He said that the priest was very cold and that he was not interested in helping anybody. What Daphne's parents say or do is their business. He refused to listen.

"What should I do now?" David asked. "I thought that ministers and priests are here to help people. They just don't care!"

I wanted to tell him about Catholicism, but I knew nothing good except the priest in the state of Maine who sent us to Richmond, Virginia, and the Latvian Catholic priest in the Oldenburg Latvian refugee camp. He had told my father, his friend, that if he had known about this Catholic religion he would never have become a Catholic priest.

So I said, "You know the library in our city. You could go there and find more about this religion."

So he left and came back with a stack of books. I noticed there was variety, including other religions, too.

It was July 15, 1971, take or add a day or two. I had to make notes after hearing what I heard, to remember the details. It was about 6:00 p.m. We were living at 1510 Madison Street, Lynchburg.

I was sitting in the new wing chair in the living room. The evening sun was streaming through the large windows and rested on the sofa and the cream-colored Chinese rug, as if saying all is well. But was it?

David came and took a seat on the sofa. He was very quiet. "Did you see Daphne?"

"No," he said, quiet again.

It was my way not to pry, unless the children wanted to talk.

Then he said, "I went to see her Catholic priest. I have been several times, but was told that he was not there. I made an appointment. Finally he saw me."

"What did the priest say?" I asked.

"Nothing," said David, "then I asked if he could help us talk to her parents. Priest said he could do nothing because we were not married. Mother, aren't ministers and priests supposed to help people? Isn't that their real mission?"

There was such searching hurt in his voice.

I was stunned, so many thoughts came to me, but what was right to say?"

"I asked the priest what was the difference between string rings and gold rings. Does God prefer gold? Is there more love and union in the metal? Will you please help us? But he refused.

"I told him that in the sight of God we were married. We went up on the mountain, tied the strings around our fingers, and in God's presence made our wedding vows, and prayed."

Hearing all this I remembered another time when we lived in the Oldenburg refugee camp. David then was almost two-years old. His father, Voldis, before Oldenburg had lived in the American zone for about three years. He told of an experience he had there.

I don't remember anymore the name of the place. There were farmlands around and a big pond. Voldis often went for a walk. He liked the view, but the stench was often bad. He met a farmer there and they would stop and talk.

"Pretty place," my husband said, and was turning to go back to camp.

"Yes," said the farmer, "but the smell is bad. It is full of babies, rotting in that pond. On that side is a cloister, where monks are living. On the other side of the pond is a nunnery. We see them dropping new born babies."

"No wonder," said my husband, "Catholic misdoings, on Sunday the priest will forgive."

Then one day Daphne's mother called me on the telephone. First I thought she wanted to speak with David, but she said, "No."

"I want speak with you," she said, and continued. "I want David to leave my daughter alone, or I will kill him myself."

I could not believe what I was hearing. No, no! No mother would or could kill any child! David never did fight with any children but outsmarted initiators in a way that they lost desire or interest to fight with him.

After thinking and praying I came to the conclusion that this woman was probably just upset, but would never do something like killing. After all, they knew David. He had been in their home. He visited them. He had been invited.

No, no! All will be well. I gained my peace.

Awhile later David said to me, "Mama, I made my mind up. I am twenty-five years old, Daphne is twenty-three. I want to meet her and ask her to make a choice; should I wait for her or just forget her?"

Since she was going to a local college, he tried meet her after class, but could not. Then one day Daphne called me and said that her mother warned her if she did not drop David, stop seeing him, that she would put her in a mental institution.

Thinking about that as an unreality just to scare the girl, I thought, no, no. It cannot be!

Later when I was working in a nursing home there were a couple of cases. One woman was in her late fifties. She had never been married. She was brought there in her mid-twenties because her choice to marry a man did not please her parents and they put her in that mental institution. I was in that nursing home taking care of her. She did not have a mental problem.

There I met one or two similar patients and not one was a mental case.

After my mother passed away, I sold my property in Lynchburg and was leaving for "Tenacre" nursing school in Princeton,

New Jersey, since I was in Christian Science and was learning about healing God's way, as Christ Jesus had done. I signed on to the class to study it.

As a young girl, when I saw children or older people sick I wished to help them so they would be happy and healthy. Now it was my possibility to learn that. For twelve positions in that school there were more than fifty candidates applying for learning. When I received the news that I was one of the twelve I was so happy and grateful to our Father.

A couple of days before leaving for Tenacre, I was staying in the home of my friend, Nancy Bartley. The next day my son David came. It was almost 12:00. He was downstairs where the piano was. He started gently playing. Nancy, being upstairs, heard it and came down.

"I did not know you play so beautifully. There on the table is more of my son's music; you can use," she said, pointing to the table on the side.

"There are records, too, if you would like to try them."

David asked me if I was going some place today and if he could get a ride with me.

I said, "Yes, soon. Where do you have to go?"

He answered, "Plaza, have to be there by 2:00 p.m."

"Sure," was my answer and I went upstairs.

He played a record, then soon another. I was ready to leave and went downstairs. A record was playing a beautiful classical piece. He was standing in the middle of the room. I asked if he was ready to go.

He smiled so tenderly. "I cannot now. I don't care about the Plaza. I will get there later, somehow."

I knew he loved music, especially the classics, like Johann Sebastian Bach, the best; Mozart; Beethoven and so on.

David was standing and listening the music. I went to my car and took off for Tenacre School in New Jersey. The weather was fine. I bypassed Washington on Rt. 7, then on Rt. 1 to Maryland and then New Jersey to Princeton and six miles to Tenacre.

The place was beautiful. There were fifty acres with trees, a bubbling brook, meadows, and a beautiful chapel between the houses and buildings for patients and nurses. One road led me to the main office. After all the papers were filled in I was shown a room upstairs in the nurses' building. It was a very small room with a window, but it was enough for me.

Next morning after breakfast we met in the class to start learning. Our teacher was Miss Siebenman. She was a Christian Science nurse from Switzerland, a very pleasant woman. We had lessons until lunchtime.

The next morning the day started the same. All was understandable and interesting. At 10:00 somebody came into the classroom and talked to the teacher, then left. The teacher came to me and said that I should go to the office, that there was a message for me. So I went.

A man from the office said, "Your son-in-law called and said that your son David was killed last night. He wants to talk to you now."

I took the telephone from his hand after the man said, "Here she is, you can talk." I heard my son-in-law's voice, "Can you hear me? I have bad news. David was killed."

"No, no! You are lying, lying!" I could not stop.

"He was killed," my son-in-law said, "at Daphne's home."

I put the telephone down. I could not believe what Wayne had just told me.

It's a lie, a lie, a bad dream! Suddenly I remembered him standing in Nancy's room, listening to that music just before I left.

No, he is alive! It is only a bad dream. I will awake and find that all is well. That night I could not sleep. It was a very black night.

In the morning, after the blackest night in my life, my heart was heavy, as I had to plan what to do now. To continue in the school now and not go back to Lynchburg or return to Lynchburg? I have nothing left there.

But I had to go back now and see my son and to take care of some of David's things regardless of how much it hurt. I called the Christian Science practitioner Ruthbun H. Dickinson, CSB teacher. I told him what happened with David and that I was leaving for Lynchburg. He promised to pray. He was very helpful and came to the airport, where I had to wait more than an hour. He asked me to call him any time if I needed him. Then the airplane came and I left for my destination.

On the flight I thought about the reminder from my teacher. Psalm 46:10 "Be still and know that I am God. Verse 11-The Lord of hosts is with us."

I learned in *Science and Health* that man is never born, therefore cannot die; God, the only creator, being Spirit, divine Principle had no material matter out of which flesh could be made man. He created His ideal man spiritually. For that reason man is deathless, a spiritual idea. David was in this world twenty-five years, "His idea."

The great "I AM" made all "that was made." Hence man and the spiritual universe coexist with God. (*S & H* 267:10). In Isaiah 43:7, "Even every one that is called by my name: for I have created him for my glory, I have formed him; yea, I have made him."

These Christly truths calmed me. Still I felt as if it was just a bad dream. I remembered how much David loved and trusted God. He loved and respected everybody. Even that girl's mother; he told me she was an intelligent woman.

I went to the funeral home and met the director of the place. He told me that David was so badly shot that he had two gallons of blood in his abdomen and the back of his head was smashed.

Yes, he was an invited guest in that woman's home several times—the woman who killed David.

Then I remembered once when David and I were talking about why some people think that if a man doesn't carry a gun he is not much of a man. Later the girl mentioned that her father had several guns around their home.

He loved the girl so much and wanted to please her. We were told that two weeks before the murder, while working in Washington, DC, he bought a 38 pistol.

David's funeral was in the Fort Hill Cemetery. Maija's husband Wayne engaged a Greek Orthodox minister from North Carolina for the service. My mother was Orthodox. Wayne could not find another.

I have to accept that David is not dead. He is with the Heavenly Father. I think that God selects for each child the parents in this world. That gives us responsibility to raise them right with the help of the Bible and to love God. David always did it, since he was walking.

None of his things were returned to me by the police including $8,000.00 he had with him. I wonder what happened to it. Stolen. Police!

When they heard about the killing, my coworkers suggested that I take the girl's mother to court. I was missing my son but the court would not bring him back to me. I could not judge that woman. God in the Bible never gave us rights to judge. When I had a problem, I turned to the Bible. That book has been the longest in this world and is written in present tense and has always satisfied me. Why not? It is God's book. He is the only creator, the only real Scientist. God's promise in that Book satisfies me.

Matthew 28:20…I am with you always, even unto the end of the world.

About the judgment it is clear in the Bible.

St. John 5:30… I can of mine own self do nothing: as I hear, I judge: and my judgment is just; because I seek not mine own will, but the will of the Father which hath sent me.

St. John 8:16 … yet if I judge, my judgment is true: for I am not alone, but I and the Father that sent me.

I had to do the best I knew how. That is completely by trust in the Father.

After David was murdered, I had no knowledge about that family. Much later somebody mentioned that Mrs. Seifert moved to Charlottesville in Virginia. I was not interested. She was God's responsibility.

It has been many years since my son left this world and is with our Father-God. Because God is the only Life, Spirit indestructible, eternal, the only creator, who created us.

I remember one day in Sunday school one-four-year-old boy said, "Teacher, I want to marry God."

I asked him, "Why?"

"Then God would be with me all the time and I with him," said the boy, "just like my mommy and daddy are together all the time."

It took me a few weeks to calm down. Then I had to decide what to do. I wanted to forget Lynchburg. I returned to "Tenacre" to nursing school to keep me busy. We had classes in the morning, then work on the floor and extra assignments in the evenings. I did them all. To my surprise it did not make me tired.

Then came my turn to be on the night duty. I thought it would be so easy because people sleep at night, but it was not so. It was not as heavy as in the daytime, but we were busy. I enjoyed working with the patients, trying to get a smile on their faces. Like the Bible says, "This is the day that the Lord has made, let us rejoice and be glad." Why not? This place was provided by God to his people he had created. He was with each of them, giving the rights to be well and to live eternally.

One year later the course was finished. We had tests and an examination. Mrs. Whitney, in charge of nursing education, was receiving reports from our teachers. We all had passed. I was complimented for my work. She wanted to know who wished to continue two more years. At this point I was a practical nurse. Two more years would give me a diploma and I could have easier work, get more pay, and work in the office. That I did not like at all. Sitting again at the desk? Being with the patients, taking care of them, doing what they needed and seeing their smiling faces made me happy.

No office work anymore! Not for me!

*Ida and her graduating class at Tenacre,*
*October 1973, Princeton, NJ,*

Then came an opportunity to be in Alexandria in Northern Virginia to see a Christian Science nursing home. It was called Lynn House. I liked the place.

My daughter and her family were moving to Woodbridge, near Alexandria, so I decided to take the job in Lynn House. With that I could join two other nurses in a three-bedroom apartment.

Since we worked different shifts and had one kitchen and one bathroom we had to be careful all the time not disturb each other. Often somebody was sleeping. Later I found another apartment in a beautiful place, which suited me better.

I worked for a while as a nurse in the nursing home, but I did not like the way some patients were treated by domestic help. Their negative remarks about patient health and chances for them to get well did not help patients.

I returned to Lynchburg, bought a house there and was listed in the *Christian Science Journal* as a nurse. Since the elderly patients did not like to be in the nursing homes, which they called "strange place," I took care of them in their own homes from Monday to Saturday. If they had any family to come and be with them, I left them for the weekend. That did improve my patient's frame of mind, that they were not forgotten but loved by the family.

I saw wonderful healings and patient's desire to live, not just exist and often saw them turn to a hobby or other activity.

I had no contact with my ex-husband for almost forty years. Then some of my friends who lived near Washington, DC, who attended the beautiful Lutheran church had seen Voldis. I was not interested to know about him or his life and did not listen to what was told about him.

A couple of years later the subject about his life was brought up again, that his wife, Mary, died and there was no one to take care of him.

I asked if he was complaining to somebody. The answer was no, but that they noticed him in the grocery store shopping and in his basket was a loaf of bread and a couple of soup cans. It's none of my business, I thought.

Still thoughts about what I had heard about him kept coming. Did I want him to be with me? No! Must I ask my daughter, my grandchildren? He did not know anything about the grandchildren. No. Maybe he was happy being alone.

Then a thought came to me. He had no family left. If he needed help, who would help him? At present the grandchildren don't know that they have a grandfather. Some day they may say to me, "He needed help, you knew that, but you did not tell us and did not help him." What will I tell them?

I had to call Voldis and ask how he was doing. So I did. We talked. He said that he had been remembering and thinking about me. He told me that Mary, his wife, died in 1992 and that he was retired. He asked if I could come and visit with him. He had an apartment in a boarding house. I said that I would think about it.

He suggested that the weather now in April is warm, a good time to travel.

I promised to visit him the next week.

In Rockville, Maryland, near Washington, DC next to the park, Latvians purchased a large piece of land. They built the Lutheran Church, a boarding house for pensioners, and other necessary gathering buildings, parking places and a park with trees and flowers.

Since I had a car I decided to drive there. I took Route 29 North and enjoyed the roads, trees, forests, and meadows here and there interrupted by small towns.

I reached Rockville about lunchtime. The place was nice and quiet. I parked my car and walked to the boarding house but did not see anybody outside. There were three cars on the lot but no people. The main doors of the boarding house had lots of glass, but were locked. On the right of the door on the wall were mailboxes for each apartment and a button to ring the bell. I rang the bell and Voldis came down to open the door to let me in. The hall was light, clean, and beautiful. Right there was the elevator. He lived on the second floor.

In no time we were on the second floor hall and inside his living room. It had a sofa, a small coffee table, a chair or two and a glass door to the balcony, with a view of the parking lot and the church.

"I am glad that you came," he said and offered me a seat on the sofa. "Would you like something to drink?"

"I think a glass of water will do," I said.

So he brought me a glass of water. We sat and talked. Then he said, "Come see this place so you will know where everything is."

From the living room we were in a small hall and on the right was his laundry room, which included an iron and ironing board. The next door was to the bathroom with tub and shower. Then there was a door to the bedroom. It had one twin-size bed and other bedroom furniture, a closet, and a window overlooking the church.

The next entrance from the hall was to the kitchen. It was small and was furnished efficiently. At the end extension was the dining room area with a table and a window.

He said that I could sleep in the bedroom and he would sleep on the sofa in the living room.

As we were sitting in the living room I asked him to go to my car and bring our dinner that we could warm up. I gave him the key to my car, asking him to lock up.

He brought it up and asked, "What is it?"

"Stew," I said, "stew with meat and vegetables and potatoes, and apple pie for dessert."

After awhile we had our meal. Voldis liked it and thanked me several times.

"You sure know how to cook."

We were looking at a program on TV and talking too. Then we said good night to each other and I went to the bedroom. He took a pillow and blanket from the closet and went to the living room to sleep.

The next morning I wanted to take a bath, but the tub was the color of the road. I had to wash it, but besides the soap and washcloth there was nothing. I used what I had, but the tub was not cleaner. Voldis was asleep. I gave up the bath. I tidied up the bedroom and took my books (Bible, *Science and Health with Key to the Scriptures* and Quarterly) to study my weekly assignment. I do it everyday, mostly in the morning. God's presence and His laws keep me healthy, wealthy, happy, and protected. It took about one hour.

Then Voldis was up. He asked me if I took a bath. I said no because I wanted to clean the tub.

"No," he said, "we don't wash it. We take a shower and the water itself runs out."

"I don't like a shower. Could we go today to some grocery store if it's not too far away? What do you eat for breakfast?"

"Cereal and milk," he said, "coffee, milk, and toast. After breakfast we can go to the store. It's only two short blocks."

He had cereal at home, so we had breakfast. Afterwards we walked to the store. Like he said, it was nearby and was a beautifully landscaped place. The store was called "Giant." It was big and had all kinds of goods.

I bought some things for cleaning the tub. I knew to have a bath one had to have a clean tub. It took a long time and hard scrubbing till the tub was clean.

I asked Voldis if he would like to move to Virginia. He was asking about my house, the city, about our daughter Maija, her husband Wayne and the grandchildren. I told him that I had several bedrooms and two bathrooms.

Since he was eighty-eight years old and did not use a car anymore, he asked about transportation in the city.

I told him we have autobus and that the bus stop is a very short distance from the street corner. He was satisfied with the information and said, "When are we to leave? I will start packing."

"We could go the beginning of next week if you can finish everything here," I said.

"I have to give up the apartment and go to the bank to transfer my pension to Lynchburg. Then we can leave."

"What will you do with your furniture?" I asked. "I have all necessary furniture in my house. I have no place for more."

"I will call the Salvation Army. They will come and take it. What shall we do with my things?" he asked.

"All the things you have we can put in my car. It is only a two-door but I am sure we can do it."

The next week everything was done. His color TV was sitting in the back seat of the car, books (he had many of them), clothes, big suitcases, it all went.

The day was warm and sunny and we took off for my home in Lynchburg. When we arrived, Voldis chose a bedroom and bathroom downstairs. Then he brought all his things inside and I helped make his bed.

Since I was living on my pension like he on his, I offered that we share our expenses together. He agreed. So he gave me $100.00 a month for his room and $250.00 a month for food, heating, electricity and so on.

Everything was all right. Since he brought with him some medicine, I asked him if he needed a physician. He said, "Yes, but not here. My doctor is in Washington, DC. When I need to see my doctor, I will go by bus."

"Well," I said, "when you make an appointment with your doctor, I will drive you to the bus terminal. We don't have city transport to that place. Then when you come back, call me and I will pick you up."

Being a farmer's son he estimated the land around the house, especially the backyard. "We can have tomatoes here," he said, pointing to a corner near the house. So we went to the nursery and bought the plants. He started digging the selected place and rested, then worked and rested. After a while he put the shovel aside and took a seat in the nearest chair.

Later I said, "I have to try the shovel, I used to have a tomato bed and other vegetables, but it was long ago."

I made the holes, planted the plants, and watered them. Voldis did not participate; he was tired. Later he cut wood sticks to support each plant.

Later we had many and very good tomatoes. Since I was the only tomato caretaker we did not plant the next year.

When Maija was told that Voldis was here, she and Wayne and Whitney, her daughter, came to visit us.

In April 1995 they invited us to visit them in Florida, and we did. They met us at the airport and took us to a beautiful hotel. We were there eight days, in Fort Myers. Later we had dinner in their three-bedroom apartment. It was nice and we had a wonderful meal.

Since they both worked long hours, we were glad to stay in the hotel, as we were free to do as we liked, see what we wanted to see. We also went to St. Petersburg to visit old friends. At that time oranges were on the trees ready to be harvested. It was so beautiful and aromatic.

In August we both decided to fly and visit our families in Latvia. We did that. They met us in the airport of Riga. It was wonderful.

Since Voldis's family home of Mezini was near Cesis, we went with his family there. His birthday was in August. They had not seen him since 1944 and were preparing there to celebrate his birthday with all the family. His sister's daughter Dace and his sister Alida took the time and prepared a feast to fit a king. The place was full of people, and all were family members.

Three days later I left Voldis there with Alida and went to Riga to stay with my relative, Zina. The next week Voldis came too.

Together we went to see old places, the central market, and the restoration of the old historical city that was bombed and destroyed by the war.

The time came to return to America. Our families took us to the airport. Saying goodbye, we were wondering when we would see each other again.

We arrived in New York. From there we continued in a smaller plane to Lynchburg.

Voldis wished to go to the eye doctor. I offered to take him to the one he chose. Since his English was minimal, I said, "I will translate between you and the doctor as you talk, but no advice from me."

He agreed. The doctor said that he might have a swelling or tumor behind the eyeball and suggested that he take the eye out and look deeper. Voldis chose to think it over. He took his time. Then he asked me to pray for him. I agreed. A few days later I noticed that he had a newspaper and was reading a long time. Then later he read some more.

At suppertime he said he was reading longer than two hours, then some more, and had no problems with his eyes. So no operation was needed. After that he continued reading and never had more problems.

When still living in Rockville he had a problem with breathing. His doctor said it was emphysema. He was told there was no medicine for healing.

Using Christian Science for all my needs and questions, I prayed about what God wanted me to know about this disease. Reading the Bible and about Jesus Christ's healings, I found no place that God ever created any disease. Then it was only illusion. Jesus Christ knew it and healed.

In the Bible, Genesis chapter 1:31..."God saw every thing that he had made, and, behold, it was very good." It proves, yes, demonstrates illusion of disease.

I don't remember when Voldis's emphysema vanished, but his lungs had no problem with breathing any more.

I noticed that Voldis had problems with his legs. At night he used an electric heater on them. He was taking some kind of blood thinner. It did not help him much. We went to the doctor. I translated. With his pants rolled up, I saw on his left leg the artery was twisted like a rope on top of the leg. The foot was purplish. It looked bad.

The doctor said it had to be operated on. I asked, "What will you replace the artery with?"

"With plastic," he said.

"What about the capillaries?" I asked.

"We have to bypass them," said the doctor. I had to translate that to Voldis and he said that we had to think about it. We left.

At home he asked me more about the operation. I had to explain to him about capillaries and told him he had to decide for himself. He did not answer. Then he said, "No operation!"

Some time passed. We did not talk about it. Here and there I was thinking. In the Bible God created man spiritually, Genesis 1:26, 27 and 31... "God saw everything that he had made and behold it was very good." *Using Science and Health with Key to the Scriptures*, by Mary Baker Eddy, I prayed as it is taught in that book. I got what I was looking for. His legs were healed. (*Message for 1900*, pg. 5-27 by M.B. Eddy.)

It was the middle of a sunny day. Voldis was sitting in the chair and reading. I came in the room to write. I took a chair at the table and noticed that he was lightly scraping his ankle.

"Is it too warm in the room for your feet?" I asked.

"No," he said, "but I feel something." He pushed the sock down and we both saw a white foot. Then he pulled up his pants leg and we saw a white leg, perfectly normal. The artery under the white of the leg was smooth like a young man's leg. He took off his sock; the purple was gone.

He did the same to the right foot; it was as perfect as the left, white, smooth. In the doctor's office it was lightly purplish.

Now I could see and he, too, God's perfect healing, *S & H* by M.B. Eddy. 310:29 Mind is God, and God is not seen by material sense, because Mind is Spirit, which material sense cannot discern.

*S & H*, 251:28 Ignorance, like intentional wrong, is not Science. Ignorance must be seen and corrected before we can attain harmony. In harmonious beliefs, which rob Mind, calling it matter and defy their own notions, imprison themselves in what they create. They are at war with Science and as our Master said, "If a kingdom be divided against itself, that kingdom cannot stand."

In 1997 my friend Aija from Riga, Latvia, came to visit me. She had a three-week vacation and never had been in America. At the same time our grandsons, Darren and Patrick, arrived from San Francisco, California. It was May and the end of Darren's school year in his law school. All three of them went to Richmond, Virginia, to see their sister Whitney, then to Williamsburg, Virginia. They very much enjoyed that place.

At the beginning of June our grandsons left for Florida and Aija returned back to Riga and her work.

In 1998 we did not go out much, only to shop for our daily needs. Voldis went once to Rockville, Maryland, for a couple of days regarding something about war veterans; he used to organize it and for many years took care of it.

1998 was election year and it was already October. We talked a lot about the election. Voldis asked if I would vote. I answered that I was not sure.

He said, "You have been talking about it."

"I have to pray more. Only God knows who is the right one," I said. I went for a walk and to pray. When I came home he asked if I had made my decision.

I said, "No, I left the choice of selection and election to our Father, knowing that it is the best."

As we sat watching TV and reading we also talked about Sunday. He was planning go to his church, Greek Orthodox, as usual. Sunday morning after breakfast he changed his mind, saying that he was feeling kind of weak. He said he would go next Sunday.

I went to my church. When I came home he was in the TV room resting on the cot. We talked about lunch, food, and the year 2000.

"Remember," I said, "we agreed to live until 2000."

"Definitely," said Voldis.

There were lots of leaves from poplar and other trees in my front yard. I raked and raked. He stood by the window, as he often did, watching me rake leaves. He did not seem to have much strength. The year before, 1997, he raked the leaves. By Friday most of the leaves were gone. Voldis was perkier, saying that this Sunday he would go to church.

His plan was to take a bath after breakfast on Saturday, but then he changed to Sunday morning. Sunday he was up early. His bedroom door was open, so he must up. All was quiet.

I went downstairs and started to prepare breakfast. Voldis came in the kitchen. His face was shaved.

"I thought you would take a bath," I said.

"Not now, later," he said.

I served him a good breakfast. He ate all of it and left, saying he was going up to change for church.

When I went upstairs he seemed to be resting on the cot. He said that he didn't feel very good. When I asked if he had pain, he said no, but something was pressing on his chest. He said he would stay at home.

I was ready to go to my church and I said, "I will be back soon."

He asked, "Would you please stay?"

Usually I would not, because the service was only one hour.

This time I felt that I should stay. He asked so gently as a prayer. I could not leave him alone.

Since I am used to being in the church at this time, I offered to read a Psalm from the Bible. He liked the idea; then I read from the New Testament. It seemed to give him peace, but when I stopped he was restless again.

I called his doctor, but we could not reach him so I decided that on Monday morning I would take him to his doctor.

After 12:00 noon my neighbors, Scotty and her husband, arrived. They said they missed me at church. We sat in the living room and talked awhile. As they left, Scotty offered for me to call her anytime that she could help.

Voldis was resting in the TV room. He had no pain, but still had the pressure in his chest. I asked if he would like something to drink or eat and brought him a cup of tea. After 3:00 o'clock I offered him soup, potatoes, meat, and vegetables.

"It would be good," he said.

I brought a tray with food and set it on the table in the living room by the big window facing the back yard and woods and went looking for him. He was in his bedroom sitting in the chair. I told him that his food was on the table in the living room and asked if he would rather eat in his room.

"No," he said, "I will come."

He stood up effortless, walked to the living room and took a chair. He took the soupspoon, used it one time, and swallowed, then moved the soup bowl away. Then he took the fork. With its tip he picked up a little potato with meat and put it in his mouth. He swallowed and then he put the fork on the tray.

He started to lean back in the chair until it was on just two legs. I was at his side, thinking if the chair fell I could not lift him up from the floor. I started to push the chair down until it stood on all four legs. I turned to the telephone on my right and called Scotty and asked her to call an ambulance.

Then I turned back to Voldis. His mouth was opened wide. A little saliva came out but not a sound. His arms stretched out to the window and back yard. His fingers stretched out as if reaching to somebody.

Then his right arm was on his lap; the other had dropped down. I lifted it and put it on his lap and said, "It is all over, all is well." His face coloring was now like a young child's.

Scotty Stratton came in. She had called the ambulance. Her husband Robert was waiting outside. Scotty offered to give Voldis CPR. Not thinking, my mouth said, "No." I just felt such peace and Christly presence that all was well. That God was there. We needed no help.

The ambulance arrived in seconds with four men. They tried to revive Voldis but with no success. They took him to the hospital emergency room. Scotty said that we had to go too because without us they would do nothing for him.

In the hospital we had to wait in separate rooms. At 7:30 a nurse and a hospital minister came and said that they couldn't revive him and that now I could see him.

Voldis was lying on the hospital "table" bed. He looked like he was just asleep. His face had no wrinkles, he had the coloring of a young child, his right arm on top of the cover was white with no wrinkles and the brown spots were gone.

After praying we all left the room. It was 8:00 p.m. When we arrived at my place, Scotty mentioned food. I was not hungry. We had not eaten all day. She suggested that she make mint tea and started heating water on the stove. Her husband Robert started to clean leftovers from the table and wash the dishes.

I put cookies and a cake on the table. Voldis liked sweets so we had plenty of them. It was about 9:00 p.m. It was quiet inside and outdoors. Suddenly I heard a noise as if somebody upstairs was closing doors. Then it sounded like somebody moving in Voldis's bedroom. Before I said anything, Scotty said, "He is back, where else would he go? He doesn't know anybody here."

"Yes," said Robert. So he heard it too, not just me. Then after some minutes there was a click in the furnace room and it started heating.

"It is the furnace this time," said Robert.

Monday I called the funeral home to find out when I could visit to see Voldis before they cremated him, as he wished. They told me that the body would be brought from the hospital to the funeral home on Tuesday, November 17. Since he died on Sunday, November 15, by Virginia law they had at least 24 hours before bringing the body to the funeral home. I could see him about 2:00 p.m.

I was there at the Diuguid Funeral Home on time and saw Voldis's body. He had the same face coloring, only a little blue color on the ear lobe. He looked so young.

Then I went to the office because they needed some information from me.

"How old was Mr. Mednicks?" a man in the office asked.

I said, "Ninety two."

The director looked at me and said, "It must be some mistake."

I said, "No."

He said it must be, probably in the birth certificate, because he doesn't look more than forty.

That Tuesday, Scotty Stratton called the funeral home about visiting with me. The director asked her how old Mr. Mednicks was. She said the same as I did. He expressed that it must be a mistake; he could not be more than early forties.

After they sent me Voldis's death certificate, he was cremated that week in Charlottesville, Virginia.

Once, after visiting my brother Misha in Riga, Latvia for about three weeks I returned to Lynchburg and started to look for work.

In the *Christian Science Monitor* I saw an advertisement for a nurse in Wisconsin, near Milwaukee. It had given my teacher's name—Miss Siebenmann. So I telephoned her. She was glad to hear that I was back from my visit and ready to work.

Within one week I left my home for Wisconsin to work there about one year. I had never been in that state, but what I saw on the road I liked. I was given a comfortable room on the second floor in the nursing house.

The patient area, a one-story building, was near the yard. It too was a nice place. Miss Siebenmann was in charge of the nursing. The place was busy, but neat and in good order. Working together, month after month, the time did not stand still.

I remember one time it was a very cold month. There was lots of snow and ice. More than three feet of it was piled on the roads and roofs.

When the shift ended at 4:00 p.m., not all of the next shift nurses arrived because of the weather. The road was in bad condition. My work was done so I left. I took off my uniform and with it and other clothes went downstairs to put them in the washer. Then I went upstairs to my room. I was tired and lay down on my bed. I hoped to rest, but my telephone was ringing. I had to respond. It was Miss Siebenmann asking me to come and help her with the work. I told her that my uniforms were washing and I had nothing to wear.

She insisted for me to come, regardless of what I wore. She had a man from an accident, wounded on the street, bleeding; another patient needed help and there were more and only one young aide had made it in because of the roads. So I had no choice and went.

Miss Siebenmann was still busy with the wounded patient. She asked me to take care of a new patient, who was vomiting. Clothes and bed had already been changed three times and now they needed to be changed again.

So the aide and I took care of this patient. Then we divided the rest of the patients. The aide would take care of patients who needed only minimal care and I would do the rest. We started at 5:00 p.m.; after 8:30 p.m. all was done. Mrs. Siebenmann was surprised at the work we had done and told me to go home and not come in for the early shift, but to come later.

I went to my room, dropped my shoes, turned on a small electric heater, and crawled into bed. My room seemed so cold. I lay on my back but could not fall asleep. I wanted to turn on my side, but could not.

I thought that maybe I could read myself to sleep. I wanted to pick up the book on the bedside table, but I was unable to lift my arm.

Then another thought came—I must turn off the heater, but I couldn't lift myself up. I wanted to call somebody, but no sound came out from my mouth.

I am dying! That's okay. I am ready. Then I remembered the patients on the floor and the need of nursing care. I prayed for each patient room by room that God would bring the necessary nurses and help in the morning, that all would be cared for and I expressed gratitude to our Heavenly Father, the creator.

Then I got up, turned off the heater and went back to bed. I was surprised at what I did.

At 6:00 a.m. I awoke with a sense of duty and went to work. Sitting at the table in the nurse's station, I suddenly felt bad.

When Siebenmann came in I asked permission to go to the nurses' restroom. There I lay on the couch and prayed. After about twenty minutes, I felt okay and went to work. I left work at the usual time at 4:00 o'clock.

At work I never was asked about that night and did not feel a need to talk about it.

As summer came and my promised time came to an end, I felt a need to return home to Lynchburg. Also my friend Margaret in Lynchburg was in the hospital. She was a widow, had no children, no family left.

Sunday after our church service I went to the Baptist hospital to visit her. She told me that at home she had a sudden stroke of apoplexy and had to go to the hospital. We had not seen each other for a while.

"You, Ida, never had any stroke or any heart trouble?" she asked.

"No," I said. Then I remembered the night in the winter. I told her about it adding that I had no pain and the next morning I went to work. "Yes," I said, "I did not feel good for a while and two more mornings, but then all was well."

We chatted a little longer, and then I left to go home. She was waiting for her doctor's visit about 5:00 p.m. He and her late husband were longtime friends.

A week later after church service I visited my friend in the hospital again. Talking about her time in the hospital and returning to her home, Marge said, "When last Sunday my doctor came I told him about your story." At first I could not understand what story. "I forgot, what story?"

Then she continued, "The doctor said that you had a massive coronary and they would have pinned you to all kinds of machinery. Three times continued bad feelings indicate that it was a massive coronary."

I am sure glad that I was there in the Christian Science place and God, being always present, healed me with no machinery as they use in hospitals.

I soon was called to do some nursing work, which I liked. Mostly they were retired and living at home. So I worked until I retired.

One morning I was reading our local paper. I noticed a story about a place near Lynchburg called Monroe, which was a home established for teenage children who needed supervision. Originally the place was built by the Catholic Church to take in young Catholic boys and train them as monks.

With God's law of progress in our life, thank you Heavenly Father, the young men chose their freedom and not what was forced on them and they left.

Then that property was acquired by the government as an educational establishment. The teenagers, girls and boys, were brought in from different cities and states. They lived in dormitories and were getting an education. They also had an opportunity to learn a craft.

In the local paper a young man expressed gratitude for that place giving him a chance to be prepared for life and work. He mentioned a desire to see more volunteers who could help other students there. Reading all that I became very interested.

I prayed to our Father about what I should do. A couple of days later I called the information given in the paper. A lady answered, and I made an appointment. She was one of the volunteers, mid-thirties, nice, active, a mother herself of two middle-school children.

After talking about all I wanted to know, we decided for me to come two days a week from 10:00 a.m. to 4:00 p.m. Her idea was that it was best to start in the cooking class. The children there were not sure of what kind of work they would like to do. Since everyone liked food, there was no harm to begin with cooking.

I noticed in the class that some were active, some were not. Some were sitting on the chairs along the back wall.

This teacher was teaching students to prepare dishes, the food, about cooking, serving, and after that cleaning up the kitchen.

Kids were permitted to ask about anything in which they were interested. A tall, nice, dark boy came to me asking if he could talk to me. Sitting next to me was a chair, "Have a seat here," and he took it.

Taylor said that he was seventeen years old and was from Delaware. His parents were working and he attended school in Delaware. When I asked if he liked it, he said yes but the teachers did not like him. They told his parents that he wasted their time.

"What do you like to do?" I asked him.

"I like to sing, but nobody cares for it," he said.

"Do you know the Bible?" I said, "It is the book about how we were created. It is about us all, you and me and our parents."

"You are talking just like my grandmother. She is in a nursing home. I visit her. My parents' work leaves no time to talk to me. I like to talk to you, Mrs. H."

"Good, we can do it anytime," I said.

In that place from the main door was the chapel, used for prayer, graduation, and student performances. At that time they had 375 students, twenty students were white, the rest dark.

The next week when I came, people were going in the chapel. So I went in too. It was full. I found a place between students. A band of four students had musical instruments ready to play and there was a small choir.

It was nice. Then I saw Taylor come in with a group and they were singing. His voice sounded wonderful. I had heard in my life many wonderful singers, but his voice was so rich and deep.

While the singing went on, students sitting in the chapel did not behave as they should. They were talking, making noise, and being generally disrespectful. After the performance was finished they all left the chapel.

Next week when talking with Taylor I mentioned his singing and his talent. He said that nobody liked his singing; that's why they made noise. He said he would not sing anymore.

"No," I said, "when we are born, our Creator God gives us talents. To you he gave a voice to sing. A beautiful voice, such as I have not heard for a long time. Don't pay attention to what other people say. God wants to hear you singing. Remember when you sing, think with gratitude and sing to God. Forget everything else."

Graduation time came for Taylor. He finished all tests and was given employment as a cook on a marine ship in San Francisco, California, with good pay.

There was a service in the chapel. Taylor conducted the small choir. Then he sang a solo. He had a deep, honey voice. It was so beautiful that one could not think about anything else, only listen. It was so still as if no one was breathing. After the song was ended the stillness was broken with great applause. Indeed, everybody was happy.

When at work at that place, walking in the hall, I heard some music. I noticed on my right side a big door, and I wondered where it could lead. Once when the door was not quite closed I opened it a little more. The place was large, and not too far from the door was a grand piano. There was sitting a young man playing on it. I recognized him. He was Lee, a student in our cooking class. I went to see him and asked what he was playing. He said that he didn't know how to play, never before had he touched a piano or any instrument, but he could sometimes hear music in his head, and at lunchtime when everybody ate he came to play.

"What about your parents?"

He said that he was from Delaware State. His mother was a nurse, working in a hospital. He didn't have a father. His mother was raped when she was fifteen. That man lives in California. He didn't know him.

"Do you go to church?"

"Yes, with my mother when she can."

"Do they have a piano?"

"Yes," he said, "but the church is small and the minister won't let anyone put a finger on it."

Later the thought came to me to see Mrs. Shelby Davis, my son's piano teacher, and tell her about Lee. She became interested and asked if I could bring him to her.

Then I noticed that no music was coming from the room. I asked Lee about it. He answered that a teacher from that place ordered him not ever to go and use the piano.

No wonder, I was thinking, they don't ask the teachers but talk to me.

They had said, "They teach us only because of money, but the volunteers, who don't get paid, come because they love us."

I found that Lee had never done anything wrong and I asked our cooking teacher to get a permit for him and also for other students to learn to play the piano.

After awhile the permit was given to Lee and a girl student to bring them to my home for a weekend. I picked them up in Monroe on Saturday morning and returned them Sunday evening.

After lunch we had a meeting with Mrs. Davis, my son David's piano teacher. When we arrived she asked if Lee would like to play something on the piano. She had an old upright Wurlitzer. When Lee asked what, she said, "Anything you like." He played and she asked, "What is it?"

"I don't know," he said, "it's just what I feel." I could see she liked what he was playing.

She had prepared five separate small booklets of music notes on music paper and gave them to him one by one to play. He did. In a half hour he had played all of them. Mrs. Davis was surprised and said, "It would take a good student six months to do what he did in a half hour."

We understood—Lee had a wonderful talent.

A young man was often sitting on a chair by the wall at the end of the room. When asked to do something he never hesitated. His name was Robert, also about seventeen, light color, and slender.

When I asked the teacher about him, she said that he was from Delaware. He was found on someone's doorstep. He seemed not to have any interest about anything. For that reason he was sent to cooking class.

I wanted to know more about Robert and was praying to our Father how and if it's possible.

About a week later the teacher asked me if I could substitute for her one day and I said, "Yes." The day came. In the morning I came and all was usual. I still had no plan about Robert. The kids were in the kitchen preparing to cook. After lunch I was called to come to the office.

The idea came to me. I told Robert that I was called to go to the office so he would have to take care of everything in the kitchen, tell the girls what to do, clean, tidy up, and put everything in the right places. I stayed at least a half hour in the office to give Robert time to do the work in the kitchen in the way I was expecting.

When I returned, the kitchen was perfect, everything was in place and there was harmony between all of them. I thanked him for his good work. I could see he liked that and then he went to sit on the chair by the wall.

By 3:00 p.m. the kids were leaving. Robert was sitting, dreaming. When I saw it was 4:00 p.m. I said to him, "It is four o'clock, we can leave."

It was just him and I alone in the room and I saw my opportunity to ask him what I wanted to know. He began walking across the room to the door and I did too. In the middle of the room I stopped, he facing me as if giving me access to the door and said, "Mrs. Harris, you don't have to help me. You don't know about me. I am nothing; I was left at some door. I have been in seventeen foster homes. I have no mother, no father."

"You are wrong," I said, "you have the best father and mother in the world, the God. He is the only Creator, Life and Love. He did not like the ones who gave birth to you, but made them leave you by the door. So He being Life and Love is with you (you are alive!) because He loves you. In the Bible, Isaiah 43:7 '... I have created him for my glory, I have formed him.' Be grateful to him, talk to him. He will guide you and provide for you. Learn to trust him. See you tomorrow," and we left.

I was at Taylor's graduation and after walking to the chapel's entrance hall to give him a present, there were so many people congratulating graduates it was hard to get through to Taylor. Then I noticed somebody else coming my way in that crowd. "Mrs. H," I heard. I did not at first recognize that happy, smiling face. He saw me and said, "It is me, Mrs. Harris. I am Robert! I have something to tell you! I am not in the kitchen anymore. I am with small engines, and I love it!"

I am grateful to our Father God, that Robert, his son had turned to him, his Creator, and will never let him go.

Then I stopped going to the Monroe place. There were some changes in my life too. I had calls for help and went into private practice. That kept me busy. In my old country there are many orphanages and I love children, and am willing to help, especially if the child has no family left. I love to help. It keeps me busy and makes me happy to see man well.

Psalm 118:16-17 the right hand of the Lord is exalted:

the right hand of the Lord doeth valiantly.

I shall not die, but live, and declare the works of the Lord.

The way is straight and narrow, which leads to the understanding that God is the only Life (*S & H*-324:13-15 by M.B. Eddy).

Controlled by the divine intelligence, man is harmonious and eternal (*S & H*-184:16-17).

# CONCLUSION

In Revelation 10:2, he had a little book open. Then 10:10, I took the little book out of the angel's hand, and ate it up; 10:11, he said unto me. Thou must prophesy again before many peoples, and nations, and tongues, and kings.

More than 125 years ago Mary Baker Eddy was entrusted to write the *Science and Health with Key to the Scriptures*, and she did.

This is the only key to the Bible that I know. It changed my life for the better.

To U.S.A.